Advances in African Economic, Social and Political Development

Africa is emerging as a rapidly growing region, still facing major challenges, but with a potential for significant progress – a transformation that necessitates vigorous efforts in research and policy thinking. This book series focuses on three intricately related key aspects of modern-day Africa: economic, social and political development. Making use of recent theoretical and empirical advances, the series aims to provide fresh answers to Africa's development challenges. All the socio-political dimensions of today's Africa are incorporated as they unfold and new policy options are presented. The series aims to provide a broad and interactive forum of science at work for policymaking and to bring together African and international researchers and experts. The series welcomes monographs and contributed volumes for an academic and professional audience, as well as tightly edited conference proceedings. Relevant topics include, but are not limited to, economic policy and trade, regional integration, labor market policies, demographic development, social issues, political economy and political systems, and environmental and energy issues.

More information about this series at http://www.springer.com/series/11885

Diery Seck
Editor

The External Sector of Africa's Economy

Springer

Editor
Diery Seck
CREPOL - Center for Research on Political Economy
Dakar, Senegal

ISSN 2198-7262 ISSN 2198-7270 (electronic)
Advances in African Economic, Social and Political Development
ISBN 978-3-319-97912-0 ISBN 978-3-319-97913-7 (eBook)
https://doi.org/10.1007/978-3-319-97913-7

Library of Congress Control Number: 2019930702

This Springer imprint is published by the registered company Springer Nature Switzerland AG
The registered company address is: Gewerbestrasse 11, 6330 Cham, Switzerland

Introduction

There is a striking contrast between the attention given by African policymakers and private sector actors to the external sector of their economies and the limited volume and scope of the existing literature, in comparison to other development-related issues. This observation serves to justify this book and the detailed studies that it includes. From the perspective of the book, external sector is viewed from two angles. At the national level, it refers to the extent to which individual countries manage the degree of openness of their economies with respect to trade, foreign direct investment (FDI), and international financial flows all of which translate into their participation in globalization. External sector also encapsulates the cross-border arrangements such as regional integration or various forms of policy harmonization like common external tariffs. The main underlying motives for increased interest in the external sector can be listed as follows. First, after more than half a century of efforts, African countries have failed to achieve their goals in domestic resource mobilization and have felt the need to look beyond their borders to finance their development.

Second, inward-looking economic policies of the 1960s and 1970s epitomized by rhetoric such as infant industry arguments or transfer of economic surplus from the agricultural sector to industry have not borne fruit. Third, the growing wave of globalization that swept the world, developed and underdeveloped, and the influence of multinational companies on the world scene have exposed African countries alike, in some instances against their will, to a higher degree of presence of their external sector than during earlier periods. The advent of globalization has also revealed the need to compete internationally, thus to focus on their comparative advantage, create sub-regional groupings and promote export-led growth strategies. Over the last three decades, several elements of evolution in the world economy have put the external sector in the forefront. They include inception of the World Trade Organization (WTO), advent of several external debt crises and programs to remedy them, economic partnerships between Africa and other world regions and the strong realization that African countries are too small and that sub-regional groupings might help improve their economic prospects. Yet, despite the failure of African countries to industrialize in particular, and to converge towards industrialized countries, new opportunities such as information and communication technologies (ICTs) give new impetus to the Continent's economic fate.

In light of the evolution described above, new questions are raised with respect to Africa's external sector and require new answers. In this respect, the stakes underlying external sector policies in Sub-Saharan Africa (SSA) can be summarized by three policy targets. First, how to secure high and steady access to development finance through debt flows and FDI? Second, how to achieve a higher level of international trade and gain more international market share? Third, how to create larger domestic markets through regional integration arrangements on the Continent?

The book examines three aspects of the external sector, namely Regional Integration, External Trade, and Macroeconomics and Political Economy.

In the first chapter, Seck assumes that economic welfare is pursued by an African country considering or evaluating its Regional Integration Arrangement (RIA) membership. He proposes an approach that assigns to inputted residuals computed from pre-integration trend lines the change in after-reform per-capita GDP and gives an estimate of the economic gain that arises from the integration initiative for each member country. The timing of the gain is also identified starting from the year of integration enactment. For the sampling period 1970–2016, the results show that members of the UEMOA benefitted significantly and rapidly from the reform of 1994 while CEMAC countries reaped a significantly lesser gain. Considerable gains also accrued to EAC members over the period 1978–2016.

In the second chapter, Chuku Chuku et al. seek to understand three main issues: first, what are the long- and short-run determinants of current account balances in West Africa; second, is there a sustainable path for the current account position that is consistent with regional integration; and if so, what has been the process of adjustment towards such a path. They address these questions by first identifying the long-term determinants of the current account, and then using the results to calculate the equilibrium sustainable targets for the current account in the region. After accounting for short-run disequilibrium adjustment processes, they show how far apart each country is from the regionally sustainable path. Their key findings are as follows: the determinants of current account dynamics differ depending on the time horizon; the real exchange rate, fiscal policy, trade openness, investment, and income levels are the key determinants in the short run; there is considerable variation by country in the deviation of each country's current account position from the regionally sustainable equilibrium path.

Doukoure analyzes in chapter "Obstacles to Strengthening Economic Integration in the West African Economic and Monetary Union" the obstacles to strengthening economic integration in the West African Economic and Monetary Union (WAEMU). Several studies show that strengthening economic integration requires an increase of intra-trade in Regional Trade Agreements (RTAs). But it is not the case in WAEMU where trade between member countries is rather low. He seeks to identify both the economic and political factors that limit economic integration in WAEMU and how they impact trade between members. In order to rank such potential obstacles, he develops an extended gravity model, using a panel dataset for WAEMU from 1996 to 2013 for all member countries. Bilateral export flows between member countries are used as endogenous variables.

In addition to the usual variables (income, population size, and distance), the effects of three factors (infrastructure, economic policy, and political tensions) are taken into account. The empirical results show that the state of infrastructure gaps—in particular, telecommunications and transport networks slow down significantly economic integration within WAEMU.

External trade is also investigated as a prime component of the external sector of African countries. In chapter "Growing External Trade, Development and Structural Heterogeneity in West Africa: Examining the Evidence", Ekpo and Omotor's study sets out to determine the extent to which West African economies are integrated and assess their take in the global value chains and some important parameters which could influence their trade flows given the perceived structural heterogeneity among them. The findings and results from the West African Enabling Trade Index, their participation in Global Value Chains and estimated simple gravity model among others suggest that trade performance of the sub-region does not sufficiently improve its export performance. Second, access to trade finance and identifying potential markets and buyers are among the most problematic factors that inhibit export trade in the region. The implication is that reducing these barriers will enable trade and contribute to prosperity and welfare.

In chapter "Driving Factors of Intra-regional Trade in Agricultural Goods: The Case of West African Economic and Monetary Union", Houeninvo et al. examine the impact of distance (transport/logistical cost) and the level of development on intra-WAEMU agricultural exports. They analyze the determinants of intra-WAEMU trade in agricultural products and therefore the variables on which policymakers could act to promote intra-regional trade. Using a panel data estimation in a gravity model over the period 1996–2013 covering seven West African countries with yearly data, they show that two gravity factors, the level of development measured by GDP as well as the distance are highly significant at 1% with the expected signs. Regarding the four control variables population (pop), foreign direct investment (FDI), political stability, and the common external tariff, all of them have the expected signs but only FDI with 2 lags is significant, at 1%.

In chapter "Trade Openness and Food Security in Africa: A Comparative Study of CEMAC and WAEMU Countries", Assoumou Ella and Eba Nguema conduct a comparative analysis of the effect of trade liberalization on food security in EMCCA and WAEMU countries with data spanning the period 1987–2014. Their findings lead to the conclusion of a negative effect in general. The beneficial effect of trade on the food situation is most visible in terms of availability. Also, it leads to lower prices. However, adverse terms of trade appear to wipe off the positive effects and lead to food insecurity. This outcome is robust for both the EMCCA and WAEMU samples. With regard to policy, these countries should implement trade policies to facilitate openness, while supporting and diversifying domestic food production.

Okah Efogo in chapter "Trade in Services for Growth and Structural Transformation in West Africa" seeks to identify the categories of services likely to foster structural transformation and economic growth in ECOWAS. With data on ECOWAS countries over the period 1995–2015, she estimates a dynamic panel model and shows that for each ECOWAS county there is at least one category of services that promotes structural transformation and/or economic growth. Services trade (imports and/or exports) could be a powerful tool for economic growth, structural transformation, and integration if the various countries rely on the appropriate service for this purpose.

Macroeconomics and political economy issues are studied in three chapters. In chapter "Macroeconomic Effects of Commodity Price Shocks in ECOWAS Members", Tule et al. examine the effect of commodity price shocks on ECOWAS member countries using a panel data analysis of 13 member countries for the period 2000–2015. Dynamic General Method of Moments (GMM) technique was adopted using an instrumental variable (IV) regression model. Their results show that precious metals are positively but insignificantly related to gross domestic product per capita. Also, there is a positive and statistically significant relationship between energy prices and the dependent variable. However, a negative relationship is observed between non-energy prices and gross domestic product per capita. In addition, the results show that 87% of the economy is susceptible to energy price shocks. This result forces a rethink of the integration agenda not only along monetary lines, but also along diversification integration.

In chapter "Is Currency Devaluation Appropriate for Improving Trade Balance in the Wamz Countries?", Englama et al. examine the appropriateness of devaluation in improving trade balance in the six West African Monetary Zone (WAMZ) countries. The motivation is largely derived from the need to reverse the deteriorating external sector of these countries which has become worrisome particularly from the latter half of 2014 on the backlash of a slump in commodity prices and tight global monetary condition. The study employs descriptive analysis, granger causality technique, and Vector Error Correction Model (VECM) to analyze the impact of devaluation on trade balance in these countries. Two other control variables, domestic and global output, are included in the model to capture the impact of domestic and global shock while the data covers the period 1980–2014. The trend analysis reveals considerable volatility in real exchange rate in all the countries with the exception of the Gambia while there is a virtual absence of co-movement between devaluation and trade balance in all the countries. All the series are integrated to the first order while Johansen cointegration test indicates the existence of long run relationship among the variables employed in the study.

Results of the normalized long run model indicate that the coefficient of real exchange rate is positively significant for only Liberia while it is negatively significant in the Gambia only. Real exchange rate is not significant in the remaining four countries, suggesting that devaluation may not lead to an improvement in trade balance in the WAMZ countries except probably in Liberia. Results from the models further suggest that external conditions like expansion in global output tend to have a positive impact on trade balance though the effect is not significant in all the countries. The variables are virtually not significant in the short-run models for all the countries while the vector error correction term suggests that the impact of shock on trade balance does not wane rapidly. The study recommends, among others, that devaluation may not be the most appropriate policy option to improve trade balance in these countries while these economies should endeavor as much as possible to improve the export content of gross domestic product in order to allow local economic conditions to drive trade balance.

In chapter "The ECOWAS–EU Economic Partnership Agreement: Towards Inclusive Development?", Acheampong and Ortsin analyze the ECOWAS-EU EPA agreement attempting to answer the question: how does the agreement foster both international trade and inclusive development by promoting investment and sustainable growth? Using evidence from countries in the ECOWAS sub-region, this discussion paper covers the following thematic areas: (1) external sector development impact of the EPA agreement and (2) the impact on fostering inclusive growth and development. Their results indicate that the EPAs will pose a number of policy challenges for West African countries as their economies increasingly integrate into the global economy. However, the EPA provides an opportunity to fast-track global trade and the regional integration agenda in West Africa. It is important that the EU treats the EPA as an instrument of development cooperation and not a conduit to pursue mercantilist corporate interests as did happen in colonial times. They also find out that balanced growth and poverty reduction are not automatic outcomes from liberalization processes, but rather these objectives must be actively promoted by complementary policies in conjunction with appropriate fiscal adjustments in order to fully gain from trade liberalization.

While the ten chapters of the book cover a broad area of the external sector in the context of SSA, it leaves unaddressed a number of key issues whose elucidation would facilitate better understanding of the challenges faced by the sub-region. First, how do external sector policies, even the most appropriate, cause economic growth and, for each individual country, which specific external sector policy would yield the best results? Second, the degree of control of countries over external sector interventions needs to be ascertained. In other words, to what extent can a country unilaterally set the level of, say, its export earnings, inbound FDI, or even external indebtedness from private sources which constitute the largest sources of debt markets in the world? There is no doubt that the external sector of SSA could contribute significantly to its economic growth but the right mix of policies to achieve that goal requires considerable more work.

Dakar, Senegal
June, 2018

Diery Seck

Contents

Part I
Introduction Regional Integration

The Economic Value of Regional Integration in Africa

Diery Seck

Contents

Abstract Economic welfare is assumed to be pursued by an African country considering or evaluating its Regional Integration Arrangement (RIA) membership. The proposed approach assigns to imputed residuals computed from pre-integration trend lines the change in after reform per-capita GDP and gives an estimate of the economic gain that arises from the integration initiative for each member country. The timing of the gain is also identified starting from the year of integration enactment. For the sampling period 1970–2016, the results show that members of the UEMOA benefitted significantly and rapidly from the reform of 1994 while CEMAC countries reaped a significantly lesser gain. Considerable gains also accrued to EAC members over the period 1978–2016.

D. Seck (✉)
CREPOL – Center for Research on Political Economy, Dakar Yoff, Senegal
e-mail: d.seck@crepol.org

D. Seck (ed.), *The External Sector of Africa's Economy*, Advances in African Economic, Social and Political Development,
https://doi.org/10.1007/978-3-319-97913-7_1

1 Introduction

Membership in regional integration arrangements (RIA) is a widespread strategy of African countries that has grown in importance over the last 25 years. The main African RIAs can be categorized as follows: 1) Customs and monetary unions: Union Economique et monétaire Ouest Africaine (UEMOA), Communauté économique et monétaire de l'Afrique Centrale (CEMAC), 2) Customs unions: East African Community (EAC), 3) Multilateral Free Trade Areas: Southern Africa Development Community (SADC), Arab Maghreb Union (AMU), Common Market for Eastern and Southern Africa (COMESA), Community of Sahel-Saharan States (CEN-SAD), 4) Developmental: Economic Community of West African States (ECOWAS), Communauté Economique des Etats d'Afrique Centrale (CEEAC) and Intergovernmental Authority for Development (IGAD). Every single country on the continent is a member of one or more RIAs.

The diversity of goals pursued by the various RIAs may help explain the multiplicity of national memberships, which raises the question on the motives for African countries to enter into specific regional integration initiatives. One of the issues that arises from this situation is to investigate the form of RIA that is most beneficial in the African context. A common yardstick is needed to assess the value of each form of RIA for the countries not only as an ex-ante decision tool, given the possibility to choose to join one form or another, but also to evaluate the welfare outcome of membership over time.[1] The approach to evaluation of the benefits of RIA membership that is used in this paper does not take into account non-economic motives such as defense or political considerations, which, arguably, may not be shared by many countries and therefore serve as common assessment tools. Consequently, economic welfare is the only goal that is assumed to be pursued by an African country considering or evaluating its RIA membership.[2]

2 The Theoretical Model

Assessment of the economic gain that accrues from regional integration is based on the theoretical model proposed by Baldwin and Venables (1995). The gain measures welfare by the level of consumption.

[1]There is debate regarding multiple membership of many African countries in more than one RIA, the African Union seeking rationalization through single membership while countries adhere to the policy of multiple membership. So far, no argumentation for or against has prevailed.

[2]There is an abundant literature on regional integration. Brenton and Hoffman (2016), Afessorgbor (2017), Draper (2010), Kritzinger-van Niekerk (undated), the East African Community (2002), the Economic Commission for Africa (2004), Lindberg and Scheingold (1971) Schiff and Winters (2003), Teunissen (1996), Volz (2011), and the World Bank examine the nature and process of regional integration. The gains from regional integration are evaluated by Fernandez (1997), Lloyd and Maclaren (1996), Mistry (1996, 2000), Mwasha (2008), and Yang and Gupta (1995).

Suppose the welfare of a representative consumer is formulated by the following indirect utility function:

$$V(p + t, n, E)$$

p = vector of border prices
t = vector of trade costs including the tariff equivalent of import barriers
n = vector of the number of product varieties available in each industry
E = Total spending on consumption

Considering that, as an accounting identity, the total of sources of income is equal to the total of applications of income (consumption and investment), consumption is equal to total income minus investment:

$$E = wL + rK + X[(p + t) - a(w, r, x)] + \alpha tm - I \tag{1}$$

Where,

L = supply of labour, K = supply of capital
r and w are factor prices for capital and labor respectively
X = production vector
a(w,r,x) = average cost that reflects the average cost and the production level in each sector
α = diagonal matrix that captures the wedge t that creates income for domestic agents given that α = 1 for a tariff or other barrier that generates domestic rent income, or α = 0 where there is no rent.
m = net imports
I = investment.

The different components of total income are:

wL + rK is total factor income, wL is labor income and rK is capital income
X[(p + t) − a(w,r,x)] is the level of profit in the economy
αtm = income accruing from import rent.

Totally differentiating the indirect utility function and dividing it by the marginal utility of expenditure gives:

$$\begin{aligned} dV/V_E &= \alpha t\, dm - m\, d[t - \alpha t] - m\, dp \\ &+ [p + t - a]\, dX - Xa_x dx + (V_n/V_E)\, dn + (R/\rho - 1)\, dI \end{aligned} \tag{2}$$

In cases of increasing returns to scale and imperfect competition

- [p + t − a] dX: is the output effect
- Xa_x dx: is the scale effect resulting from changes in average costs as firm scale changes
- (V_n/V_E) dn: is the variety effect, i.e. happens when the number of differentiated consumer products changes

- $(R/\rho - 1)$ dI: is the profitability of investment where R is the social rate of return, ρ is the social discount rate so,

  If $R > \rho$ then a positive change in investment will result in higher profits.

3 Case of African Country: Small Economy and Fixed Prices

African countries have small economies and do not enjoy a high degree of international competitiveness. They also trade very little with each other. As a result, most RIAs that they enter into seek to increase their intra-regional trade, some form of protection through high external tariff and other external trade barriers. Given their limited influence on international markets, they are price takers and face fixed prices. In other words, the following conditions apply to them: $\alpha = 1$, $t - \alpha t = 0$ and $dp = 0$

Given these three conditions, Eq. (2) reduces to

$$\begin{aligned} dV/V_E &= \alpha t\ dm \\ &+ [p + t - a]\ dX - Xa_x dx + (V_n/V_E)\ dn + (R/\rho - 1)\ dI \end{aligned} \tag{3}$$

The analysis below focuses on the welfare effect caused by changes in the factors that can result from the RIA, namely increase in imports (dm), increase in production (dX), increase in investment (dI), increase in number of sectors (dx) and increase in number of consumer products (dn). If there is economic value in regional integration, it will materialize through one or more of them.

Based on the model the conditions for positive economic value of regional integration are: $dm > 0$, $dX > 0$, $dI > 0$, $dn > 0$ and $dx < 0$.

4 The Empirical Evidence

Empirical assessment of the economic value of regional integration is conducted at the level of individual countries considering that they decide to enter or leave a RIA. Given the relatively large number of RIAs in Africa and the need to measure as accurately as possible their impact through stronger attribution of the endogenous economic variables, the cases of advanced integration are examined. In this regard, the analysis will focus on the UEMOA and CEMAC, which are customs and monetary unions, and the EAC, a customs union. The analysis will use a before-after approach which consists in comparing the levels of the endogenous variables during the years before the year of inception of the RIA and the years after its creation. Welfare is measured by Per Capita Growth Domestic Product (GDP). Considering that economic variables may change irrespective of the RIA status of the country, the residual imputation approach is used. It consists in estimating the trend of the endogenous variables for the period preceding inception of the RIA and comparing their actual values with the values that are obtained if the pre-RIA trend is extended.

The residuals that are calculated, difference between actual and trended values are considered to be the impact of the RIA; Clavaux (1969), Truman (1969). The underlying rationale is that the residuals are fully attributed to the impact of the RIA although, in reality other factors including shocks, may also be at play. Econometric techniques are proposed in the literature to address this issue but require considerable data that are not available for most African countries. As a result, the residual imputation approach is utilized in the present study despite the criticism that is leveled at it.[3]

In order to conduct the empirical inquiry two questions are investigated. The first one is whether there is an economic gain that arises from the RIA and its size. The second question addresses the speed of accrual of the gain that follows inception of the RIA.

5 Existence and Size of the Economic Gain

The measure of economic welfare that is most common in developing economies is the Per Capita GDP. Statistical data related to it are readily available from a number of sources in a standardized form. Therefore, the Per Capita GDP in constant 2010 Dollars published by the World Bank's World Development Indicators (WDI) is used in this study. As stated earlier, African countries with the most advanced agenda for regional integration are included in the sample. Specifically, they cover UEMOA countries: Benin, Burkina Faso, Côte d'Ivoire, Guinea Bissau, Mali, Niger, Senegal and Togo; CEMAC countries: Cameroon, Central African Republic, Chad, Republic of Congo, Equatorial Guinea and Gabon; and East African Community (EAC): Burundi, Kenya, Rwanda and Uganda. Tanzania has been left out for lack of data.

The technique of residual imputation is used to measure the economic gain. The Per Capita GDP trend line is computed for the years prior to the inception of the RIA. The trend equation is used to extend the trend over the RIA years thus giving projected value of the Per Capita GDP. The difference between the actual value of the Per Capita GDP and the projected value gives the imputed residual for each year in the RIA period. The rationale is that gain from RIA is attributed to the imputed residual. It is noteworthy that, at the single country level, other factors such as policy changes or shocks that are independent from regional integration could affect Per Capita GDP. However, imputed residuals can be a convenient way of assessing the

[3]Alternative econometric techniques are proposed by Aitken and Lowry (1973), Balassa (1974), Resnick and Truman (1973), Winters (1984), Coe and Moghadam (1993), Carrere (2004), Tegoum et al. (2013), Afesorgbor (2017).

economic value of regional integration if there is congruence between different countries of the same integrated zone.

Table 1 presents the results of the calculation of economic gains accruing to the member countries based on the imputed residuals. For the UEMOA the mean imputed residual, calculated over the RIA period, 1994–2016, shows a strongly significant economic gain for all the countries except for Guinea Bissau that experienced a civil war in 1998 and 1999, immediately after it became a member of UEMOA in 1997. CEMAC fared more modestly with three of the six sampled countries showing a significant gain while three others had negative mean imputed residuals. The countries, Cameroon, Congo and Gabon, have the three largest economies. This is puzzling unless one considers that the adjustment sought with

Table 1 Statistics of the mean imputed residuals

	Mean imputed residual	Standard error	t Value	Signif.	Ratio mean imputed residuals/actual values
Union economique et monétaire de Ouest Africaine (UEMOA)					
Benin	75.52	5.72	13.20	***	0.099
Burkina Faso	93.65	14.27	6.56	***	0.168
Côte d'Ivoire	324.45	55.64	5.83	***	0.246
Guinea Bissau	−176.04	14.42	−12.21		−0.331
Mali	51.49	8.20	6.28	***	0.091
Niger	115.94	17.06	6.79	***	0.327
Senegal	173.35	26.67	6.50	***	0.175
Togo	45.00	10.01	4.50	***	0.086
Communauté economique et monétaire de l'Afrique Centrale (CEMAC)					
Cameroon	−591.64	13.31	−44.44		−0.508
Central African Rep.	65.47	11.75	5.57	***	0.157
Chad	258.98	44.66	5.80	***	0.308
Congo, Republic	−1230.56	49.25	−24.99		−0.482
Equatorial Guinea	10,944.62	1367.69	8.00	***	0.862
Gabon	−1758.36	208.79	−8.42		−0.188
East African Community (EAC)					
Burundi	0.103	0.017	6.06	***	0.103
Kenya	83.469	26.206	3.19	***	0.078
Rwanda	263.12	27.95	9.41	***	0.421
Uganda	102.07	13.13	7.77	***	0.175

Note: Confidence levels are 99% (***) and 95% (**). Sampling periods are 1970–2016 for UEMOA and CEMAC countries and 1978–2016 for EAC countries except for Equatorial Guinea, 1980–2016 and Uganda 1982–2016. RIA periods are 1994–2016 for UEMOA and CEMAC and 2000–2016 for EAC. However, for Guinea Bissau the RIA period is 1997–2016. For Rwanda and Burundi it is 2007–2016 the reform underlying the RIA initiative was adequate for UEMOA countries than for CEMAC countries.

An alternative explanation could be that the economies of Cameroon, Congo and Gabon were close to their full GDP potential prior to the RIA and that after inception of the reform its costs were higher for them than its benefits. It is worth noting that Equatorial Guinea has scored a very large mean imputed residual during the RIA period, most likely owing to the very high increase in revenues from oil, its main export commodity. The East African Community has recorded results similar to UEMOA's because all four countries (Tanzania being excluded) display positive and significant mean imputed residuals.

The last column of Table 1 reports the size of the economic gain of the RIA accruing to each country. The mean Ratio of imputed residuals over Actual Values of Per Capita GDP provides the proportion of the Actual Per Capita GDP that is contributed by the RIA. In the case of UEMOA, the RIA contributed sizable shares of the Per Capita GDP, especially for Niger: 32.7%, Côte d'Ivoire: 24.6%, Senegal: 17.5% and Burkina Faso: 16.8%. As for Guinea Bissau, it lost one third (−33.1%) of its Per Capita GDP mostly owing to its civil war in 1998 and 1999.

Results of the CEMAC sub-region are more diverse, ranging from a reduction of −50.8% of Per Capita GDP of Cameroon imputed to the onset of the RIA and −48.2% for Congo to a sharp increase of 86.2% for Equatorial Guinea. Such results call into question the uniform adequacy of the reforms underlying inception of CEMAC for its member countries and, by extension, as compared to member states of UEMOA which underwent the same measures. Therefore, out of a total of 14 countries (8 for UEMOA and 6 for CEMAC) that experienced the same RIA measures, 10 recorded a significantly positive mean imputed residual which is tantamount to a positive impact of the integration initiative. Apart from the case of Guinea Bissau which saw a debilitating civil war early during its membership years, more study is needed to investigate the factors that prevented the central African countries of Cameroon, Congo and Gabon from benefitting from their RIA.

The East African Community recorded a uniform outcome of its RIA on its members. All the countries benefitted from the RIA and, except for Kenya that had a modest mean ratio of 7.8%, the mean value was considerably higher for Burundi (10.3%), Uganda (17.5% and Rwanda (42.2%). In summary, 18 African countries from various parts of the Continent were investigated and 14 reported a positive economic impact of regional integration based on the imputed residual approach.

6 Speed of the Economic Gain from Regional Integration

Assessment of the economic gain that accrues to African countries that participate in a RIA is based on identification of the year during which Actual Per Capita GDP departs significantly and consistently from the predicted values after inception of the RIA. Speed is measured by the lag between the date of inception and the beginning of departure, itself captured by the rising (or declining) imputed residual over time.

For all the figures presented below, for UEMOA, CEMAC and EAC, the inception date is indicated by a vertical line drawn in the inception year. UEMOA and CEMAC were created on the same day, in January 1994. Bissau Guinea joined UEMOA in 1997. The East African Community was operational in July 2000, and Rwanda and Burundi acceded in July 2007.

Figures 1, 2, 3, 4, 5, 6, 7, and 8 depict the evolution over time of the imputed residuals of the UEMOA countries. Except for Guinea Bissau that experienced a severe civil war in 1998–1999, an upturn starting in 1994 or the year after is the most

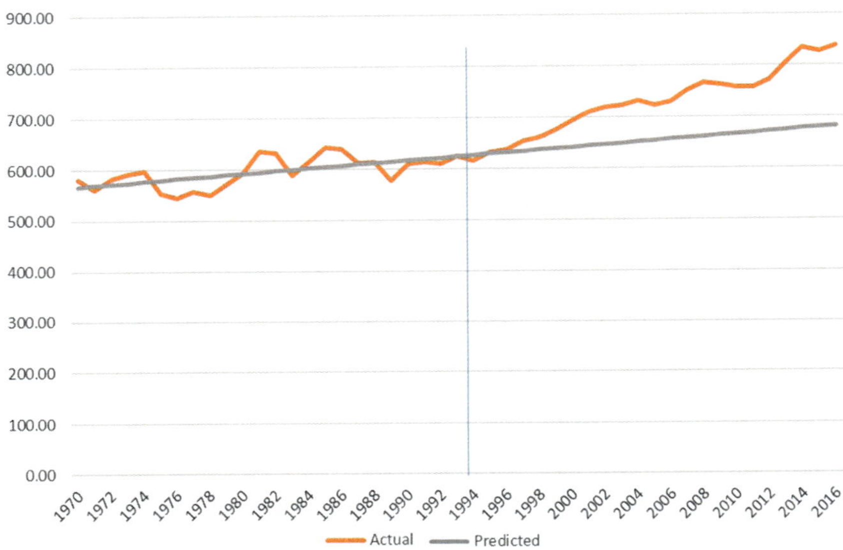

Fig. 1 Per capita GDP: Benin

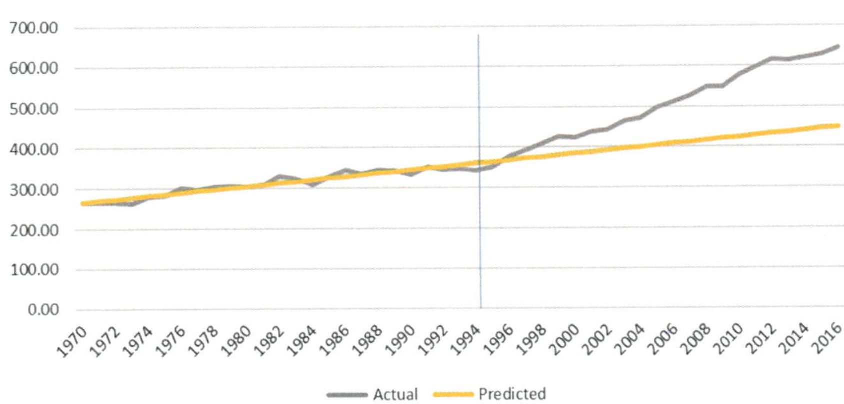

Fig. 2 Per capita GDP: Burkina Faso

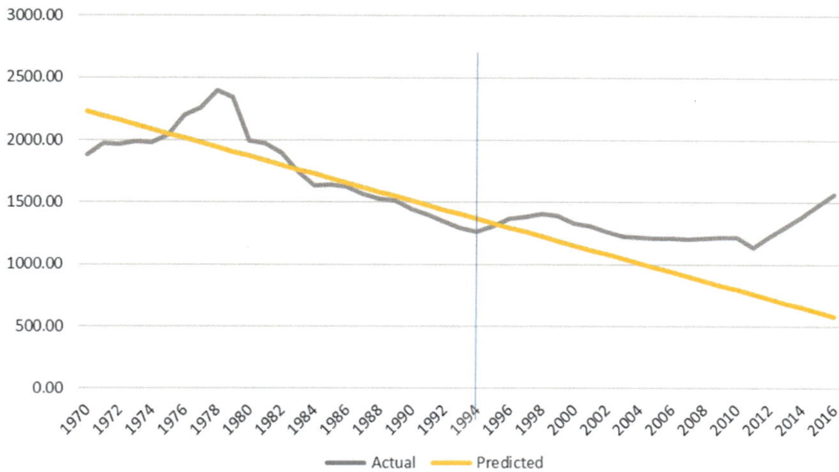

Fig. 3 Per capita GDP: Côte d'Ivoire

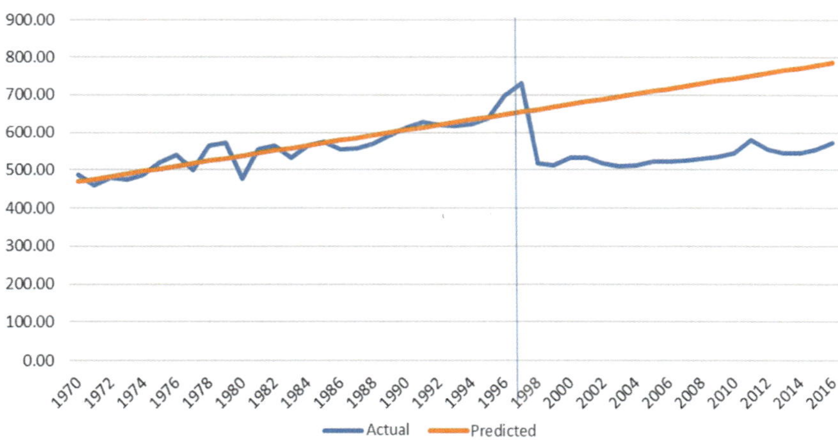

Fig. 4 Per capita GDP: Guinea Bissau

common characteristic of the countries' Per Capita GDPs. This is true even for countries, notably Côte d'Ivoire, Niger, Senegal and Togo that were on a sharp downward trend during the years prior to enactment of UEMOA. The speed of the economic gain captured by a positive and consistent imputed residual can be considered fast because the upturn is observed in 1994 for all countries, even for Guinea Bissau after the 2-year hiatus of the civil war, although to a lesser extent. Furthermore, for most countries, the speed remained constant during the 24 years after inception of UEMOA, the implicit trend line of the Actual Per Capita GDP

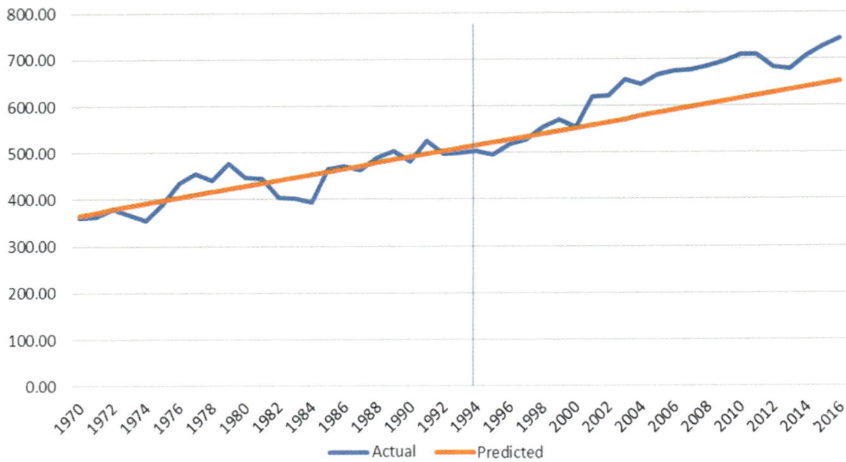

Fig. 5 Per capita GDP: Mali

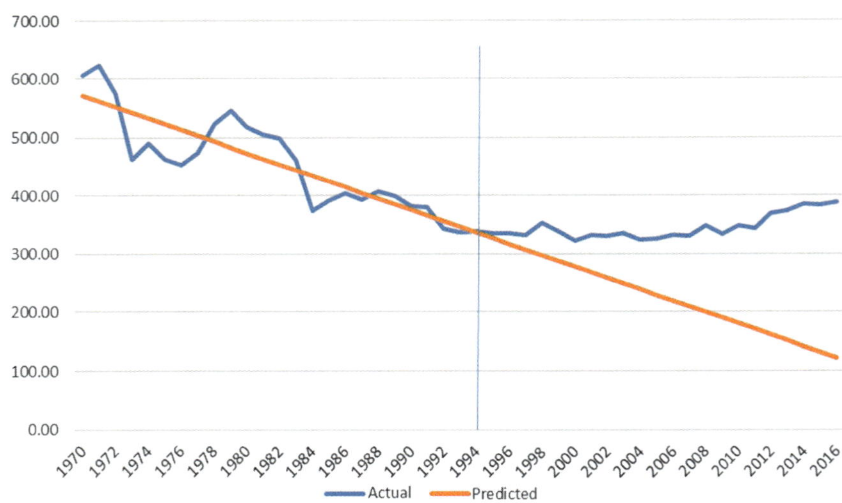

Fig. 6 Per capita GDP: Niger

having stayed relatively linear during the period 1994–2016, thus a linear increasing imputed residual over time.

Speed of the economic gain for CEMAC countries is captured in Figs. 9, 10, 11, 12, 13, and 14. Unlike in UEMOA, starting inception in 1994, these countries experienced mild variations in the imputed residuals which showed modest speed. For many countries, Cameroon, Central African Republic, Chad and Gabon, the residuals were constant for several years after 1994, and equal to zero in some cases,

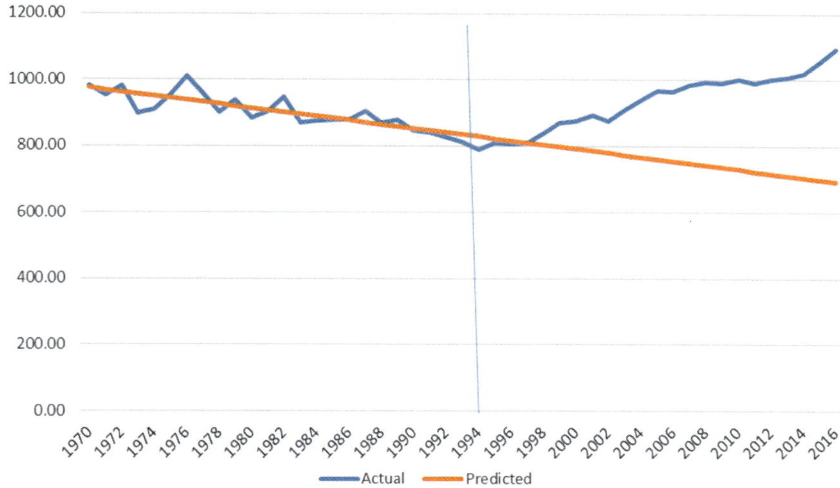

Fig. 7 Per capita GDP: Senegal

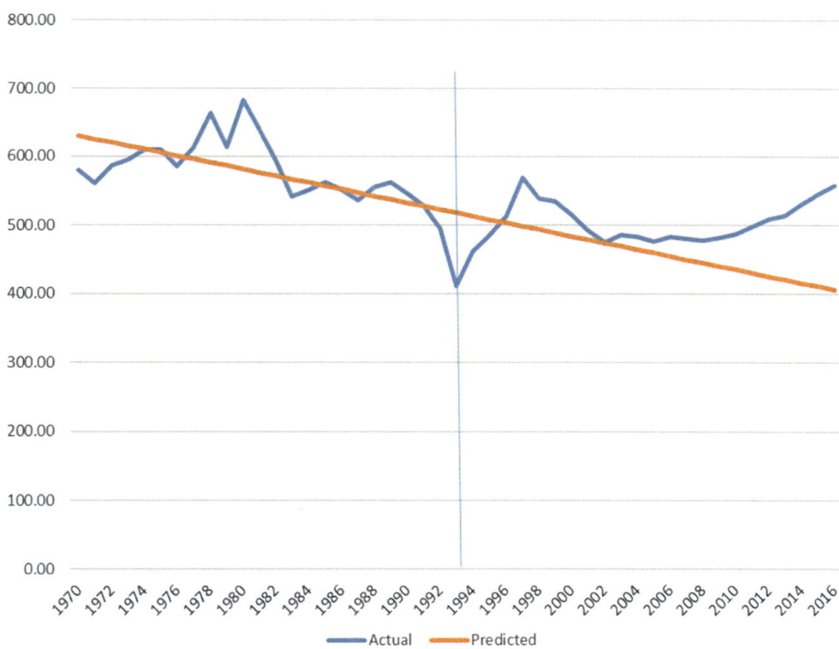

Fig. 8 Per capita GDP: Togo

thus showing slow economic gain. Finally, it can be argued that for Gabon and to a lesser extent the Central African Republic, no economic gain accrued from the CEMAC RIA.

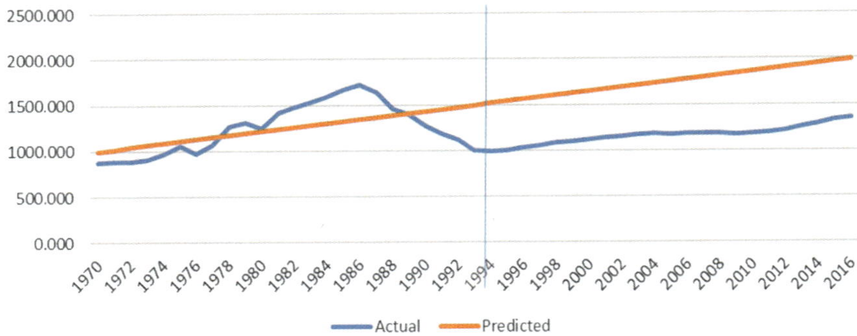

Fig. 9 Per capita GDP: Cameroon

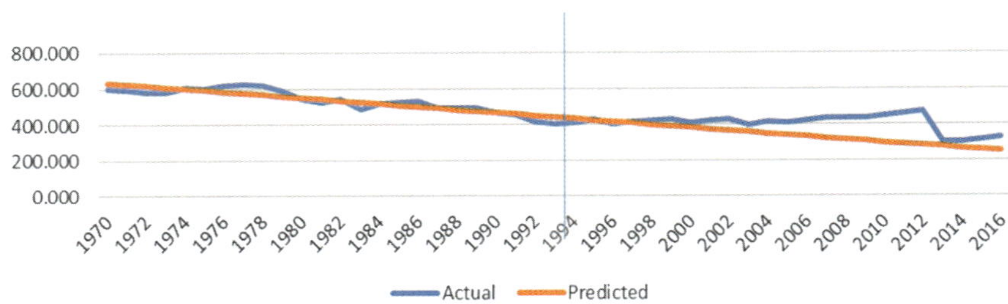

Fig. 10 Per capita GDP: Central African Republic

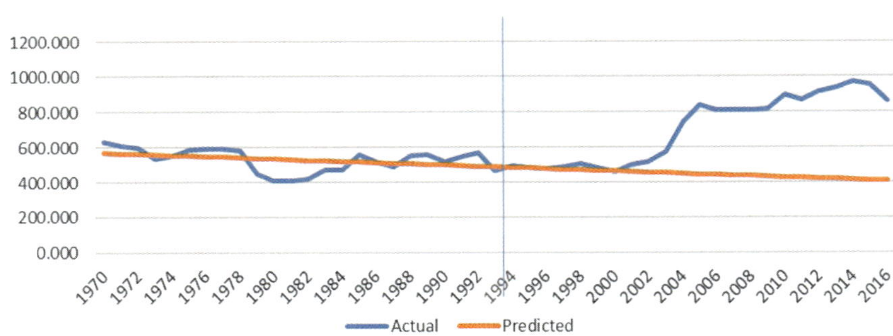

Fig. 11 Per capita GDP: Chad

Figures 15, 16, 17, and 18 display the evolution of the imputed residuals for EAC countries. Two countries, Kenya and Uganda, joined EAC in July 2000, and two others, Rwanda and Burundi, acceded in July 2007. Kenya took 4 years and Uganda 1 year to show an upturn and start benefitting from the RIA but, once the imputed residual turned positive, it increased fast almost in a straight line as can be seen from

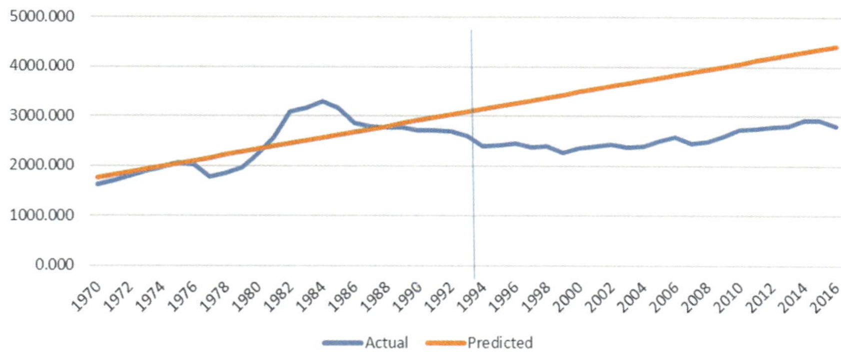

Fig. 12 Per capita GDP: Congo Republic

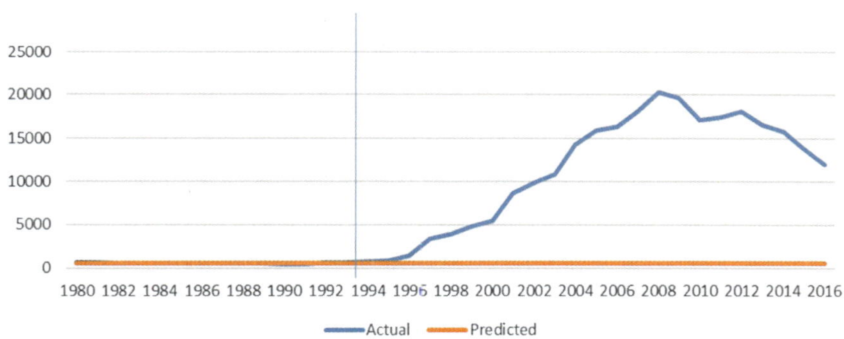

Fig. 13 Per capita GDP: Equatorial Guinea

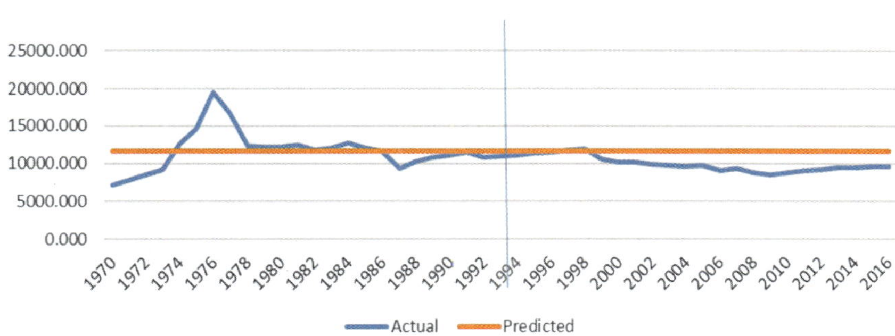

Fig. 14 Per capita GDP: Gabon

the difference between Actual and Predicted Per Capita GDP starting in 2004 for Kenya and 2001 for Uganda. The new entrants, Burundi and Rwanda, recorded an even faster economic gain following their accession in 2007, their respective imputed residuals growing linearly, albeit with a little drop following the political crisis that has afflicted the former over the last 3 years. It is noteworthy that Rwanda

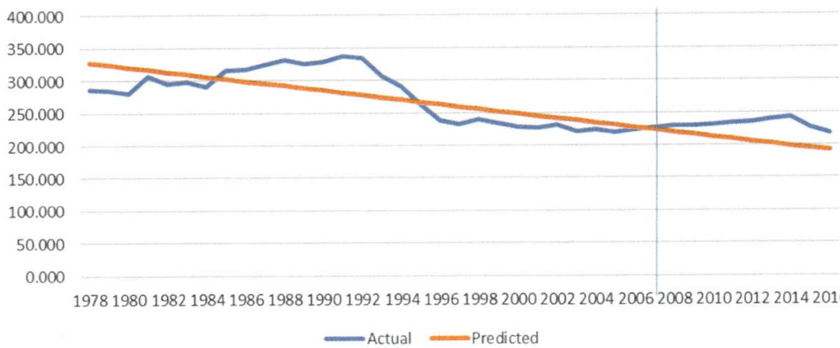

Fig. 15 Per capita GDP: Burundi

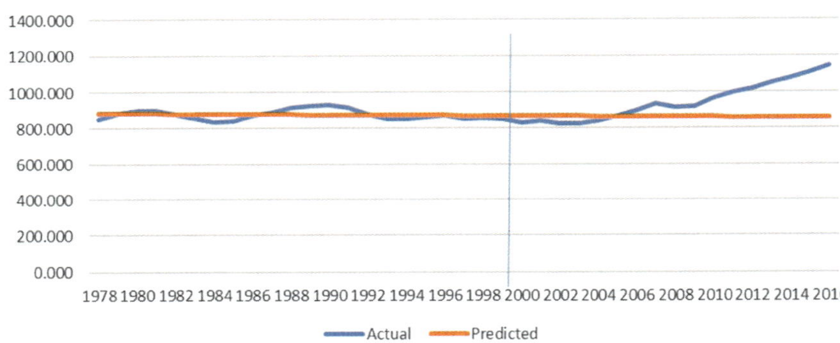

Fig. 16 Per capita GDP: Kenya

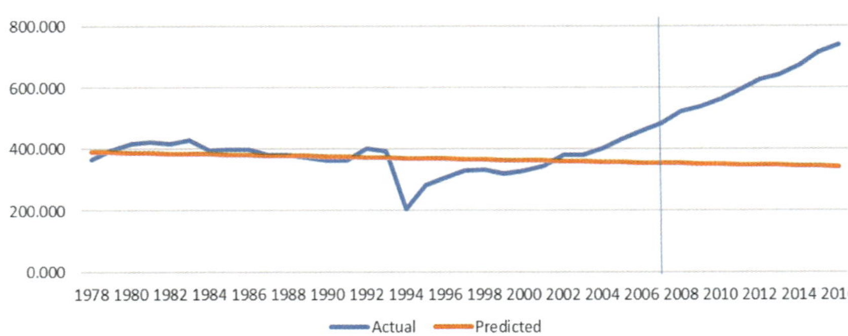

Fig. 17 Per capita GDP: Rwanda

began a fast increasing imputed residual immediately after its civil war in 1994 and kept the same pace after joining EAC, which raises the question of the relative role of the RIA in its Per Capita GDP growth relative to its own efforts, a topic for another study.

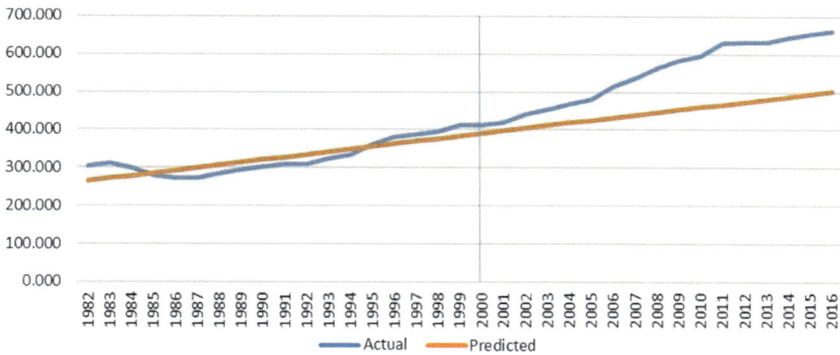

Fig. 18 Per capita GDP: Uganda

7 Conclusion

The present study sought to answer two questions regarding the economic value of regional integration in Africa. First, do African countries gain from Regional Integration Arrangements (RIA) of which they are members and what is the size of that gain? Second, how fast does the gain materialize after accession to RIA membership? The three sub-regions with the most advanced integrative agendas, UEMOA, CEMAC and EAC, were sampled. The residual imputation technique was used to compute the gain. Out of the 18 countries included in the study, 14 recorded a significant economic gain, which represented a sizable percentage of their actual Per Capita GDP after inception of the RIA. Except for Guinea Bissau that experienced a civil war immediately after it joined UEMOA, all the UEMOA and EAC countries gained from regional integration. For CEMAC, only three out of six countries benefitted from RIA although the reform measures were identical and adopted simultaneously with UEMOA. This result leads to the question whether those reforms were more attuned to the economies of the UEMOA sub-region than to those of CEMAC.

With respect to the speed of the economic gain, most UEMOAS countries had an immediate reaction, within a year or two, to the RIA enactment and benefitted from that new source of growth for a sustained period. Benin, Burkina Faso, Mali and Senegal had the fastest reactive gains. The speed of the gain was more modest for CEMAC countries and, except for Chad and Equatorial Guinea that benefitted mostly from a sharp increase in their oil revenues, they did not show immediate economic gains and recorded unchanged Per Capita GDP over several years after inception of the RIA. Accrual of the gain for EAC countries was uniformly immediate, not unlike in the case of UEMOA. The upturn of the Per Capita GDP during the year of accession to EAC membership was significant for all countries while Rwanda maintained previously strong growth well before joining the RIA, in fact immediately after its 1994 civil war.

Results of the present study have given empirical evidence that there is economic value in regional integration in Africa, most sampled countries having benefitted from it in several sub-regions of the Continent. However, several questions remain unanswered. First, considering Eq. (3), what factors are the main determinants of the economic gain that arises from regional integration? Second, why did some countries that had no specific adverse shock such as civil war fail to benefit from regional integration? Third, would more advanced integrative agendas yield higher gains for participating countries? Finally, would alternative measurement techniques give results that differ from the ones obtained through residual imputation? Clearly, investigation of the economic value of regional integration in Africa is of significant interest and calls for more studies.

References

Afessorgbor, S. K. (2017). Revisiting the effect of regional integration on African trade: Evidence from meta-analysis and gravity model. *The Journal of International Trade and Economic Development, 26*, 133–153.

Aitken, N., & Lowry, W. (1973). A cross-sectional study of the effects of LAFTA and CACM on Latin American trade. *Journal of Common Market Studies, 11*, 326–336.

Balassa, B. (1974). Trade creation and trade diversion in the European common market: An appraisal of the evidence. *Manchester School of Economic and Social Studies, 42*, 93–135.

Baldwin, R. E., & Venables, A. J. (1995). Regional economic integration (Chapter 31). In: G. Grossman & K Rogoff (Eds.), *Handbook of international economics* (Vol. III, pp. 1597–1644). Elsevier Science B.V.

Brenton, P., & Hoffman, B. (2016, February). *Political economy of regional integration in Sub-Saharan Africa*. World Bank Group, 154 pp.

Carriere, C. (2004). African regional agreements: Impact on trade with or without currency unions. *Journal of African Economies, 13*, 199–239.

Clavaux, F. (1969). The import elasticity as a yardstick for measuring trade creation. *Economia Internazionale, 22*, 606–612.

Coe, D., & Moghadam, R. (1993). Capital and trade as engines of growth in France: An application of Johansen's cointegration methodology. *International Monetary Fund Staff Papers, 40*, 542–566.

Draper, P. (2010). *Rethinking the (European) foundations of sub-Saharan African regional economic integration*. OECD Development Center. Working Paper.

East African Community. (2002). *The treaty for the establishment of the East African community*. EAC: 2002 xiv, EAC Publication No. 1, Arusha, Tanzania.

Economic Commission for Africa. (2004). *Assessing regional integration in Africa*. Ethiopis: Addis Ababa.

Fernandez, R. (1997). *Returns to regionalism: An evaluation of nontraditional gains from regional trade agreements*. World Bank Research Working Paper No. 1816.

Kritzinger-van Niekerk, L. (Undated). *Regional integration: Concepts, advantages, disadvantages and lessons of experience*. World Bank, 12 pp.

Lindberg, L., & Scheingold, S. A. (1971). *Regional integration: Theory and research*. Cambridge: Harvard University Press.

Lloyd, P. J., & Maclaren, D. (1996). Gains and losses from regional trading agreements: A survey. *The Economic Record, 80*(251), 445–467.

Mistry, P. S. (1996). *Regional integration arrangements in economic development, Panacea or Pitfall?* The Hague: FONDAD.

Mistry, P. S. (2000). Africa's record of regional cooperation and integration. *African Affairs, 99*, 553–557.

Mwasha, O. (2008). The benefits of regional economic integration for developing countries in Africa: A case of East African community. *Korean Review of International Studies, 11*(1), 69–92.

Resnick, S. A., & Truman, E. M. (1973). An empirical examination of bilateral trade in Western Europe. *Journal of International Economics, 3*, 305–335.

Schiff, M., & Winters, L. A. (2003). *Regional integration and development*. World Bank.

Tegoum, P. J. N., Nakelse, P., & Ngwesse, R. (2013). Growth and convergence in Africa: A dynamic panel approach. In *Wealth through integration and poverty-reduction strategies in Africa* (pp. 43–68). New York: Springer.

Teunissen, J. J. (1996). *Regionalism and the global economy, The case of Africa*. The Hague: FONDAD.

Truman, E. M. (1969). The European economic community: Trade creation and trade diversion. *Yale Economic Essays, 9*, 201–257.

Volz, U. (2011). *Regional integration, economic development and global governance*. Cheltenham: Edward Elgar.

Winters, L. A. (1984). Separability and the specification of foreign trade functions. *Journal of International Economics, 17*, 239–263.

Yang, Y., & Gupta, S. (1995). *Regional trade arrangement in Africa: Past performance and the way forward*. IMF Working Paper WP/05/36.

Current Account Im(balances) and Adjustments to Targets for Regional Integration in West Africa: One Step Forward, Two Steps Backwards

Chuku Chuku, Johnson Atan, Felix Obioesio, and Kenneth Onye

Contents

Abstract In this paper, we seek to answer three main questions: first, what are the long- and short-run determinants of current account balances in West Africa; second, is there a sustainable path for the current account position that is consistent with regional integration; and if yes, what has been the process of adjustment towards such a path. We address these questions by first identifying the long-term determinants of the current account, and then using the results to calculate the equilibrium sustainable targets for the current account in the region. After accounting for short-run disequilibrium adjustment processes, we show how far apart each country is from the regionally sustainable path. The key findings are as follows: the determinants of current account dynamics differ depending on the time horizon; the real

C. Chuku (✉)
Department of Economics, University of Uyo, Uyo, Nigeria

Macroeconomic Policy, Forecasting and Research Department, African Development Bank, Abidjan, Ivory Coast
e-mail: c.chuku@afdb.org; chukuchuku@uniuyo.edu.ng

J. Atan · F. Obioesio · K. Onye
Department of Economics, University of Uyo, Uyo, Nigeria

D. Seck (ed.), *The External Sector of Africa's Economy*, Advances in African Economic, Social and Political Development,
https://doi.org/10.1007/978-3-319-97913-7_2

exchange rate, fiscal policy, trade openness, investment, and income levels are the key determinants in the short run; there is considerable variation in the deviation of each countries' current account position from the regionally sustainable equilibrium path. Some implications for policy are highlighted.

1 Introduction

Current account (im)balances and the process of adjustment to desirable and sustainable levels that are consistent with the regional integration objectives of the West African Monetary Zone (WAMZ) are two key aspects of regional economic integration that have received little or no attention from the research and policy communities. For the West African sub-region, the problem is more compounded because, although there is some knowledge about what the structural determinants of the current account is elsewhere—for example, in industrial and developing economies, see Chinn and Prasad (2003), and for Europe, Belke and Dreger (2013); Gosse and Serranito (2014)—there is hardly any evidence on the structural determinants of the current account in West Africa.[1]

Understanding the factors that influence the fluctuation of the current account in the short and long-term is important primarily because it is a crucial indicator of the relative health of the external sector of an economy, and it is a key dimension for proper policy guidance towards achieving the economic integration goals of the West African region. This is particularly so because the sustainability of current account positions has been indicted severally as having contributed to the recent macroeconomic instability that has been experienced by the European and East Asian regional economic blocks (see Obstfeld and Rogoff 2009; Gruber and Kamin 2007). The implication, therefore, is that if the behaviour of the current account is not properly understood and carefully managed in the region, it could as well be the source of severe macroeconomic instability in the West African region, if it has not already been.

Moreover, a carefully stylized characterization of the region reveals unique structural peculiarities: alarming levels of current account deficits in recent years, poor rates of growth, heavy reliance on imports and foreign aid, low savings and financial mobilization, high concentration of imports of primary commodities, and large macroeconomic distortions (see Calderon et al. 2007). Given these realities, knowledge of the current account levels that may be considered to be 'sustainable' for regional integration based on the macroeconomic, political and demographic characteristics of countries in the region would be a vital part of the information set

[1]Osakwe and Verick (2007) and Calderon et al. (2007) are exceptions in the sense that they consider the determinants for Africa as a whole.

required for policy synchronization to achieve better regional economic integration in West Africa.

In the light of the above, we are interested in three main questions: first, what are the long- and short-run determinants of current account balances in West Africa; two, is there a sustainable path for the current account position that is consistent with regional integration; and if yes, what is the process of adjustment towards such a path? To address these questions, we follow a two-prong approach. In the first stage, we seek to identify the long-term determinants of current account balances in West Africa, using newly developed panel cointegration techniques that particularly account for cross-sectional dependencies (Westerlund 2007). Secondly, we use the results from the first stage to do three things: first, we calculate the joint long-run targets, which are interpreted as the equilibrium sustainable target of the current account variable for the region; second, we account for short-run disequilibrium adjustment processes; and third, we separate the series country-by-country and show how far apart each country is from the regionally sustainable path for the current account.

The main contribution of the paper goes beyond the fact that we use second-generation panel unit root and cointegration testing schemes, which improves on the power and size limitations of conventional first-generation tests. But more importantly, the policy-relevant exercise of showing the current account (im)balances for each country, and comparing the actual values to the regionally sustainable equilibrium path, using recent methodologies applied by Gosse and Serranito (2014) and Lane and Milesi-Ferretti (2012) distinguishes the paper from many other studeis. These results shed light on the policy implications of current account dynamics for regional integration, not only in terms of magnitudes, but also in terms of the direction for policy.

The main results of the paper can be summarized as follows: (i) the determinants of current account dynamics in West Africa are different in the short and long run, in particular, the effects of a depreciation in the real exchange rate and an increasing national income work to worsen the current account balance in the long term; whereas, it works to improve it in the short term; (ii) fiscal policy is a significant determinant of the current account both in the long run and short run and the 'twin deficits' hypothesis does not necessarily hold for West African economies; (iii) the process of adjustment back to equilibrium is relatively fast, with an estimated 'half-life of around 1½ years; (iv) there is considerable variation by country in the deviation of the current account positions from the equilibrium targets.

The balance of the paper is as follows. In Sect. 2, we present a stylized characterization of current account balances and their postulated structural determinants in West Africa, focusing on the unconditional correlations, densities, and their between- and within-sample properties. In Sect. 3, we explore the literature review, making a clear demarcation between theoretical and empirical contributions, and also contributions between industrial and developing economies. Section 4 contains the empirical strategy, with a brief description of data sources. In Sect. 5, the results from the empirical exercises are reported and discussed, including some policy implications. Section 6 contains the conclusion of the paper.

2 Stylized Facts and Unconditional Relationships

In this section, we descriptively interrogate the data on current account balances (as a ratio of GDP) and some identified structural determinants of the current account, with a view to gaining intuition about the unconditional relationships that exist between the current account balance and some macroeconomic variables in West Africa.

In Fig. 1, we plot the trend of the current account positions of selected countries in the region. Just by eye-balling the chart, it is obvious to see that most of the countries in the region have consistently maintained significant current account deficits. In particular, countries like Benin, Burkina-Faso, Ghana, Guinea-Bissau, Niger, Senegal, Sierra Leone, and Togo have had persistent and large current account deficits since the 1980s until recently. One possible explanation for the observed protracted deficit positions is the persistent deterioration of the terms of trade conditions for many of these economies. Nigeria, however, seems to be an exception, as the current account position has been switching almost evenly from surplus to deficit positions over the same period. This is understandable, especially given the oil component of Nigeria's export composition, which is likely to be driven by booms and busts in the international price of crude oil. Cote d'Ivoire has, however, had some sustained episodes of current account surpluses in recent years, this could be as a result of the return of peace in the country, and the booming tourism sector.

The next question we ask is whether the current account positions of countries in the region could tell us something about the nature of the cross-sectional growth performance in the region. To answer this question we plot a cross-sectional scatter chart of the current account positions and growth performance of countries in the region for the year 2011 in Fig. 2. From the figure, it is not obvious that any conclusion can be made about the relationship between the current account and growth performance of West African economies. For example, we see a situation where it is possible for a country to have a current account surplus and yet record poor growth rates. This is the case for Cote d'Ivoire with a surplus current account balance and a growth rate of around −5.00% in 2011. This is in contrast with Nigeria, which had a surplus current account balance and a positive growth rate in 2011—somewhere around 7%.

On the other hand, we also see a situation where countries with significant current account deficits achieve high growth rates e.g., Ghana, and at the same time, some others achieve very low growth rates, e.g., The Gambia. We are, however, careful not to impose any structural interpretation on these patterns, especially because it is only a snapshot of the relationship at a specific time. However, we are able to conclude that the growth performance of countries in the region does not necessarily depend on their current account positions, it is more likely that the current account interacts with several other structural variables to determine individual country growth rates in the region.

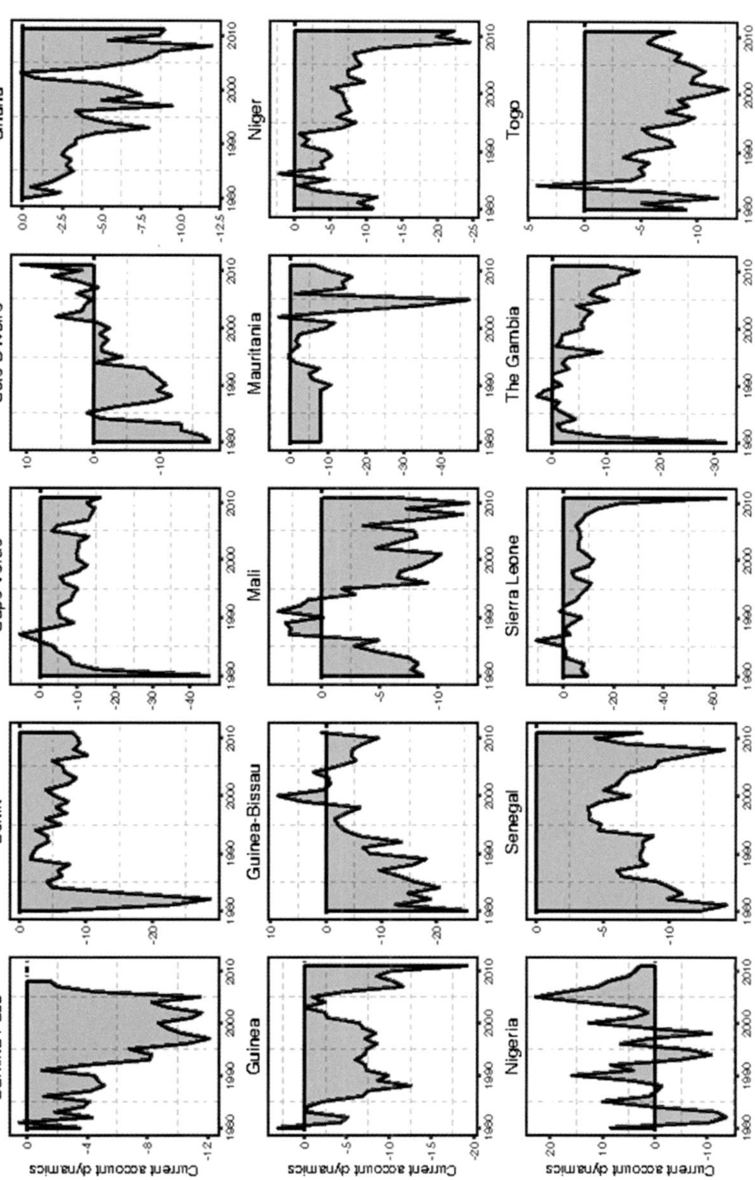

Fig. 1 Trend of current account/GDP in West African Countries

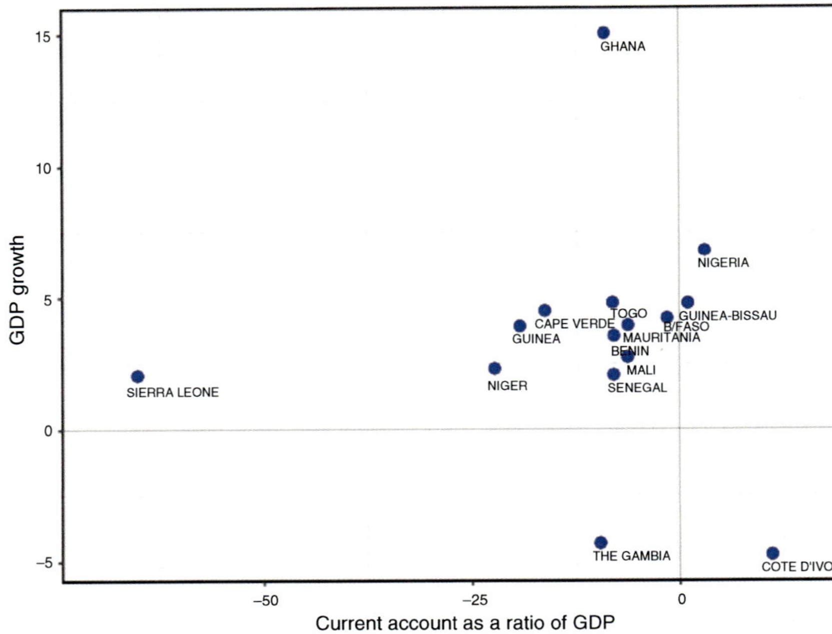

Fig. 2 Current account and GDP growth in West Africa: cross section at 2011

Next, we consider the unconditional correlations between the current account and some hypothesized drivers of the current account. In Fig. 3, we plot the scatter plots for the current account and some selected macroeconomic variables, superimposing a non-parametric regression line to help us understand the bilateral nature of the relationships without imposing linearity restrictions. The plot also contains the histograms of the variables, to help us examine the nature of the individual distributions of the variables, and finally, the unconditional correlation matrix for each pair.

By looking at Fig. 3, it is possible to validate the results from the previous section. In particular, when we look at the scatter plot between the current account (CA) and the growth rate (GDPG), we observe a near horizontal line (no relationship) pattern with a correlation coefficient of 0.06; hence, it is difficult to tell a priori the relationship between the current account and economic growth in the region. This is in contrast with the stylised characterization in Calderon et al. (2007), which shows that the current account is negatively correlated with growth in a pooled sample of all African economies.

The correlation between the current account and real exchange rate is negative but low, approximately −0.17, and there is no evidence of a non-linear relationship when we examine the fitted regression lines from the scatter plot. As for the fiscal balance, the correlation coefficient is negative, approximately −0.21, however, from

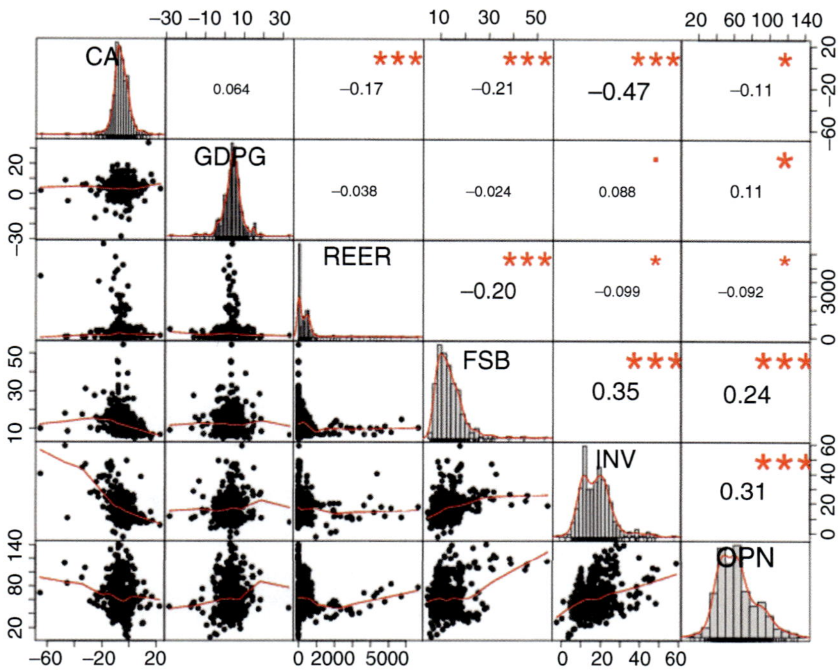

Fig. 3 Scatter plots, correlation matrix and histograms of structural determinants. Note: Illustration is based on data from WEO and WDI. The lower triangular matrix contains the scatter plots with a non-parametric fitted regression line, the diagonal displays the histograms (density) of the variables, and the upper triangular matrix contains the Spearman's correlations, which gets bolder with larger positive values and smaller with more negative correlations

the pairwise scatter plot, it is clear that this relationship is not linear—at lower levels of the current account, the relationship seems to be positive.

Finally, investment and openness have a monotonic and statistically significant negative relationship with the current account at with a correlation coefficient of −0.47 and −0.11 respectively. In addition, the histogram of the openness variable seems to suggest that the variable has a bi-modal distribution. In summary, what we find is that the relationship between the current account and its potential structural determinants in West Africa seems to be slightly different from what has been observed in developing countries and the entire African sample at large. There is also some evidence to suggest non-linearities and bimodality in the distribution of some variables. Other summary statistics including means and standard deviations by country and for the entire panel for each variable is presented in Table 1.

Table 1 Country level descriptive statistics of the current account and its structural determinants

	CA		lnGDP		REER		FSB		INV		Finop		OPN		INFL	
	Mean	SD	Mean	SD	Mean	SD	Mean	SD	Mean	SD	Mean	SD	Mean	SD	Mean	SD
Burkina Faso	−5.730	(3.694)	5.774	(0.202)	3.614	(2.097)	19.89	(4.151)	19.18	(2.755)	0.223	(0.108)	37.04	(4.336)	3.993	(5.648)
Benin	−7.393	(5.597)	6.201	(0.0763)	452.1	(143.0)	13.14	(2.009)	17.52	(4.313)	0.284	(0.125)	51.86	(7.166)	3.506	(7.049)
Cape Verde	−9.313	(8.122)	7.148	(0.584)	82.66	(17.91)	10.04	(3.443)	15.34	(12.34)	0.162	(0)	83.71	(12.70)	4.699	(3.302)
Cote D'ivoire	−3.535	(6.904)	6.969	(0.136)	452.1	(143.0)	11.96	(4.260)	12.27	(4.228)	0.238	(0.116)	75.08	(10.80)	5.122	(5.242)
Ghana	−4.719	(3.023)	6.062	(0.187)	0.417	(0.496)	10.89	(2.260)	17.45	(7.602)	0.539	(0.416)	60.69	(30.87)	31.52	(26.80)
Guinea	−6.263	(4.424)	5.827	(0.347)	1788.9	(1861.1)	10.41	(3.600)	19.18	(4.089)	0.162	(0)	64.79	(17.01)	13.02	(6.249)
Guinea-Bissau	−7.288	(7.837)	6.109	(0.108)	309.6	(266.6)	11.01	(7.042)	21.31	(12.39)	0.151	(0.0567)	49.58	(8.641)	22.67	(23.11)
Mali	−5.060	(4.620)	5.925	(0.162)	452.1	(143.0)	12.30	(2.723)	20.82	(3.844)	0.284	(0.125)	57.95	(9.596)	3.662	(5.186)
Mauritania	−9.137	(9.610)	6.526	(0.0814)	20.75	(7.743)	21.17	(8.218)	25.37	(10.41)	0.169	(0.0434)	104.0	(23.04)	5.925	(2.811)
Niger	−7.573	(5.840)	5.669	(0.135)	452.1	(143.0)	13.86	(2.175)	15.90	(9.166)	0.263	(0.119)	47.07	(10.01)	3.443	(8.647)
Nigeria	3.132	(8.857)	6.476	(0.220)	64.87	(58.35)	10.12	(3.756)	12.97	(8.075)	0.249	(0.0643)	55.35	(16.71)	20.69	(18.46)
Senegal	−7.742	(2.817)	6.571	(0.0669)	452.1	(143.0)	15.87	(3.052)	20.50	(3.371)	0.284	(0.125)	65.25	(9.357)	4.348	(7.037)
Sierra Leone	−7.753	(11.90)	5.828	(0.160)	1345.0	(1366.6)	9.585	(1.979)	10.70	(7.261)	0.246	(0.133)	45.92	(12.31)	4.998	(3.976)
The Gambia	−5.517	(6.584)	6.069	(0.0372)	13.81	(9.260)	16.33	(11.65)	16.28	(9.018)	0.699	(0.358)	79.74	(25.13)	9.540	(10.39)
Togo	−7.255	(3.123)	6.016	(0.0949)	452.1	(143.0)	13.08	(3.613)	16.74	(3.463)	0.162	(0)	87.51	(14.08)	4.915	(8.221)
Panel	−6.076	(7.234)	6.211	(0.476)	422.8	(776.2)	13.31	(6.013)	17.44	(8.307)	0.274	(0.220)	64.37	(23.62)	9.470	(14.37)

Notes: SD is the standard deviation of the variables which are reported in parenthesis. CA is current account as a ratio of GDP, lnGDP is the log of GDP per capita, REER is the real effective exchange rate, FSB is the fiscal balance, INV is for investments, Finop is a measure of financial openness, OPN is for trade openness, and INFL is for inflation

3 What Drives Current Account Balances?

Within the theoretical literature there exist some robust analysis and models that try to explain the determinants of CA dynamics. However, these different models offer diverse proposals on the predictions about the factors underlying the CA dynamics and consequently provides dissimilar economic policy implications. In general, three notable theoretical frameworks have been widely used in modelling current account determinants: the absorption approach, the elasticity approach, and the intertemporal approach.

The elasticity approach treats the current account balance as the sum of trade balance and net international investment income. It is mainly based on the analysis of price elasticity of demand for imports and that of demand for exports, with respect to changes in exchange rate. In a typical elasticity approach, the current account balance is mainly determined by the real exchange rate, domestic output and foreign output. This approach is largely applied to evaluate the effect of currency depreciation or appreciation on the current account balance. In particular, it is used to examine if currency depreciation can help improve the current account balance. Therefore, the elasticity approach highly emphasizes the role of exchange rate and trade flows in current account adjustments (Cheung et al. 2010).

The absorption approach considers the current account balance as the difference between income and absorption, or equivalently, the difference between savings and investment. It is also known as the saving-investment balance approach. This approach is a macroeconomic approach. It investigates the effect of exchange rate change on trade balance through the absorption channel whereby income and relative prices change and adjust. This approach states that if an economy spends more than it produces (i.e. absorption exceeds income), it must import from other countries for its excess consumption and spending—this economy thus runs a current account deficit. On the other hand, if this economy spends less than it produces (i.e. income exceeds absorption), it runs a current account surplus. Since the sum of current account and capital account must equal zero, ex-post in a flexible exchange rate regime, shocks that occur first in the capital account will eventually affect the current account and vice versa (Dornbusch and Fischer 1980; Cheung et al. 2010).

The intertemporal approach, which is derived from the absorption approach, also considers the current account balance from a saving-investment perspective. This approach suggests that an economy runs a current account surplus if national income is temporarily high or investment temporarily low. However, the intertemporal approach is a microeconomic-based analysis, while the absorption approach is a macroeconomic based analysis. To be more specific, it recognizes the current account balance as the result of optimization decisions of economic agents. This approach achieves a synthesis between the trade and financial flow perspectives by recognizing how macroeconomic factors influence future relative prices and how relative prices affect saving and investment decisions (Obstfeld and Rogoff 1995).

Analysing CA dynamics from an intertemporal saving-investment perspective has become the dominant approach in modern empirical literature following the work of Sachs (1981) and its generalization by Obstfeld and Rogoff (1994, 1995), which is now arguably the 'workhorse' model of modern international macroeconomics. The main insight offered by this approach is that intertemporal utility maximization of a representative household or profit-maximizing firm, infinitely lived agents lead to smooth consumption paths, where the CA via the savings rate acts as a buffer against temporary income shocks. A direct implication of the model is that CA deficits are likely whenever investment is high or income is temporarily low.

The empirical findings from previous studies on CA dynamics allow a rough classification in two groups: on the one hand, Ghosh and Ostry (1995), Glick and Rogoff (1995), Nason and Rogers (2006), and Giuliodori (2004), among others, have implemented the intertemporal model by means of vector autoregressions; on the other hand, regression-based studies have been used by Debelle and Faruqee (1996), Calderon et al. (2007), Chinn and Prasad (2003), and Bussiere et al. (2004). The latter contributions concentrate on panel techniques (mainly between and dynamic FE regressions) to uncover the determinants of the CA. The typical approach is to regress the CA measured as a ratio of GDP on a set of variables, thought to determine saving or investment rates. Apart from addressing the impact of cyclical output and price changes (exchange rates, terms of trade), this strand of the literature refers to a broad set of intertemporal models. Firstly, the so-called 'twin deficits hypothesis', which states that there is a positive relationship between the fiscal balance and the CA in the absence of (perfect) Ricardian off-setting.

Secondly, a postulated connection between CA positions and the stage of a country's economic development also exists. According to this argument countries at some early stage of development have a high marginal productivity of capital and, hence, tend to accumulate external debt to finance economic growth. At later stages of development, these countries have to repay their debts, leading to CA surpluses for mature economies. Finally, life-cycle considerations have given rise to the hypothesis that countries with a relatively large share of dependents to total population tend to have worse CA positions since dependents are unable to accumulate savings.

The result emanating from these works have been mixed. Again while some studies point to some factors as significantly correlated with CA dynamics, others only treat such factors peripherally. Khan and Knight (1983) investigate the evolution of the current account balances for 32 non-oil developing countries over the period 1973–1980 by using a pooled time-series cross-section data and adopting an Ordinary Least Square (OLS) estimation approach. Their results indicate that both internal factors (the increase in fiscal deficits and the appreciation in real effective exchange rates) and external factors (the deterioration in terms of trade, the decline of economic growth, and the increase in foreign real interest rates) are important in explaining the deterioration of the current account of the countries under review.

Debelle and Faruqee (1996) try to explain both short-run dynamics and long-run variations of the current account by using a panel data of 21 industrial countries over the period 1971–1993 and also an extended cross-section data that includes an additional 34 industrial and developing countries. They adopt a saving-investment perspective to motivate empirical specifications that contain the structural determinants of current accounts. Their work finds that relative income, government debt, and demographic factors play a significant role in the long-run variation of the current account in the cross-section, while fiscal surplus, terms of trade and capital controls do not. Also, by estimating partial-adjustment and error-correction models using panel data, they find that fiscal policy has both short-run and long-run impacts on the current account in the time series. Furthermore, they find that the real exchange rate, the business cycle and the terms of trade also have short-run effects on the current account.

Calderon et al. (2002) attempt to extend the work of Debelle and Faruqee (1996) by applying more advanced econometric techniques to control for joint endogeneity and by distinguishing between within economy and cross-economy effects. They used a panel data of 44 developing countries over the period 1966–1995 to examine the empirical links between current account deficits and a broad set of economic variables proposed in the literature. By adopting a reduced-form approach rather than holding a particular structural model, they find that current account deficits in developing countries are moderately persistent. Higher domestic output growth, increase in the terms of trade and the real exchange rate appreciation tend to worsen the current account deficit. On the other hand, increases in the public and private savings, higher growth rates in industrial countries and higher international interest rates have favourable impacts on the current account balance.

Chinn and Prasad (2003) investigate the medium-term determinants of current accounts by adopting a structural approach that highlights the roles of the fundamental macroeconomic determinants of saving and investment. Their basic data set has annual data for 18 industrial and 71 developing countries and covers the period 1971–1995. Both cross-section and panel regression techniques are used in their study to examine the properties of current account variation across countries and over time. They find that initial stocks of net foreign assets and government budget balances have positive effects on current account balances. In addition, they also find that measures of financial deepening are positively correlated while indicators of openness to international trade are negatively correlated with current account balances among developing countries.

Gruber and Kamin (2007) assess some of the explanations that have been put forward for the global pattern of current account imbalances that have emerged in recent years, particularly the large U.S. current account deficit and the large surpluses of the developing Asian economies. Their work is based on that of Chinn and Prasad (2003), using a panel data of 61 countries over the period 1982–2003 and including the standard current account determinants (per capita income, relative growth rates, fiscal balance, demographic factors and international trade openness). They find that the Asian surpluses can be well explained by a model that incorporates, in addition to standard determinants, the impact of financial crises on current accounts. However, their model fails to explain the large U.S. current account deficit even when the model is augmented by measures of institutional quality.

In an attempt to ascertain the empirical short and medium term link between CA balance and some economic variables for the Middle East and North African countries, Aristovnik (2007) employed the dynamic panel regression technique to account for the characterization of the variation in the CA balance in the selected countries. His results are generally consistent with theoretical and previous empirical analyses and indicate that higher (domestic and foreign) investment, government expenditure and foreign interest rates have a negative effect on the current account balance. He further submits that a more open economy, higher oil prices, and domestic economic growth generate an improvement in the external balance, whereas the latter implies that the domestic growth rate is associated with a larger increase in domestic savings than investment. Finally, the results show a relatively high persistence of current accounts and reject the validity of the stages of development hypothesis as poorer countries in the region reveal a higher current account surplus (or lower deficit) relative to their richer counterparts.

To the best of our knowledge, only Oshota and Badejo (2015) have, in recent times, made concerted effort to uncover the key determinants of CA dynamics in West Africa. The conclusion reached by this study indicates that in the long run, GDP per capita, investment (*INV*), broad money supply (M_2) and DER in PMG model positively impact CA balance while the real effective exchange rate (*REER*) has a negative and statistically significant long-term effect on CA balance. The results of the DFE model employed by the study suggest that an increase in *GDP* per capita and M_2 increases CA balance in the long run while, in the short run, *INV* exert positive impact on CA balance in the two models. An increase in *REER* has a significant negative impact on CAB. The presence of a long-run relationship between the CA balance and some of its determinants as shown by Oshota and Badejo (2015) implies the effectiveness of targeting one of the variables in influencing the long run behaviour of other variables by policy makers. However, this study fails to account for the transitory adjustment of the CA balance to its equilibrium state. It also does not stipulate the degree of persistence of CA deficits in the result. Our main proposition in the current paper is to ascertain factors that account for transitory and persistent changes in the CA balance in West Africa.

3.1 Industrialized Versus Developing Economies

Within the literature, there exists a dichotomy concerning the factors that typically determine CA dynamics in developed and developing economies. This dichotomy is clearly shown in the study by Chinn and Prasad (2003) which indicates that CA dynamics systematically differ across developed and developing countries. Some of the key factors for developing countries, as pointed out by Khan and Knight (1983) and Calderon et al. (2007), include worsening terms of trade position, sluggish economic activities in industrialized economies, rising cost of capital (interest rate) and financial assets in the international credit market, poor domestic adjustment to external shocks, high deficit fiscal balance, and sharp appreciation in real effective exchange rate. Though not exhaustive, this list effectively captures the fundamental variables that have been identified in the literature.

The list of determinants can be classified into two broad categories: external and domestic factors. For explanatory purposes, it may be convenient to view the first three factors in the list above as external due to the fact that these factors are exogenous to developing countries. Analogously, the latter three factors can be classified as the domestic factors to the extent that the national authorities can significantly control their outcome. In the present context of the study, we will further enrich the existing empirical model utilized by previous studies by including the standardized variables that succinctly typify the countries under study.

4 Empirical Strategy

The empirical methodology applied in this study is similar to those of Gosse and Serranito (2014), Lane and Milesi-Ferretti (2012), and Belke and Dreger (2013). In particular, it involves three distinct stages. In the first stage, we use a second-generation type panel cointegration estimation frameworks to identify the long-run determinants of the current account in West Africa. In the second stage, we apply linear projection techniques on the results from the first stage and use them to calculate 'equilibrium' long-run targets for the current account in the region. Finally, in the third stage, we account for short-run dynamics by estimating equilibrium corrections versions of the long-run relationship.

We start with a specification of a reduced form version of the determinants of the current account thus,

$$\mathrm{CA}_{it} = \delta_i + \sum_{j=1}^{M} X_{i,t}^{j}\beta + \mu_{i,t}; \quad i = 1, 2, \ldots, N; \quad t = 1, \ldots, T, \tag{1}$$

where CA is the current account to GDP ratio, δ_i are the fixed effects, $X_{i,t}^{j}$ are the theoretically and empirically suggested structural determinants of the current account, highlighted in the literature review earlier, and M are the number of regressors.

Following Lane and Milesi-Ferretti (2012), and Gosse and Serranito (2014), a measure of current account imbalances can be computed as the error term from the long-run reduced form equation in (1). In other words, the difference between the fitted values from Eq. (1) and the actual values can be treated as a measure of current account imbalances, while the fitted values serve as the long-run equilibrium relationship.

If we find the existence of at least one cointegrating relationship in the reduced form long-run equation, then it is possible to account for the short-run dynamics by estimating an error correction model (ECM), which will enable us to capture the speed of adjustment of any deviations from the long-run path of the current account back to its equilibrium path. The estimation equation for this short-run adjustment path is given as follows

$$\Delta\mathrm{CA}_{it} = \delta_i + \sum_{j=1}^{M} \theta_i \Delta X_{i,t}^{j} + \gamma ECT_{i,t-1} + \mu_{i,t}, \tag{2}$$

where as before δ_i is a country fixed-effect, Δ is a difference operator, and ECT_{it} is the error-correction term which is the measure of current account imbalances retrieved as the error-term from the long-run cointegrating relationship in Eq. (1). In other words, the error-correction term is given as $ECT_{i,t-1} = \mathrm{CA}_{it-1} - \widehat{\delta}_i +$

$\sum_{j=1}^{M} X_{i,t-1}^{j}\widehat{\beta}$. The estimated value of γ is then interpreted as the adjustment coefficient which measures the speed of convergence, and is used to calculate the half-period required for full equilibrium to be restored after a current account imbalance.

4.1 Data Sources

We retrieve data from two main sources, the Word Development Indicators (WDI) of the World Bank, and the International Financial Statistics (IFS) of the IMF. The data covers the period from 1980 until 2014 and is collected at the annual frequency. The sample is made up of all the 15 West African countries with consistently available data up to at least 15 points for the period covered. Overall, we have a panel dataset with 15 countries and 510 annual observations for the period 1980–2014 for each of the variables used in the analysis. The details of the variables used in the analysis, a brief description, and the source of the variable is contained in Table 2.

Table 2 Description of variables

Variable	Code	Description	Source
Current Account	CA	Current Account Balance as a ratio of GDP	World Development Indicators
Real Per-capita GDP	GDPpc	Gross Domestic product divided by the total population size	World Development Indicators
Trade Openness	OPN	The sum of exports plus imports as a ratio of GDP	World Development Indicators
Investment	INV	Public plus private sector investments as a ratio of GDP	World Development Indicators
Fiscal Balance	FSB	This is the net value of government budget revenue and expenditure take as a percentage of GDP	World Development Indicators
Financial Openness	Finop	This is the degree of openness of the financial sector to the external sector, measured as net foreign assets (NFA) as a ratio of GDP.	World Development Indicators
Real Exchange Rate	REER	REER is the multilateral real exchange rate computed using the following formula: $REER = (P/e)/\left[\Pi_k(P_k/e_k)^{\delta_k}\right]$, where e is the exchange rate (in unit of local currency per US$), P is the consumer price index (CPI) of the domestic country, and e_k and P_k are exchange rates and CPIs for trading partners, respectively.	International Financial Statistics (IFS)
Terms of Trade	TOT	Terms of trade is computed as the ratio of export prices to import prices, base year of 2005	International Financial Statistics
Inflation	INF	Inflation is measured by the consumer price index which is simply the annual percentage change in the CPI.	International Financial Statistics

5 Results

5.1 Panel Data Properties and Diagnostics

We start by interrogating the time series variables used for the analysis in such a way that allows us to better understand their integration and cointegration properties. This then informs the specific variables to be included and the nature of the structural specification to be employed. Table 3 contains a battery of panel unit root tests with different specifications for the variables used in the estimation procedure. The choice of a battery of tests is particularly appropriate because of the known size and power limitations of standard unit root tests; an up-to-date survey with examples can be found in Baltagi (2008).[2] We consider two main categories of panel unit root tests: so-called first-generation tests, e.g., Levin et al. (2002) (LLC) test, Breitung and Das (2005) (Breitung) test, Im et al. (2003) (IPS) test, and Hadri (2000) (Hadri) test; and second-generation tests, e.g., Pesaran (2007) (Pesaran) test. The major difference between the two generations of tests is ability of the second-generation tests to account for cross-sectional dependence and heterogeneity in the panels.

The specification used to compute the LLC, Breitung, and IPS tests are very similar. In particular, these tests make the simplifying assumption that all the panels share the same autoregressive parameter. In addition, we demean the series by subtracting the cross-sectional averages which helps mitigate the impact of cross-sectional dependence. The optimal lag structure for the autoregression is selected automatically in such a way that minimizes the Akaike information criterion (AIC).

The results as presented in columns 1–3 of Table 3 are mixed. The rejection of the null hypothesis for most of the variables seems to depend on whether or not we include only a constant, or constant and trend, in the specification of the test. For example, the current account in GDP, openness, investments, and fiscal balance when using these tests are often stationary ($I(0)$) at levels when we use a specification that includes only a constant term. However, when the specification that includes a constant term and trend is used, they lose their stationarity in levels and only become stationary after a first-difference transformation. This tenuous behaviour of the tests is however not surprising, especially when we consider the study by Breitung and Das (2005), which uses simulation exercises to show that the power of the LLC and IPS tests are very sensitive to the specification of the deterministic terms in the model.

Some other well-known limitations of this category of tests that have manifested in the mixed results we have now obtained in Table 3 are: the fact that the test crucially depends on independence assumption across the cross-sections, which would not be a valid assumption if cross-sectional correlation is present; secondly, the null hypothesis is constructed in an absolute and restrictive sense, that is, it assumes that all cross-sections have or do not have a unit root (Baltagi 2008).

---

[2]Recall that the power of a test lies in its ability to reject the null hypothesis when it is not true; and the size of a test is the probability of rejecting the null hypothesis when it is actually true.

Table 3 Battery of panel unit root tests

Variable	Specification	First-generation tests				Second-generation test
		LLC	Breitung	IPS	Hadri	Pesaran
CA	Constant	−1.71**(0.04)	−1.49*(0.06)	−4.50***(0.00)	5.87***(0.00)	−1.85(0.37)
	Constant & trend	0.06(0.52)	1.65(0.95)	−6.29***(0.00)	3.76***(0.00)	−2.11(0.37)
ΔCA	Constant	−12.85***(0.00)	−3.56***(0.00)	−12.96***(0.00)	2.52***(0.00)	−3.58***(0.00)
	Constant & trend	−6.45***(0.00)	−2.28**(0.01)	−12.94***(0.00)	5.59***(0.00)	−3.58***(0.00)
lnGDPpc	Constant	6.78(0.99)	5.92(0.99)	5.77(0.99)	11.59***(0.00)	−1.34(0.96)
	Constant & trend	1.74(0.95)	2.54(0.99)	−1.24(0.11)	9.01***(0.00)	−2.18(0.74)
ΔlnGDPpc	Constant	−35.15***(0.00)	−5.17***(0.00)	−10.36***(0.00)	6.23***(0.00)	−3.14***(0.00)
	Constant & trend	3.03(0.99)	−7.02***(0.00)	−11.40***(0.00)	2.91***(0.00)	−3.14***(0.00)
Openness	Constant	−3.98***(0.00)	−2.61***(0.00)	−2.79***(0.00)	5.50***(0.00)	−2.11(0.16)
	Constant & trend	0.37(0.64)	−0.96(0.16)	−3.26***(0.00)	5.59***(0.00)	−2.09(0.74)
ΔOpenness	Constant	−17.05***(0.00)	−8.76***(0.00)	−13.00***(0.00)	−0.30(0.62)	−2.88***(0.00)
	Constant & trend	−13.27***(0.00)	−7.59***(0.00)	−13.13***(0.00)	3.09***(0.00)	−2.95***(0.00)
Investments	Constant	−2.95***(0.00)	−1.77**(0.03)	−2.57***(0.00)	6.61***(0.00)	−2.21**(0.03)
	Constant & trend	1.67(0.95)	−0.01(0.49)	−3.69***(0.00)	6.60***(0.00)	−2.91***(0.00)
ΔInvestments	Constant	−13.32***(0.00)	−6.58***(0.00)	−12.71***(0.00)	2.14**(0.01)	−3.29***(0.00)
	Constant & trend	−1.54*(0.06)	−6.59***(0.00)	−13.19***(0.00)	3.89***(0.00)	−3.41***(0.00)
Fiscal Balance	Constant	−4.69***(0.00)	−0.75(0.22)	−3.51***(0.00)	7.51***(0.00)	−2.12*(0.07)
	Constant & trend	5.74(0.99)	−1.88**(0.02)	−4.52***(0.00)	6.71***(0.00)	−2.29(0.58)
ΔFiscal Balance	Constant	−0.45(0.32)	−3.38***(0.00)	−12.72***(0.00)	1.21(0.11)	−3.28***(0.00)
	Constant & trend	6.84(0.99)	−4.87***(0.00)	−13.05***(0.00)	3.16***(0.00)	−3.26***(0.00)
Fin Openness	Constant	−1.31*(0.09)	−0.21(0.41)	−0.67(0.24)	9.51***(0.00)	−0.98(0.99)
	Constant & trend	−1.55*(0.06)	−1.84**(0.03)	−3.52***(0.00)	4.12***(0.00)	−1.54(0.99)
ΔFin Openness	Constant	−14.04***(0.00)	−12.15***(0.00)	−12.68***(0.00)	−0.65(0.74)	−1.71(0.58)
	Constant & trend	−10.06***(0.00)	−11.42***(0.00)	−12.78***(0.00)	3.61***(0.00)	−2.02(0.92)
REER	Constant	2.23(0.98)	3.99(0.99)	14.71(0.99)	10.72***(0.00)	−1.35(0.99)

	Constant & trend	1.72(0.95)	2.35(0.99)	3.31(0.99)	9.01***(0.00)	−1.37(0.99)
ΔREER	Constant	−9.54***(0.00)	−4.35***(0.00)	−9.03***(0.00)	9.48***(0.00)	−2.34***(0.00)
	Constant & trend	−8.24***(0.00)	−3.61***(0.00)	−10.62***(0.00)	6.79***(0.00)	−3.42***(0.00)
TOT	Constant	9.41(0.99)	−0.79(0.21)	−2.37***(0.00)	4.39***(0.00)	−1.53(0.82)
	Constant & trend	9.94(0.99)	−0.45(0.32)	−3.59***(0.00)	4.42***(0.00)	−2.19(0.73)
ΔTOT	Constant	−7.96***(0.00)	−5.79***(0.00)	−11.97***(0.00)	0.18(0.42)	−2.85***(0.00)
	Constant & trend	−3.41***(0.00)	−5.91***(0.00)	−12.97***(0.00)	2.28**(0.01)	−3.41***(0.00)

Keys: LLC is for the levin2002unit test; Breitung is for the breitung2005panel test; IPS is for the im2003testing test; Hadri is for the hadri2000testing test and Pesaran is for the pesaran2007simple test, which accounts for cross-sectional dependence and heterogeneity. The keys for rejection of the null hypothesis are *, ** and *** for the 10%, 5% and 1% confidence levels respectively

Further, among the first-generation tests, we also consider the Hadri (2000) test, which is a residual-based Lagrange multiplier (LM) test where the null hypothesis is that of stationarity; i.e., there is no unit root in any of the series in the panel, similar in spirit with the Kwiatkowski–Phillips–Schmidt–Shin (KPSS) times series tests. The results here seem to be more stable, as we are able to reject the null hypothesis of stationarity in the level of most of the variables.

Given the limitations and non-dependability of the conclusions from the first-generation unit root tests, we mostly rely on the results from Pesaran (2007)'s second-generation unit root test to arrive at a conclusive decision about the stationarity property of the panel time series. More so, because the latter category of tests are robust to the limitations of the first-generation tests earlier highlighted, especially when one is working with a panel framework where heterogeneity is suspected, and the size of the *T* variable does not necessarily go to infinity, i.e., there is a relatively small time frame—in our context, just over three decades of data.

Overall, the results show that apart from the financial openness measure, we are not able to reject the null hypothesis of a unit root at the 1% critical value for all the other variables; current account/GDP, log of GDP per capita, trade openness, investments, fiscal balance, real effective exchange rate, and the terms of trade variable in levels.[3] Stationarity is, however, induced when we consider the first-difference transformations of these variables. The correct time series property of the financial openness measures remains a bone of contention as the results are generally different for the different tests and the specifications used.

5.2 Equilibrium Cointegrating Relationships

Following the results of the unit root tests, which conclusively indicates that all, but one, of the variables are integrated of order one, it becomes instructive to further investigate the existence of cointegrating relationships between the current account balance and its fundamental determinants. In testing for panel cointegration relationships, we deviate from the norm of using residual-based tests, for examples Pedroni (1999, 2004), which, although able to accommodate heterogeneous dynamics, endogenous regressors, and individual-specific constants and trends, have been shown to have low power (see Ho 2002), mainly because they require the long-run cointegrating vectors for the variables in their levels to be equal to the short-run adjustment process for the variables in their differences. A requirement commonly referred to as the common-factor restrictions which often does not hold.

Our approach to cointegration testing is to use the relatively newer and more robust test statistics developed by Westerlund (2007). The beauty of the test lies in the fact that it is based on testing the null of no cointegration in the structural rather

[3]The result for the inflation variable also indicates that it is stationary in levels, however, we do not report the result in the table for lack of space, the results are available upon request.

Table 4 Panel and group-mean cointegration tests

	Structural specifications	Westerlund test statistic $\mathscr{P}_{\tau}$	p-val	$\mathscr{P}_{\alpha}$	p-val
1	CA, TOT, OPN, REER, Finop, GDPpc, FSB	−5.27	(0.99)	−5.66	(0.99)
2	CA, TOT, OPN, REER, Finop, FSB	−14.7***	(0.00)	−9.27	(0.82)
3	CA, OPN, REER, GDPpc, FSB, INV	−16.03***	(0.00)	−20.35***	(0.00)
4	CA, TOT, OPN, REER, GDPpc, FSB, INV	−6.07	(0.99)	−5.78	(0.99)
5	CA, OPN, REER, GDPpc, FSB	−15.47***	(0.00)	−21.03***	(0.00)
6	CA, TOT, OPN, REER, Finop, GDPpc, INV	−4.63	(0.99)	−2.51	(0.99)
7	CA, OPN, REER, FSB, GDPpc, Finop	−14.25***	(0.00)	−19.34***	(0.00)
8	CA, OPN, REER, FSB, Finop, INV	−15.99***	(0.00)	−21.65***	(0.00)

Notes: The test statistic $\mathscr{P}_{\tau}$ is based on Westerlund (2007) asymptotic results. $\mathscr{P}_{\alpha}$ is the test statistic after normalization by cross-sectional averages of the effective number of observations per country. The keys for rejection of the null hypothesis of no cointegration are *, **, and *** for the 10%, 5%, and 1% confidence levels respectively. The probability values of the test statistics are based on 399 bootstrap resampling, and are reported in parentheses

than residual dynamics and therefore does not require the common-factor restriction. The procedure involves testing the null by inferring whether the error-correction term in a conditional error-correction model is equal to zero; if this is rejected, then the null hypothesis of no cointegration is also rejected (Westerlund 2007). What is more, the test is able to accommodate individual specific short-run dynamics, serially correlated error terms, individual-specific intercepts, trends, and slope parameters with bootstrap resampling methods used to account for cross-sectional dependence.

The results for the panel and group mean cointegration tests for eight different combinations of current account and its structural determinants are presented in Table 4.[4] Note that two different test statistics are reported: the standard $\mathscr{P}_{\tau}$, and the $\mathscr{P}_{\alpha}$, which accounts for cross-sectional dependence. All the probability values are based on 399 bootstrap resampling. From the results in Table 4, we notice that once the terms of trade variable (TOT) is included, we are not able to reject the null hypothesis of no cointegration especially when we account for cross-sectional dependence. This result may be explained by the well-known result in the literature, see for example Gosse and Serranito (2014), that exchange rates rather than the terms of trade is more likely to be a fundamental determinant of the current account, as it represents a better proxy for price competitiveness in West African countries.

We find that there are four different combinations of the current account and its structural determinants for which there is a cointegrating relationship, i.e., where we reject the null hypothesis of no cointegration. These include: specification number 3 (CA, OPN, REER, GDPpc, FSB, INV); specification number 5 (CA, OPN, REER, GDPpc, FSB); specification number 7 (CA, OPN, REER, FSB, GDPpc, Finop); and

[4]The results for the group mean tests are suppressed, especially because we are only specifically interested in the equilibrium relationships that are consistent with integration for the entire region and not for individual countries.

Table 5 Estimates of the cointegrating vectors by DOLS: dependent variable CA/GDP

	Structural specifications			
	Model 3	Model 5	Model 7	Model 8
Openness	0.0130	−0.0210	−0.0208	0.0130
	(0.024)	(0.028)	(0.029)	(0.024)
REER	−0.163***	−0.378	−0.361	−0.444
	(0.001)	(0.573)	(0.576)	(0.467)
lnGDPpc	−0.521	0.637	0.676	
	(2.469)	(2.951)	(2.958)	
Fiscal Balance	−0.162**	−0.337***	−0.330***	−0.154**
	(0.077)	(0.097)	(0.097)	(0.078)
Investments	−0.359***			−0.379***
	(0.048)			(0.047)
Fin. Openness			0.413	−2.140
			(3.548)	(2.865)

Note: The long-run cointegrating vectors are fitted by dynamic OLS for cointegrated panel data with homogeneous long-run covariance structure across cross-sectional units, as in Kao and Chiang (2000). Standard errors of the estimates are in parenthesis, and the keys *, ** and ***, are for the 10%, 5%, and 1% confidence levels respectively. The model numbers correspond to the numbering of the structural specifications in Table 4

specification number 8 (CA, OPN, REER, FSB, Finop, INV). These results imply that there are at least four different combinations of equilibrium targets for the current account that would be consistent with regional integration. Next, we estimate the cointegrating vectors for the significant cointegrating relationships.

Given the observed cointegration between the current account and selected structural variables in the West African panel, it is possible to estimate the long-run equilibrium relationship which could serve as an indicator of targets that would be consistent with regional integration. In Table 5, we present the results for the long-run cointegrating vector for the four structural specifications for which we observe the existence of a cointegrating relationship. The cointegrating vectors are obtained by dynamic OLS (DOLS), following Kao and Chiang (2000), as opposed to the commonly employed fully modified OLS (FM-OLS) as in Pedroni (2000). Our choice of this approach is motivated by the final sample property results in Kao and Chiang (2000), which shows that: (i) the OLS estimator has a non-negligible bias in finite samples, (ii) the FM estimator does not improve over the OLS estimator in general, and (iii) the DOLS estimator may be more promising than the OLS or FM estimators in estimating the cointegrated panel regressions.

From the results in Table 5, we use the number of statistically significant variables, and the consistency of the sign of the coefficients with theoretical expectations to inform selection of the appropriate cointegrating vector for the equilibrium target in West Africa. Model 3 stands out from the rest, as the signs on the coefficients for REER and investments are both negative and statistically significant as expected. Although the sign of per capita income in Model 3 is not significant, it is negative, which is what we expect, and this is in contrast with the positive sign that it assumes on in Models 5, 7, and 8.

The sign for the openness variable is ambiguous in the literature, so a positive but not significant value is not very indicative of the situation in West Africa. The only slightly puzzling result is that of the fiscal balance variable, although there are no conclusions about the theoretical expectation of this variable; previous empirical work for other regions have often shown that this variable positively affects current account dynamics, see for examples, Gosse and Serranito (2014), Chinn and Ito (2008), Lane and Milesi-Ferretti (2012), Abbas et al. (2011).

5.3 Equilibrium Relationships and Estimated Adjustment Paths

Focusing on the most plausible equilibrium relationships between the current account and its fundamental determinants established in the previous section, we now concentrate on investigating how disequilibrium in the established long-run relationships are corrected in the short run. Specifically, we estimate panel error correction models, which in addition to showing how the structural determinants affect the current account, also shows the speed of adjustment back to the equilibrium relationship. We use three different panel data estimators: pooled OLS (POLS), the fixed effect (FE) estimator and the random effect (RE) estimator, and discriminate between the FE and RE based on the Hausman specification test.

The results for the disequilibrium correction estimates are presented in Table 6. Columns (1) to (3) reports the results for the short-run determinants when we use exactly the same variables that are relevant in the long run from Model 3 in Table 5; whereas, in columns (4) to (6), we include two additional short-run determinants—inflation and financial openness—to improve the fit. Because results do not significantly change with the different estimators, we concentrate on discussing the results from the fixed effect estimation, especially because the Hausman test does not discriminate against it.

One of the fascinating results we see from Table 6 is that the effect of a depreciation of the exchange rate on current account seems to be switching from negative in the long-run, (see column 1 in Table 5), to positive in the short-run. The value in the short-run ranges between 1.2 and 3.1, and 2.2 for the FE estimates, implying that a depreciation of the real exchange rate improves the current status in the short-run by around 2%. However, in the long-run, a depreciation of the rear exchange rate leads to a worsening of the current account balance by around 0.52% in West Africa. Although relatively higher, this result is comparable to similar studies elsewhere. For example, the estimated long-run effect of the exchange rate on OECD countries in Gosse and Serranito (2014) is −0.11 and for European countries, it is around −0.16 in Belke and Dreger (2013). On the other hand, the short-run enhancing effect of real exchange rate depreciation is also lower for West

Table 6 Disequilibrium adjusted estimates: dependent variable CA/GDP

	(1)	(2)	(3)	(4)	(5)	(6)
	POLS	FE	RE	POLS	FE	RE
ΔOpenness$_t$	−0.0437**	−0.0477**	−0.0437**	−0.0448**	−0.0492**	−0.0448**
	(0.023)	(0.023)	(0.023)	(0.023)	(0.023)	(0.023)
ΔREER$_t$	1.200	2.202*	1.200	2.134*	3.109**	2.134*
	(1.098)	(1.251)	(1.098)	(1.225)	(1.336)	(1.225)
ΔlnGDPpc$_t$	8.739***	8.574***	8.739***	9.297***	9.089***	9.297***
	(3.295)	(3.475)	(3.295)	(3.307)	(3.478)	(3.307)
ΔFiscal Balance$_t$	−0.170**	−0.163**	−0.170**	−0.173***	−0.166**	−0.173***
	(0.074)	(0.076)	(0.074)	(0.074)	(0.076)	(0.074)
ΔFiscal Balance$_{t-1}$	−0.0745	−0.0728	−0.0745	−0.0871	−0.0880	−0.0871
	(0.071)	(0.073)	(0.071)	(0.072)	(0.074)	(0.072)
ΔInvestments$_{t-1}$	−0.387***	−0.384***	−0.387***	−0.386***	−0.381***	−0.386***
	(0.043)	(0.044)	(0.043)	(0.043)	(0.044)	(0.043)
Inflation$_{t-1}$				−0.0278*	−0.0366**	−0.0278*
				(0.016)	(0.019)	(0.016)
ΔFin. Openness$_{t-1}$				0.306	0.873	0.306
				(3.036)	(3.104)	(3.036)
ECT$_{t-1}$	−0.423***	−0.417***	−0.423***	−0.424***	−0.417***	−0.424***
	(0.043)	(0.043)	(0.043)	(0.043)	(0.043)	(0.043)
Constant	−0.102	−0.190	−0.102	0.0672	0.0632	0.0672
	(0.231)	(0.239)	(0.231)	(0.251)	(0.272)	(0.251)
R^2	0.31	0.31	0.31	0.33	0.33	0.32
Country effects	No	Yes	Yes	No	Yes	Yes

Time effects	No	Yes	No	No	Yes	No
Hausman: FE vs. RE		4.27			6.17	
p-value		(0.748)			(0.723)	
Half-life of adjustment	1.26	1.28	1.26	1.25	1.28	1.26

Note: The error correction term, ECT, is computed from the structural long-run equation of Model 3 in Table 5. POLS, FE, and RE are abbreviations for the pooled OLS, fixed effect, and random effect estimators respectively. The estimated half-life of the adjustment (in years) back to equilibrium is computed as ln (0.5)/ ln $(1 - \gamma)$. Standard errors of the estimates are in parenthesis, and the keys *, ** and ***, are for the 10%, 5%, and 1% confidence levels respectively

Africa when compared to OECD countries for which Gosse and Serranito (2014) find that the effect on the one period lag of the real exchange rate is around 3.78.

As expected, trade openness worsens the current account position in the short-run, whereas, the effect in the long-run seem to be ambiguous. The short-run effect is, however, minuscule, somewhere around −0.04%. This result is intuitive in the sense that it could be explained by the differences in the structural composition of trade patterns from West Africa. Whereas the region exports more primary commodity with little or no technical embodiment, the nature of imports is more of tertiary goods—industrial, manufacturing and services—with higher net value.[5] Hence, the worsening impact of trade openness on current account balances.

As for the effect of GDP per capita on the current account, the long-run cointegrating vector suggests that there is a countercyclical effect, which is consistent with the prediction of equilibrium real-business-cycle theory that aggregates demand-side shocks typically raises income through the net increase in domestic investments by more than real national savings, which typically leads to a current account deficit (see Barro 2007). The short-run effect is, however, positive and statistically significant as we see that the average effect is around 9%, which is difficult to rationalise in the short-run. The result for the investment variable is in line with the predictions of equilibrium open-economy business-cycle theory that rising investments as a result of a demand-driven shock would lead to a worsening of the current account position.

The discussion of the role of fiscal balance is based on the "twin deficits" hypothesis Salvatore (2006). The twin deficit hypothesis postulates that under certain conditions, the expected effect of a fiscal deficit is to decrease the CA balance. Barro (2007, p. 439) explains that this would be the case when the budget deficit reduces national savings, however, in the Ricardian case, where a budget deficit does not affect real national savings, this worsening effect should not be expected to hold. This caveat highlighted by Barro (2007) seems to be the case in West Africa, where we observe that fiscal balance actually improves current account situations both in the long and short-run.

In the short run, the average improving effect of fiscal balance is around −0.17%; this result suggests that government spending in the region crowds out private spending, and since government is a major participant in most economies, by crowding out private spending the pressure on imports would be dampened and result in improvements in the current account situation. Thus, in conclusion, there is no evidence of the twin-deficits for West African economies. When we include other short-run determinants such as inflation and financial openness, the overall results do not change in any significant way. What we find however is that inflation negatively and statistically affects the current account balance in the short run, that is, economic instability worsens the current account position as expected.

[5]This phenomenon could also be explained by the relatively high and inelastic marginal propensity to import that has been observed in many countries in the region especially for Nigeria.

Turning to the disequilibrium adjustment mechanism, we observe that the coefficient of the error correction term is negative and significant for all the models, with an average of around −0.42. This coefficient implies that every year, around 42% of the disequilibrium in current account dynamics of the previous year is corrected. Although this is relatively fast when compared to the adjustment coefficient of 15% for OECD countries estimated by Gosse and Serranito (2014), it does say something about the potential to achieve the equilibrium targets consistent with regional integration in a relatively medium to short-term period.

For concreteness, we also estimate the "half-life" of the period required for full adjustment back to equilibrium current account levels consistent with regional integration.[6] The results indicate that it is somewhere around 1½ years (1.3). We, however, caution that this result cannot be generalized in a straightforward manner to mean that in the following 4 years or so, countries would have fully adjusted to a regionally consistent path for external balances. The reason is that the adjustment is faster in the beginning periods and slows down in percentage terms as time elapses and the gaps get narrower. Moreover, during the process of convergence back to the steady state, a new shock could set in and cause another disequilibrium which exacerbates the first one, and then the adjustment process would have to start all over again.

In Fig. 4, we plot the actual path of the current account (AP, blue solid lines), the estimated adjustment path (EAP, black dot-dash lines), and the long-run structural equilibrium path (LRP, red dashed lines) for all the countries in the sample. The plots give a visual sense of where each individual country currently is, when compared to the regionally consistent long-run target for the current account, and what the adjustment process for each country looks like. The figure generally shows that there is considerable variation by country in the nature of the responses. In particular, we see that countries like Cape Verde, Guinea-Bissau, Mauritania, Niger, Sierra Leone and the Gambia, have adjustments paths that are closer to the regional long-run equilibrium path, whereas, Burkina Faso, Ghana, Guinea, Mali, Senegal, and Togo have paths that are relatively far away from the equilibrium targets, thus faster adjustments and synchronization would be required in the latter group of countries.

The result for Nigeria is slightly different from the others, this is so because although the actual and adjustment paths are both close to the equilibrium path, the level of volatility is pretty much the highest, and we recognize that this may be driven by the volatility in oil prices, coupled with macroeconomic instability. Thus, for Nigeria, what is required is a stabilization mechanism or effective macroeconomic shock absorbers such as a carefully implemented Sovereign Wealth Fund to help mitigate the volatility in the actual path of current account balances for Nigeria.

[6]Note that the "half-life" is defined as the number of periods it takes to close half of the disequilibrium. It is computed as $\ln(0.5)/\ln(1-\gamma)$.

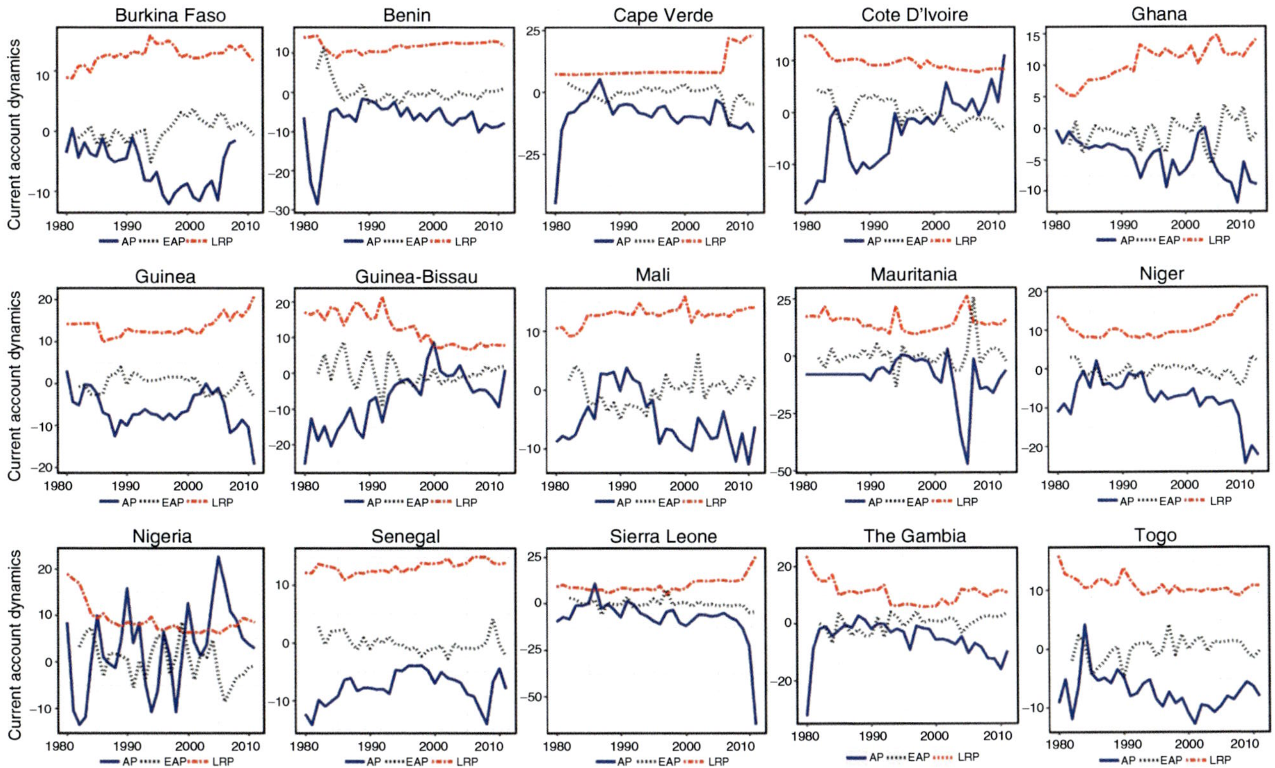

Fig. 4 Actual, equilibrium and estimated adjustment path of the current account in West African countries. Note: The keys AP, EAP, and LRP are for the Actual Path, Estimated Adjustment Path, and the Long-run path of the current account in West Africa, respectively. Estimates of the long-run path are based on the cointegrating vector of Model 3 in co_vector, while the estimated adjustment path is based on the fixed effect equilibrium correction estimates of Column 5 in vecm

6 Conclusion

In this study, we were concerned about three main issues: first is the long- and short-run determinants of the current account in West African economies, second is the existence of a sustainable path for the current account that is consistent with regional integration, and third is the process of adjustment towards such a path. To address these concerns, we use mainly second-generation panel cointegration tests that have the advantage of detecting cross-sectional dependencies among countries, which is a useful property for inference among countries that are partially regionally integrated.

The key findings from our analysis are as follows. First, the effect of the determinants of the current account in the long run and short run are not the same. In many cases, e.g., for real exchange rate and the level of income, the effect switches between being positive and negative depending on the time dimension of the analysis. Secondly, there are five main determinants of the current account in the short run—trade openness, real exchange rate, level of income, fiscal policy and investments. Thirdly, the speed of adjustment towards the regional equilibrium path for the current account is relatively fast, somewhere around a half-life of 1½ years. Finally, there is considerable variation in the deviation of countries from the regionally sustainable path.

In spite of the robustness of our results and the conclusions that follow, there are still potential opportunities for extending the analysis presented here. One way is by considering potential asymmetries in the process of adjustment back to equilibrium. For example, what is the nature of the adjustment process for countries that have surplus current account imbalances, compared to those that have deficit imbalances? This could potentially provide interesting results on the West Africa experience that could speak to the recent evidence on the nonlinear nature of the current account dynamics: for OECD economies, see Gosse and Serranito (2014); for European economies Arghyrou and Chortareas (2008); and for the US economy see Holmes (2011).

References

Abbas, S. A., Bouhga-Hagbe, J., Fatas, A., Mauro, P., & Velloso, R. C. (2011). Fiscal policy and the current account. *IMF Economic Review, 59*(4), 603–629.

Arghyrou, M. G., & Chortareas, G. (2008). Current account imbalances and real exchange rates in the Euro area. *Review of International Economics, 16*(4), 747–764.

Aristovnik, A. (2007). *Short- and medium-term determinants of current account balances in the Middle East and North Africa countries.*

Baltagi, B. (2008). *Econometric analysis of panel data.* Wiley.

Barro, R. (2007). *Macroeconomics: A modern approach.* Cengage Learning.

Belke, A., & Dreger, C. (2013). Current account imbalances in the Euro area: Does catching up explain the development? *Review of International Economics, 21*(1), 6–17.

Breitung, J., & Das, S. (2005). Panel unit root tests under cross-sectional dependence. *Statistica Neerlandica, 59*(4), 414–433.

Bussiere, M., Fratzscher, M., & Muller, G. J. (2004). *Current account dynamics in OECD and EU acceding countries-an intertemporal approach*. ECB Working Paper.

Calderon, C. A., Chong, A., & Loayza, N. V. (2002). Determinants of current account deficits in developing countries. *Contributions in Macroeconomics, NBER, 2*(1).

Calderon, C., Chong, A., & Zanforlin, L. (2007). Current account deficits in Africa: Stylized facts and basic determinants. *Economic Development and Cultural Change, 56*(1), 191–221.

Cheung, Y.-W., Chinn, M. D., & Fujii, E. (2010). China's current account and exchange rate. In *China's growing role in world trade* (pp. 231–271). University of Chicago Press.

Chinn, M. D., & Ito, H. (2008). Global current account imbalances: American fiscal policy versus East Asian savings. *Review of International Economics, 16*(3), 479–498.

Chinn, M. D., & Prasad, E. S. (2003). Medium-term determinants of current accounts in industrial and developing countries: An empirical exploration. *Journal of International Economics, 59*(1), 47–76.

Debelle, G., & Faruqee, H. (1996). *What determines the current account? A cross-sectional and panel approach*. IMF working paper.

Dornbusch, R., & Fischer, S. (1980). Exchange rates and the current account. *The American Economic Review, 70*(5), 960–971.

Ghosh, A. R., & Ostry, J. D. (1995). The current account in developing countries: A perspective from the consumption-smoothing approach. *World Bank Economic Review, 9*(2), 305–333.

Giuliodori, M. (2004). Nominal shocks and the current account: A structural VAR analysis of 14 OECD countries. *Review of World Economics, 140*(4), 569–591.

Glick, R., & Rogoff, K. (1995). Global versus country-specific productivity shocks and the current account. *Journal of Monetary Economics, 35*(1), 159–192.

Gosse, J.-B., & Serranito, F. (2014). Long-run determinants of current accounts in OECD countries: Lessons for intra-European imbalances. *Economic Modelling, 38*, 451–462.

Gruber, J. W., & Kamin, S. B. (2007). Explaining the global pattern of current account imbalances. *Journal of International Money and Finance, 26*(4), 500–522.

Hadri, K. (2000). Testing for stationarity in heterogeneous panel data. *The Econometrics Journal, 3* (2), 148–161.

Ho, T.-w. (2002). A panel cointegration approach to the investment-saving correlation. *Empirical Economics, 27*(1), 91–100.

Holmes, M. J. (2011). Threshold cointegration and the short-run dynamics of twin deficit behaviour. *Research in Economics, 65*(3), 271–277.

Im, K. S., Pesaran, M. H., & Shin, Y. (2003). Testing for unit roots in heterogeneous panels. *Journal of Econometrics, 115*(1), 53–74.

Kao, C., & Chiang, M. H. (2000). On the estimation and inference of a cointegrated regression in panel data. *Advances in Econometrics, 15*, 179–222.

Khan, M. S., & Knight, M. D. (1983). *Determinants of current account balances of non-oil developing countries in the 1970s: An empirical analysis* (pp. 819–842). Staff Papers-International Monetary Fund.

Lane, P. R., & Milesi-Ferretti, G. M. (2012). External adjustment and the global crisis. *Journal of International Economics, 88*(2), 252–265.

Levin, A., Lin, C.-F., & Chu, C.-S. J. (2002). Unit root tests in panel data: Asymptotic and finite-sample properties. *Journal of Econometrics, 108*(1), 1–24.

Nason, J. M., & Rogers, J. H. (2006). The present-value model of the current account has been rejected: Round up the usual suspects. *Journal of International Economics, 68*(1), 159–187.

Obstfeld, M., & Rogoff, K. (1994). *The intertemporal approach to the current account* (Tech. Rep.). National Bureau of Economic Research.

Obstfeld, M., & Rogoff, K. (1995). *The mirage of fixed exchange rates* (Tech. Rep.). National Bureau of Economic Research.

Obstfeld, M., & Rogoff, K. (2009). *Global imbalances and the financial crisis: Products of common causes*.

Osakwe, P., & Verick, S. (2007). *Current account deficits in sub-Saharan Africa: Do they matter?* (pp. 201–220). United Nations Commission for Africa.

Oshota, S. O., & Badejo, A. A. (2015). What drives current account balance in West Africa states: Evidence from panel ARDL. *Journal of International and Global Economic Studies, 8*(2), 91–105.

Pedroni, P. (1999). Critical values for cointegration tests in heterogeneous panels with multiple regressors. *Oxford Bulletin of Economics and Statistics, 61*(S1), 653–670.

Pedroni, P. (2000). Fully modified OLS for heterogeneous cointegrated panels. In *Nonstationary panels, panel cointegration, and dynamic panels* (Vol. 15(03), pp. 93–130).

Pedroni, P. (2004). Panel cointegration: Asymptotic and finite sample properties of pooled time series tests with an application to the PPP hypothesis. *Econometric Theory, 20*(03), 597–625.

Pesaran, M. H. (2007). A simple panel unit root test in the presence of cross-section dependence. *Journal of Applied Econometrics, 22*(2), 265–312.

Sachs, J. D. (1981). *The current account in the macroeconomic adjustment process.*

Salvatore, D. (2006). Twin deficits in the g-7 countries and global structural imbalances. *Journal of Policy Modeling, 28*(6), 701–712.

Westerlund, J. (2007). Testing for error correction in panel data. *Oxford Bulletin of Economics and Statistics, 69*(6), 709–748.

Obstacles to Strengthening Economic Integration in the West African Economic and Monetary Union

Doukouré Charles FE

Contents

Abstract This paper analyses the obstacles to strengthening economic integration in the West African Economic and Monetary Union (WAEMU). Several studies show, firstly, that strengthening economic integration requires an increase of intra-trade in Regional Trade Agreements (RTAs). But it is not the case WAEMU where trade between member countries is rather low. This work identifies both the

D. C. FE (✉)
Ecole Nationale Supérieure de Statistique et d'Economie Appliquée (ENSEA), Abidjan, Côte d'Ivoire

Cellule d'Analyse des Politiques Economiques du Cires (CAPEC), Abidjan, Côte d'Ivoire
e-mail: fe.doukoure@ensea.ed.ci

D. Seck (ed.), *The External Sector of Africa's Economy*, Advances in African Economic, Social and Political Development,
https://doi.org/10.1007/978-3-319-97913-7_3

economic and political factors that limit economic integration in WAEMU and how they impact trade between members.

In order to rank such potential obstacles, the study develops an extended gravity model, using a panel dataset for WAEMU from 1996 to 2013 for all member countries. Bilateral export flows between member countries are used as endogenous variable.

Beside the classic variables (income, population size and distance), the effects of three factors (infrastructure, economic policy and political tensions) were taken into account. The empirical results show that the state of infrastructure gaps—in particular telecommunications and transport networks greatly—slow down economic integration within WAEMU.

1 Introduction

The World Trade Organization (WTO) agreements are intended to assist stakeholders in international trade to pursue their activities in order to obtain the maximum benefit. Since 1995,[1] the regional economic communities (RECs) proliferated as a response from member countries to strengthen their comparative advantages in an increasingly liberalized environment.

Thus, these RECs by the trade-creation effects, hope to increase the volume of trade between their members and create economic growth for a harmonious and sustainable development. To do this, each RECs should follow a process described by Balassa in five steps: (i) create a zone of free—trade by reducing or removing barriers to trade among the members in order to facilitate trade between members, (ii) enhance trade integration by setting up a customs through the establishment of a common external tariff, (iii) facilitating the movement of factors of production, (iv) harmonize economic policies for more efficiency and (v) lead to the economic and monetary integration using a same currency.

This process should lead to economic growth through the revitalization of trade, both with member countries and the rest of the world. The West African Economic and Monetary Union (WAEMU[2]) is not out of this process. It has made significant advances on the process of economic integration, but, trade between the members remains low compared to other RECs in sub-Saharan Africa and in the world. Between 2012 and 2014, intra members of the WAEMU trade stagnates between 14% and 15% of the total trade of the area. This performance is not very far from that

[1]The creation of the World Trade Organization.

[2]The West African Economic and Monetary Union is a Regional Economic Community (REC) of eight West African states. It was established to promote economic integration among countries that share the CFA franc as a common currency. WAEMU was created by a Treaty signed in Dakar, Senegal, on 10 January 1994, by the heads of state and governments of Benin, Burkina Faso, Côte d'Ivoire, Mali, Niger, Senegal, and Togo. On 2 May 1997, Guinea-Bissau, a former Portuguese colony, became the organization's eighth (and only non-Francophone) member state.

of the entire sub-Saharan Africa with 17% in 2012, 18% in 2013 and 2014 (UNCTAD), 2016.

In sub-Saharan Africa, the EAC (East African Community) for its part has respectively 21%, 18% and 18% of intra trade over the same period. The SADC (the Southern African development community) intra trade represents 18%, 19% and 19% in 2012, 2013 and 2014, respectively. Other RECs in sub-Saharan Africa have poor performance in terms of intra trade like WAEMU's. In the rest of the world, among developed countries, the situation is quite different. For example, ASEAN (Association of South East Asia nations) has recorded between 2012 and 2014, respectively 26%, 26% and 25% intra trade. NAFTA (North American free trade agreement) and the EU (European Union) of the 28 are still better with respectively 49%, 49% and 50% of trade between members and 62%, 61% and 63% of intra trade from 2012 to 2014 (UNCTAD 2016). Why WAEMU's intra trade is too little? Are there any obstacles to expanding it?

The paper analyzes the potential obstacles to strengthen intra WAEMU trade. It focuses on the economic, political and infrastructural factors and assesses their impact on intra WAEMU exports. We consider a panel over the period 1996–2013. The contribution of this paper is to assess the impact of factors such as the availability of infrastructure, political stability and macroeconomic policy, on intra WAEMU trade running unit root test in panel before the estimation. Doing so, we correct potential bias into estimated coefficients due to non-stationary variables. Besides, the classic variables (income, population size and distance), the effects of these three factors (infrastructure, economic policy and political stability) were taken into account. The empirical results show that the state of infrastructure gaps—in particular telecommunications and transport networks greatly—can slow down economic integration within WAEMU.

The paper is organized as follows. Section 2 reviews some results from the literature about potential obstacles to expand intra African trade while Sect. 3 introduces the empirical implementation. Section 4 presents the results and Sect. 5 concludes.

2 Literature Review

Regional Economic Communities (RECs) will produce more welfare gains if the share of intra trade in the total trade is larger than the share of trade with the rest of the world (Bhagwati 1971; Amr 2013). Looking at intra African trade, many authors have highlighted some factors that inhibit the expansion of intra trade. Most of empirical papers on this question have identified some of them: the infrastructure (Limão and Venables 2001), in particular gaps in telecommunications networks and transport, trade policies and economic management (Longo and Sekkat 2004; Francoisa and Manchin 2007). According to Rodrik (1997), the slow growth of African economies. The trade barriers also slow down intra African trade (Norehan et al. 2014). The institution quality of both the importer and exporter (Anderson and

Marcouiller 2002; Linders et al. 2005; Levchenko 2007; Francoisa and Manchin 2007).

Longo and Sekkat (2004) analyzed the determinants of intra-African trade in order to assess the potential barriers to their expansion. They show that the State of infrastructure, in particular gaps in telecommunications networks and transport, greatly inhibits trade. On the other hand, the adoption of sound economic policies and good management of exchange rates promote intra regional trade. The infrastructure (the quality and quantity) and other services to exporters is a source of positive externalities. It contributes to the reduction of transaction costs and economic agents become more competitive than those that do not benefit from such externalities. It does have evidence that improvements in transportation services and infrastructure can lead to improvements in export performance.

Limão and Venables (2001) find that in Sub-Saharan Africa, the quality of infrastructure has a strong explanatory power for the limited growth of trade in 1990. Particularly they showed that poor infrastructure damage trade because deterioration in infrastructure raises transactions costs and reduces trade flows. Infrastructure and institutional quality are significant determinants not only for export levels, but also for exports which may take place.

When the level of infrastructure of member countries reaches one of the best endowed countries of the union, intra WAEMU potential trade is high (Cahérine et al. 2013). These authors estimated the effects in terms of exports to harmonize the level of infrastructure within WAEMU in 2006. They show that the potential gains from trade in terms of exports is very high. According to Rodrik (1997), the long-term decline in Africa's participation in the world trade is due to the slow growth of African economies.

A higher GDP increases trade while a longer distance inhibits trade. Larger population also results in higher trade. In terms of trade openness, the results show that the trade barriers are found to be positively and significantly correlated with openness (Norehan et al. 2014). The levels and similarities of market size, domestic R&D stock and inward FDI stock are positively related to the volume of bilateral trade, while the distance between trading countries has a negative impact (Wang et al. 2010).

The institutions quality of both the importer and exporter increases the amount of bilateral trade (Linders et al. 2005). Levchenko (2007) suggests that differences in institutions quality can themselves be a source of comparative advantage, finding that institutional differences across countries are important determinants of trade patterns. Using a gravity model, Anderson and Marcouiller (2002) find that bilateral trade volumes are positively influenced by the trading countries' institutional quality. Other authors have pointed out the same results. They support the notion that export performance, and the propensity to take part in the trading system at all, depends on institutional quality and access to well-developed transport and communications infrastructure (Francoisa and Manchin 2007).

Agbodji (2007) displayed that the membership of common monetary zone and the implementation of the economic reforms have had significant effects in terms of imports and exports diversion. However, the economic distortions, considered as incentives for trading through unofficial channels, significantly reduced official bilateral trade in the Union. WAEMU integration increases substantially the trade among member countries after economic reforms (Gbetnkom and Avom 2005). These reforms positively impacted the flow of trade within the union, but this impact tends to decrease over the years. The results highlight the heavy dependence of the economy of WAEMU and particularly of its trade towards Côte d'Ivoire (BAD 2013a, b). We extend theses previous results taking into account economic, political stability and infrastructural factors. This study is based on Longo and Sekkat (2004).

3 Methodology

The methodology revolves around two points: descriptive statistics and econometric analysis. The descriptive statistics consist in presenting summary statistics, calculating correlation coefficient between the endogenous variable and variables of interest, making graphs and tables. Without forecasting a causal relationship, descriptive statistics tools will help to understand the association between the endogenous variable and the variables of interest. It helps us to carry out some intuitions that should be assessed by the econometrics analysis. The rest of this section focuses on the econometric analysis. It is organized in two subsections: (i) the econometric specification and estimation issues and (ii) the data used to implement this analysis.

3.1 Econometric Specifications and Estimation Issues

The study develops a transformed gravity model to analyze the potentials obstacles to expanding WAEMU intra exports. In its original form, a gravity function contains *GDP* and the transaction and transportation cost variables only and is conventionally specified as:

$$Trade_{ij,t} = A\frac{GDP_{it}{}^{\theta}GDP_{jt}{}^{\vartheta}}{D_{ij}^{\mu}}e^{\gamma X_{ijt}} \quad (1)$$

$Trade_{ij,t}$ is the value of bilateral exports between country i and country j at time t. GDP_i and GDP_j are GDP of countries i and j respectively. D_{ij} is a measure of the distance between the two countries, which captures transaction and transportation costs and X_{ijt} is a set of traditional gravity model and over control variables.[3]

A is often treated as a constant in previous literature. Following Wang et al. (2010) we treat A as a function because of the existence of heterogeneity across

[3]See appendix for more details about those variables.

countries. In fact, in this study individual country effects are allowed to vary across countries and specified as a function of its exporting capabilities to its trading partner. Thus A is specified as a function of the interaction between the availability of the infrastructure, the stability of the political environment, the management of economic policy both in the exporter countries and in their partners (Balasubramanyam et al. 1996; Coe and Helpman 1995; Coe et al. 1997; Wang et al. 2010). We assume that, these factors are closely related to a country's export capabilities. So that A is specifies as followed:

$$A_{ij,t} = e^{\alpha} FDI_{i,t}^{\beta_1} FDI_{j,t}^{\beta_2} PS_{i,t}^{\beta_3} PS_{j,t}^{\beta_4} RD_{i,t}^{\beta_5} RD_{j,t}^{\beta_6} Mob_{i,t}^{\beta_7} Mob_{j,t}^{\beta_8} \tag{2}$$

Where political stability index (*PS*), percentage of paved road in total road (*RD*), *Mobile phone subscriptions per 100 people (Mob)* and *Foreign Direct Investisment (FDI) net inflows* are the main variables of interest.

In addition, we consider the similarity index (*Sim*) as another indicator. It is given by the following formula (Wang et al. 2010):

$$Sim_{ij} = 1 - \frac{GDP_i^2}{\left(GDP_i + GDP_j\right)^2} - \frac{GDP_j^2}{\left(GDP_i + GDP_j\right)^2} \tag{3}$$

This variable measures the similarity in the levels of GDP in the trading partners, capturing the relative size of two countries in terms of GDP. It is clear that the total volume of trade should be higher, the larger the overall market size (i.e. *GDP*), which is equivalent to the average GDP, for given relative size and factor endowments. It varies within 0 and 0.5. The value 0 corresponds to an absolute divergence in country size and 0.5 equal country size). The larger this measure is, the more similar the two countries in terms of GDP, the higher the share of intra-industry trade. Then, the Eq. (2) becomes:

$$A_{ij,t} = e^{\alpha} FDI_{i,t}^{\beta_1} FDI_{j,t}^{\beta_2} PS_{i,t}^{\beta_3} PS_{j,t}^{\beta_4} RD_{i,t}^{\beta_5} RD_{j,t}^{\beta_6} Mob_{i,t}^{\beta_7} Mob_{j,t}^{\beta_8} Sim_{i,t}^{\beta_9} Sim_{j,t}^{\beta_{10}} \tag{4}$$

We draw on Longo and Sekkat (2004) combining Eq. (1) and Eq. (4) in log the final specification is:

$$Ln\left(Trade_{ijt}\right) = \ln A_{ijt} + \theta lnGDP_{it} + \vartheta lnGDP_{jt} - \mu lnD_{ij} + \gamma X_{ijt} + \varepsilon_{ijt} \tag{5}$$

With $\varepsilon_{ijt} = \mu_{ij} + \mu_t + \mu_{ijt}$, where μ_{ij} represents the error due to the pairs of countries which does not depend on the time variation, μ_t the error due to time variation only which does not depends on the country pairs, and μ_{ijt} the error due to both the pairs of countries and the time variation.

Drawing on Santos-Silva and Tenreyro (2006, 2011) we estimate Eq. (5) using Poisson Maximum Likelihood method. This method has the advantage of correcting the data are truncated at zero and the potential bias generated by log linearization of original gravity model. Before the estimation, we test for stationarity of every series in the panel (Wang et al. 2010).

3.2 *Data*

We use annual data for all the WAEMU member countries (Benin, Burkina Faso, Côte d'Ivoire, Guinea Bissau, Mali, Niger, Senegal and Togo) and their partners in the union from 1996 to 2013. We set a panel over this period. The sample size is 56 pairs of countries during the period of the study. Hence, our dataset consists of 1008 (56×18) observations of bilateral exports flows. Apart from the traditional variables of the gravity model, we focus on three categories of variables in this analysis: infrastructure, political stability and economic policy. This section presents the indicators measuring these variables of interest and the data source. Note that variables are considered for both exporter and the partner.

3.2.1 Infrastructure Variables

Infrastructure quality and other business services are key determinants for the success of manufacturing and agricultural firms. These are also factors catalysts of economic activities by reducing transaction costs. In this analysis the focus is on the availability of economic infrastructure and communication facilities. Two variables were retained: *Mobile phone subscriptions per 100 people* (World Development Indicators) and the percentage of paved road (*paved Roads, % of total roads*[4]) from the World Development Indicators (WDI). The major part of trade between the member States of WAEMU is done by road. Thus the availability of good quality of roads remains a factor promoting the dynamism of these transactions. A good communication network fosters economic transactions and trade by reducing transaction cost. In fine the gap in telecommunication network and transport is an important source of comparative advantages both for importers and exporters.

3.2.2 Political Stability Variable

The political environment influences economic activities. A stable environment with absence of violence reduces the risk and promotes further development of economic activities. To measure this variable, the indicator *Political Stability and Absence of Violence (PS)*, has been selected from the World Governance Indicators (WGI), missing values have been replace by the nearest value 1997 by 1996; 1999 by 1998 and 2001 by 2000. We suppose that the situation remains the same between

[4]Missing values have been replace by the geometric mean over the period 1996–2013.

the two consecutive years in the sample. The unit value rang from approximately −2.5 to 2.5, with higher values corresponding to better outcomes. For easier interpretation, the variable has been transformed according to the following formula:

$$PS_i = \frac{ps_i - Min_{Value}}{Max_{Value} - Min_{Value}} \tag{6}$$

With PS_i the new value ranges from 0 to 1 corresponding to strong political stability and, ps_i the old value, Min_{Value} and Max_{Value} are respectively the minimum and the maximum value in the old sample of the indicator. Then in order to take the log, we take the transformed value and we add one. The stability of the political environment and the absence of violence contribute to promote economic transaction.

3.2.3 Economic Policy Variable

We consider *Foreign Direct Investment* (*FDI*) net inflows as a proxy of the confidence in a country economic management and growth outlook (Longo and Sekkat 2004). This variable captures the adequacy of macroeconomic policy. We suppose that if a given country is more attractive, it is because economic authorities manage economic policies very well. The *Foreign Direct Investment* (*FDI*) net inflows, annual, in US Dollars at current prices and current exchange rates in millions, are published by United Nations Conference on Trade and Development (UNCTAD).

FDI inflows comprise capital provided (either directly or through other related enterprises) by a foreign direct investor to a FDI enterprise, or capital received by a foreign direct investor from a FDI enterprise. Data on FDI flows are presented on net bases (capital transactions' credits less debits between direct investors and their foreign affiliates). Net decreases in assets or net increases in liabilities are recorded as credits (with a positive sign), while net increases in assets or net decreases in liabilities are recorded as debits (with a negative sign). Hence, FDI flows with a negative sign indicate that at least one of the three components of FDI is negative and not offset by positive amounts of the remaining components. These are called reverse investment or disinvestment.

4 Results

This section presents the results of the analysis. It is organized into two parts. The first focuses on the results of the descriptive analysis and unit root test. The second part presents the results of unit root test and Hausman test of specification before presenting the final estimations results and interpretations.

4.1 Descriptive Statistics

Here we focus only on the variable of interest: FDI net inflows, number of mobile phone subscriber per 100 habitants, road paved in percentage of total road, politic stability and their relationship with the bilateral trade flows within WAEMU member country. This section is organized as follow: descriptive statistics are presented in the first part and the unit root test results are shown in the second part.

Graphs in Fig. 1 present the relationship between exports in value and the four main variables of interest of the analysis: net inflows of FDI, the percentage of people using the mobile phone, the percentage of paved road and political stability index. Concerning the two first variables mentioned, a clear relationship seems to emerge with the intra WAEMU exports. Intra WAEMU exports increase with the value of FDI net inflows. So the more economic agents are confident in each country the more intra WAEMU exports increase. Likewise intra WAEMU exports are fostered by the average percentage of people using mobile phones. In addition, intra WAEMU exports seem to increase with the percentage of paved road on average. Finally, the gap in telecommunication network and transport seems to be a strong determinant of intra WAEMU exports. The correlation coefficient between exports total value and the FDI net inflows, and the percentage of mobile phone subscribers on average are positive and significant. It's respectively around 0.15 and 0.3. On the contrary, intra WAEMU exports lower with the index of political stability. This curve suggests that within the union, the political stability and the absence of violence in a country leads to the lowering of the values of exports on average. Yet the relationship would be more obvious. Intuitively, the relationship is

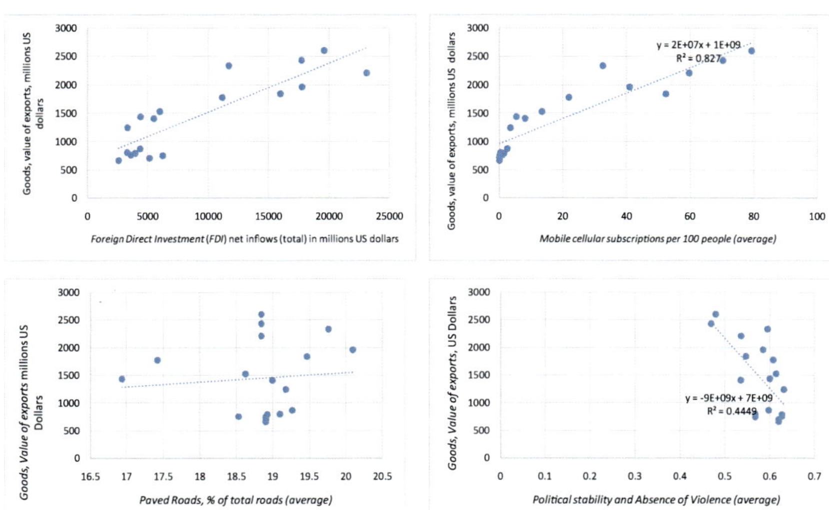

Fig. 1 The scatter plot of exports in value and the main variables of interest. Source: Authors

Table 1 Descriptive statistics for the main interest variables

Indicators	Political stability and absence of violence	Paved, roads, (% of total roads)	Foreign direct investment net inflows, in millions US dollars	Mobile phone subscriptions per 100 people
Mean	−0.415	18.862	163.96	21.81
Mediane	−0.311	17.480	63.714	6.36
Standard deviation	0.696	7.748	209.57	28.91

Source: Author

expected to be positive: if the political environment is better, intra WAEMU trade shall increase.

But this correlation coefficient is significant and negative for the percentage of paved road (−0.096) and the index of political stability (−0.27). This result may reflect the absence of linear relationship between these variables and certainly a non-linear relationship involving, for example, the existence of a threshold beyond which the quality of the political environment and road infrastructure have a positive impact on intra WAEMU exports.

Table 1 shows the summary statistics of the variables of interest. In General, between 1996 and 2013, WAEMU was confronted with political instabilities. The *coup d'état* of December 1999 in Côte d'Ivoire and the armed rebellion of 2002 that has turned into a political and military crisis until 2011, are troubled periods for the union. The instability in Côte d'Ivoire affects the economic performance of the union, including trade performance (Nayo and Egoumé-Bossogo 2011). The indicator of political stability and absence of violence is negative with a median as negative. It is clear that in periods of political instability economic transactions are slowed. Signs in regression should be that a strengthening of the political stability both in the exporter country and the importer country would encourage exports. Regarding the percentage of paved roads in the union, the figures in Table 1 show a small proportion of the total of the roads within the WAEMU (approximately 19% on average, with a median of 17%). This figure (Table 1) shows that over the period 1996–2013, road infrastructure facilitating provision prior's road transport of goods is low. This could result in additional costs of transaction in trade relations among member countries because the bulk of the trade is done by road.

Thus the trade partner, availability of quality infrastructure would reduce transaction costs and increase trade to the countries of the union.

FDI net inflows are on average about 163.96 with a large standard deviation (209.57 million USD on average from 1996 to 2013). This denotes that the distribution of the net inflows of FDI is not homogeneous. There are countries that attract larger proportions of FDI in WAEMU. Analyzing the Mobile phone subscriptions per 100 people, it appears that the level is low. Only 22% use a mobile phone. The standard deviation is greater than the mean so that there is heterogeneity among mobile phone users within WAEMU form 1996 to 2013.

4.2 Unit Root Tests

In general, conventional statistical methods in econometrics have been designed for stationarity series whose statistical properties do not change over time. The most common unit root tests in panel are those of Im, Pesaran and Shin (IPS) and Levin-Lin-Chu (LLC). Hurlin and Mignon (2004) point out that the implementation of early generations of tests such as Levin and Chu have limitations: they assume an inter independence residues. The second generation of tests such as Im, Pesaran Shin corrects this deficiency. It is this test that is used because not only is it efficient but it is also stable. The null hypothesis of this test assumes that all series are non-stationary against the alternative hypothesis that only a fraction of the series is stationary. IPS and Maddala and Wu (MW) test a heterogeneous alternative in which at least one series in the panel is stationary. We focus on the IPS results because this test assumes cross-section dependence is in form of a single unobserved common factor. Table 2 shows the results of unit root test. As we can see, GDP, Mobile phone subscriptions per 100 people, Political stability index, Similarity index and Population are non-stationary.

Table 2 Unit test root results in level

	Panel unit root test (MW) (Maddala and Wu 1999)		Panel unit root test (IPS) (Im et al. 2003)		
Variables	Without trend	With trend	Without trend	With trend	Conclusions
Goods, value exports, US dollars	261.611***	324.88***	−6.21***	−3.22***	Stationary
GDP in millions, US dollars	0.729	116.09	1.001	3.99	Non stationary
Foreign direct investment net inflows, in millions US dollars	175.426***	217.531***	−6.612***	−3.113***	Stationary
Mobile phone subscriptions per 100 people	0.218	9.243	−4.325***	−3.268***	Stationary
Political stability and absence of violence	105.694	102.432	1.480	1.784	Non stationary
Political stability index	105.694	102.432	1.480	1.784	Non stationary
Paved roads % of total roads	304.407***	203.230***	−3.742***	−0.485	Stationary without trend
Similarity index	227.289***	207.442***	4.058	0.608	Non stationary
Population	0.016	830.190***	22.781	11.768	Non stationary

***Significant at 5% level

Very often, what is thought to be a deterministic trend is actually a stochastic trend. In all series, we assume that there is a stochastic trend without losing any generality (Wang et al. 2010). For this reason we compute the first difference of all non-stationary variable before plugging them into the final estimated equation.

4.3 Hausman and Specification Tests

The Hausman test[5] leads to retain the random effects model design. The result suggests that the random effects model suit for the estimation. Then we run the specification test. It appears that the model passes the RESET test.[6] In addition, the value of the critical probability associated with the WALD statistic in the estimation of the gravity model is 0. This indicates the quality of the estimated relationship in the panel.

4.4 Estimations Results and Discussions

Table 3 presents the results of the model without (Model 1) and with (Model 2) a time-fixed effects. We suppose that over the period, the macroeconomic reforms and trade policies in order to strengthen economic integration vary over time. Then all these reforms can modify the value of coefficients. In all estimations results, the coefficients of all variables are significant. But they all have not the expected signs. The results suggest that the economic similarity, market size, economic growth, FDI net inflows, political stability and absence of violence, percentage of road paved and the proportion of mobile phone subscriber per 100 people are the powerful determinants of bilateral trade among WAEMU member countries.

In Model 1, the rate of growth of the exporting country has a positive and significant impact on exports of the latter towards the countries of the union. It is similar to macroeconomic policy; the number of people using a mobile phone; political stability and the similarity between the Member countries. As indicated in Table 3 1% increase of GDP in the exporting country causes a rise in exports into the countries of the union of 0.75%.This result is consistent with several gravity model based on empirical studies (Wang et al. 2010).

The results show also a positive and significant relationship between the level of FDI net inflow and similarity of GDP and trade flows. The results suggest that FDI and trade are generally complementary. 1% increase in inward FDI toward the exporter country leads to respectively 0.156% and 0.221% increase in intra WAEMU exports respectively without controlling time specific effect and

[5]We first perform the hausman test to select between a fixe effect and random effect model. The results suggest that the random effect is better: chi2(1) = 0.00, Prob>chi2 = 0.9983.

[6]chi2(1) = 2.7e+08, Prob > chi2 = 0.0000.

Table 3 Estimation results

Variables are in log, D is the delay operator	Model (1)	Model (2)
D(GDP of exporting country)	0.758***	−0.780***
	(0.000)	(0.000)
D(GDP of importing country)	−0.097***	−1.843***
	(0.000)	(0.000)
Distance	−0.794	−0.813
	(0.664)	(0.665)
D(Population of exporting country)	44.303***	36.500***
	(0.005)	(0.006)
D(Population of importing country)	28.819***	21.817***
	(0.005)	(0.005)
FDI net inflow in exporting country	0.156***	0.221***
	(0.000)	(0.000)
FDI net inflow in importing country	0.033***	0.060***
	(0.000)	(0.000)
Mobile phone subscription per 100 people in exporting country	0.055***	0.054***
	(0.000)	(0.000)
Mobile phone subscription per 100 people in importing country	0.089***	0.112***
	(0.000)	(0.000)
Road paved % of total roads in exporting country	−0.844***	−0.917***
	(0.000)	(0.000)
Road paved % of total roads in importing country	0.049***	−0.005***
	(0.000)	(0.000)
Political stability index in exporting country	0.054***	0.187***
	(0.000)	(0.000)
Political stability index in importing country	0.079***	0.199***
	(0.000)	(0.000)
D(Similarity index)	0.204***	1.231***
	(0.000)	(0.000)
Constant	21.562***	22.396***
	(4.612)	(4.624)
Observations	842	842
Log likelihood	−2.218e+09	−2.072e+09
Wald chi2(14)	4.33e+09	4.47e+09
Prob > chi2 (Wald chi2(14))	0.0000	0.0000
Number of individus	56	56
Alpha	5.311	5.265
	(0.812)	(0.806)
Likelihood-ratio test of alpha = 0, Prob ≥ chibar2	0.000	0.000
Time fixed-effects	No	Yes

Note: p value at significativity level in parentheses
***$p < 0.01$, **$p < 0.05$, *$p < 0.1$
Source: Authors

controlling time specific effects. The same positive relationship has been set considering the FDI net inflows in the partner country: 1% increase in inward FDI toward the partner country leads to 0.033% and 0.06% increase in bilateral trade within member countries. These results are consistent with Egger and Pfaffermayr (2004), Wang et al. (2010), BAD (2013a, b).

Talking about GDP similarity index, there is also a positive relationship with bilateral trade flows. 1% increase in the GDP similarity index leads to 0.204% and 1.231% increase in intra WAEMU trade respectively in Model 1 and Model 2. When controlling time specific effect, the impact of GDP similarity index is higher.

The results suggest also that strengthening political stability increases bilateral trade flows between WEAMU member countries.

However, an increase in the GDP in 1%-importing countries reduced exports in the direction of the union of 0.097% (Longo and Sekkat 2004). This reflects the fact that economic growth in importing countries of the union creates a need for property we covered by offers from WAEMU exporters. So these importing countries have the possibility to be provided with the needed products from the other countries of the union. This is not a brake as such to the expansion of trade in intra zone. This could translate the existence of trade diversion effect. The distance is not a factor limiting trade intra WEAMU. This result should be an asset for member countries in terms of reducing the costs of transaction between Member countries. The costs of transaction between Member countries would not constitute an obstacle to the expansion of trade intra WEAMU.

The results show that the growth of the population both in the importer country and the exporter country is an asset for the expansion of trade in intra WEAMU. It is clear that an increase in the rate of population growth of 1% led the increase in exports to the area. The positive effect is less important with time fixed-effect: 36.5% against 44.3% in the exporting country and 21.8% from 28.9% in the importing country. The population growth rate appears here as the existence of opportunities for exporting commodity in the area. Thus a population increase corresponds to an increase of the potential demand. Faced with this potential demand increase, companies will adjust their supply. The adjustment of this offer translates into an increase of exports. What could explain the positive sign associated with the variable population growth rate?

Considering the political stability and the absence of violence, the results show that the strengthening of political stability and the elimination of violence both in the exporting and importing country promote trade among the Member countries of WAEMU. Increased political stability of 1 point index causes an increase in exports intra zone of the order of 0.19%. This positive result was highlighted by Longo and Sekkat (2004). Indeed the stability of the political environment and the absence of violence reduce the risk of failure of the economic agents and encourage economic operators to invest in economic transactions. The environment is favourable, exporters develop their activities and intensify exchanges with WEAMU partners.

Concerning the level of road infrastructure, the sign associated with the coefficient is intuitive. But, analysis of the correlation shows a coefficient admittedly low, but negative and significant at 5% threshold of significance. However, the *expected*

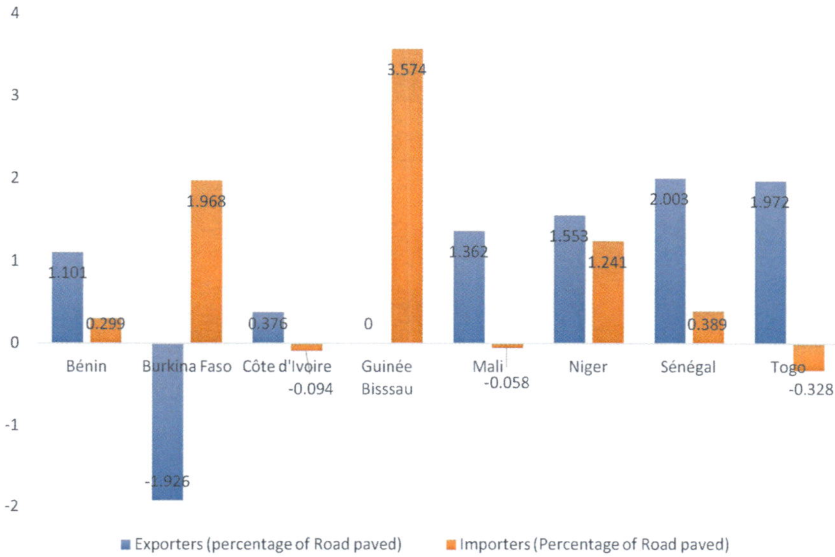

Graph 1 Impact of paved road (% of total road) on intra WAEMU exports by country. Source: Author estimations

sign of the coefficient should be positive. Because the existence of quality road infrastructure contributes to the reduction of transaction costs. However, the analysis of the results by country (Annexes 1 and 2) shows that among the eight countries of the area only Burkina Faso spring with a negative coefficient associated with the road infrastructure variiable. The result of the other countries shows a strong positive relationship between the percentage of paved roads and trade flows in WEAMU. Indeed, the availability of quality infrastructure contributes to the reduction of transaction costs. This reduction in the costs of transaction boosts trade between the partner countries. The following graph (cf. Graph 1) shows the value of the coefficient for each country over the panel. On the exporters side, an increase of the percentage of paved road leads to an increase of exports when we consider each country as exporters except in the case of Burkina Faso. On the importers side, increasing the percentage of paved road has a negative impact in the case of Côte d'Ivoire, Mali and Togo. The situation of the percentage of paved road in WAEMU on average, presents a stable trend over the period (see Annex 3). And Côte d'Ivoire has the highest level of this indicator and the lowest level appears in Togo. The more this indicators is lower the more it appears as an obstacle to expand trade because the lack increases transaction costs and slows down exports dynamic (Mali and Togo). In the case of Côte d'Ivoire, this country doesn't import much from other WAEMU member countries. It is the main supplyer for most of them.

Another variable of infrastructure considered in the analysis is the number of mobile phone subscribers. The use of the phone allows economic agents to gains time. These new technologies are involved to reduce the distance between the operators, thus lowering transaction costs. The results in the table show that both the exporter and the importer, an increase of 1 percentage point of the number of subscriber of the mobile phone (respectively in the importing country) leads to an increase of intra WAEMU exports in the order of 0.055% (respectively of 0.112%). These results are consistent with the results of Longo and Sekkat (2004).

5 Conclusion

The aims of this paper is to analyze the obstacles to the strengthening of trade intra WAEMU. It focuses on the economic, political and infrastructural factors in explaining the level of trade between the Member countries of the WAEMU between 1996 and 2013. We estimate an extended gravity model in a panel specification to assess the impact of these variables on the whole intra WAEMU trade from 1996 to 2013.

The results suggest that the economic similarity, market size, economic growth, FDI net inflows, political stability and absence of violence, percentage of paved road and the proportion of mobile phone subscriber per 100 people are the powerful determinants of bilateral trade among WAEMU country members. In others words, these results show the issues of improvement projects and construction of transport and telecommunications infrastructure, political environment stability and good management of macroeconomic policies in each member countries in strengthening the economic integration in WAEMU (Cahérine et al. 2013).

Improving domestic macroeconomic policies may raise intra WAEMU trade and hence contribute to regional spillovers (Longo and Sekkat 2004; Wang et al. 2010). As WAEMU is engaged in a process of economic reform and promotes openness, more outcomes in terms of increasing intra trade are expected. The regional economic program is a great initiative to improve infrastructure as this is pointed out as a key factor for regional take-off. So our results suggest that initiatives investing in infrastructures should be followed up, in managing and regulating infrastructure at regional level. As a recommendation about infrastructure, policy makers should develop trade-related infrastructure in order to facilitate the movement of goods and services within the union.

Another result stands for improving political environment. As the literature shows that improving governance fosters exports (Sekkat and Varoudakis 2000), it is necessary to avoid political instability. The results show that both in exporting countries and importing countries, political stability and absence of violence have a direct impact on intra trade flows. As recommendation, it will be necessary to establish and maintain a climate of political stability and good governance conducive to trade. We can extend this analysis by estimating the same equation year by year in order to assess the impact of reforms and the regional economic program over year.

Annex 1: Estimations by Country Part 1 (Benin, Burkina Faso, Côte d'Ivoire et Guinea Bissau)

Variables are in log, D is the delay operator	Benin		Burkina Faso		Côte d'Ivoire		Guinea Bissau	
	(1)	(2)	(1)	(2)	(1)	(2)	(1)	(2)
D(GDP of exporting country)	3.690***	3.625***	−0.627***	5.899***	1.181***	1.107***	−88.841***	−79.269***
	(0.001)	(0.002)	(0.001)	(0.002)	(0.001)	(0.001)	(0.058)	(0.069)
D(GDP of importing country)	−2.033***	−2.779***	3.637***	0.902***	−0.922***	−0.646***	101.283***	91.211***
	(0.001)	(0.002)	(0.001)	(0.002)	(0.001)	(0.001)	(0.068)	(0.081)
Distance	−0.575	−0.582	−5.515**	−5.373**	−1.257	−1.269	0.883	0.222
	(0.955)	(1.017)	(2.532)	(2.409)	(0.975)	(0.982)	(1.631)	(2.502)
D(Population of exporting country)	73.222***	−1183.319***	−695.319***	−1571.359***	53.139***	367.486***	−3486.075***	−2210.100***
	(0.037)	(0.960)	(0.125)	(1.064)	(0.010)	(0.068)	(3.859)	(5.745)
D(Population of importing country)	52.647***	38.587***	−26.672***	−68.752***	−5.376***	−11.590***	−1379.925***	−1286.385***
	(0.038)	(0.040)	(0.023)	(0.024)	(0.008)	(0.008)	(0.655)	(0.738)
FDI net inflow in exporting country	−0.054***	−1.457***	0.224***	0.661***	0.153***	−0.848***	4.906***	3.888***
	(0.000)	(0.001)	(0.000)	(0.000)	(0.000)	(0.000)	(0.004)	(0.006)
FDI net inflow in importing country	0.035***	0.031***	0.247***	0.350***	−0.001***	−0.001***	−0.315***	−0.449***
	(0.000)	(0.000)	(0.000)	(0.000)	(0.000)	(0.000)	(0.000)	(0.001)
Mobile phone subscription per 100 people in exporting country	0.079***	−4.663***	−0.115***	2.237***	0.253***	−2.676***	−1.699***	−2.485***
	(0.000)	(0.004)	(0.000)	(0.001)	(0.000)	(0.000)	(0.001)	(0.006)
Mobile phone subscription per 100 people in importing country	0.138***	0.124***	0.375***	0.402***	−0.048***	−0.041***	4.044***	4.743***
	(0.000)	(0.000)	(0.000)	(0.000)	(0.000)	(0.000)	(0.002)	(0.006)

(continued)

Variables are in log, D is the delay operator	Benin		Burkina Faso		Côte d'Ivoire		Guinea Bissau	
	(1)	(2)	(1)	(2)	(1)	(2)	(1)	(2)
Road paved % of total roads in exporting country	1.101***	13.683***	−1.926***	−7.144***	0.376***	5.711***	0	0
	(0.000)	(0.010)	(0.000)	(0.004)	(0.000)	(0.001)	0	0
Road paved % of total roads in importing country	0.299***	0.365***	1.968***	1.861***	−0.094***	−0.108***	3.574***	−10.892***
	(0.000)	(0.000)	(0.000)	(0.000)	(0.000)	(0.000)	(0.008)	(0.017)
Political stability index in exporting country	−5.957***	−19.792***	3.415***	13.113***	−0.126***	0.060***	−41.618***	−26.358***
	(0.002)	(0.014)	(0.000)	(0.002)	(0.000)	(0.000)	(0.048)	(0.066)
Political stability index in importing country	−0.249***	−0.299***	−0.157***	0.054***	0.125***	0.150***	2.051***	0.733***
	(0.000)	(0.000)	(0.000)	(0.000)	(0.000)	(0.000)	(0.002)	(0.003)
D(Similarity index)	−8.413***	−15.764***	−31.545***	−28.166***	0.286***	−0.791***	121.521***	104.950***
	(0.004)	(0.004)	(0.003)	(0.004)	(0.001)	(0.001)	(0.081)	(0.097)
Constant	10.054	34.383***	71.370***	104.046***	23.925***	24.245***	62.055***	98.197***
	(6.558)	(6.983)	(17.128)	(16.299)	(6.708)	(6.752)	(11.596)	(17.942)
Observations	111	111	111	111	105	105	76	76
Number of ind	7	7	7	7	7	7	7	7
Time fixed-effects	No	Yes	No	Yes	No	Yes	No	Yes

Standard errors in parentheses
***$p < 0.01$, **$p < 0.05$, *$p < 0.1$
Source: Authors

Annex 2: Estimations by Country Part 2 (Mali, Niger, Sénégal et Togo)

Variables are in log, D is the delay operator	Mali		Niger		Sénégal		Togo	
	(1)	(2)	(1)	(2)	(1)	(2)	(1)	(2)
D(GDP of exporting country)	−1.344***	1.507***	−5.012***	6.698***	0.375***	−0.070***	−4.055***	−32.920***
	(0.003)	(0.006)	(0.004)	(0.019)	(0.001)	(0.003)	(0.001)	(0.003)
D(GDP of importing country)	0.672***	2.212***	5.168***	1.321***	1.213***	1.552***	7.000***	9.253***
	(0.003)	(0.004)	(0.004)	(0.005)	(0.001)	(0.001)	(0.001)	(0.002)
Distance	−4.927*	−5.007*	−1.060	−1.064	−1.448	−1.424*	−1.068	−1.242
	(2.926)	(2.992)	(3.219)	(3.302)	(0.889)	(0.864)	(0.722)	(0.916)
D(Population of exporting country)	−342.628***	1088.434***	218.604***	1761.953***	56.669***	197.835***	−588.813***	−29,713.778***
	(0.127)	(1.203)	(0.269)	(4.247)	(0.017)	(0.965)	(0.122)	(3.111)
D(Population of importing country)	88.230***	57.064***	173.114***	153.567***	91.565***	94.222***	45.169***	31.385***
	(0.094)	(0.108)	(0.061)	(0.066)	(0.011)	(0.012)	(0.013)	(0.012)
FDI net inflow in exporting country	0.050***	0.471***	−0.203***	1.383***	0.101***	0.716***	0.037***	1.449***
	(0.000)	(0.000)	(0.000)	(0.005)	(0.000)	(0.003)	(0.000)	(0.000)
FDI net inflow in importing country	−0.034***	−0.028***	−0.237***	−0.235***	0.031***	0.059***	0.156***	0.143***
	(0.000)	(0.000)	(0.000)	(0.000)	(0.000)	(0.000)	(0.000)	(0.000)
Mobile phone subscription per 100 people in exporting country	0.056***	2.233***	−0.318***	−4.796***	−0.057***	−0.626***	0.424***	−23.170***
	(0.000)	(0.002)	(0.000)	(0.013)	(0.000)	(0.004)	(0.000)	(0.002)
Mobile phone subscription per 100 people in importing country	0.314***	0.351***	0.505***	0.549***	0.160***	0.091***	0.052***	0.279***
	(0.000)	(0.000)	(0.000)	(0.000)	(0.000)	(0.000)	(0.000)	(0.000)

(continued)

Variables are in log, D is the delay operator	Mali		Niger		Sénégal		Togo	
	(1)	(2)	(1)	(2)	(1)	(2)	(1)	(2)
Road paved % of total roads in exporting country	1.362***	−0.088***	1.553***	1.892***	2.003***	4.060***	1.972***	29.741***
	(0.001)	(0.001)	(0.002)	(0.045)	(0.000)	(0.009)	(0.000)	(0.003)
Road paved % of total roads in importing country	−0.058***	0.170***	1.241***	1.564***	0.389***	0.313***	−0.328***	0.107***
	(0.001)	(0.001)	(0.001)	(0.001)	(0.000)	(0.000)	(0.000)	(0.000)
Political stability index in exporting country	0.141***	−0.588***	0.250***	−2.202***	0.141***	0.974***	−0.440***	−11.799***
	(0.000)	(0.000)	(0.001)	(0.008)	(0.000)	(0.004)	(0.000)	(0.002)
Political stability index in importing country	0.367***	0.341***	−0.890***	−0.633***	−0.108***	−0.155***	0.290***	0.407***
	(0.001)	(0.001)	(0.000)	(0.000)	(0.000)	(0.000)	(0.000)	(0.000)
D(Similarity Index)	−11.205***	−15.712***	−8.53***	−6.583***	−3.547***	−3.799***	14.197***	17.734***
	(0.008)	(0.008)	(0.012)	(0.012)	(0.001)	(0.001)	(0.003)	(0.003)
Constant	51.039**	−1.115	0.839	−60.134***	15.024**	2.988	30.304***	802.030***
	(20.138)	(20.594)	(22.385)	(22.965)	(6.468)	(6.282)	(4.913)	(6.231)
Observations	111	111	106	106	111	111	111	111
Time fixed-effects	No	Yes	No	Yes	No	Yes	No	Yes

Standard errors in parentheses
$^{***}p < 0.01$, $^{**}p < 0.05$, $^{*}p < 0.1$
Source: Authors

Annex 3: Percentage of Road Paved in Each Country from 1996 to 2013

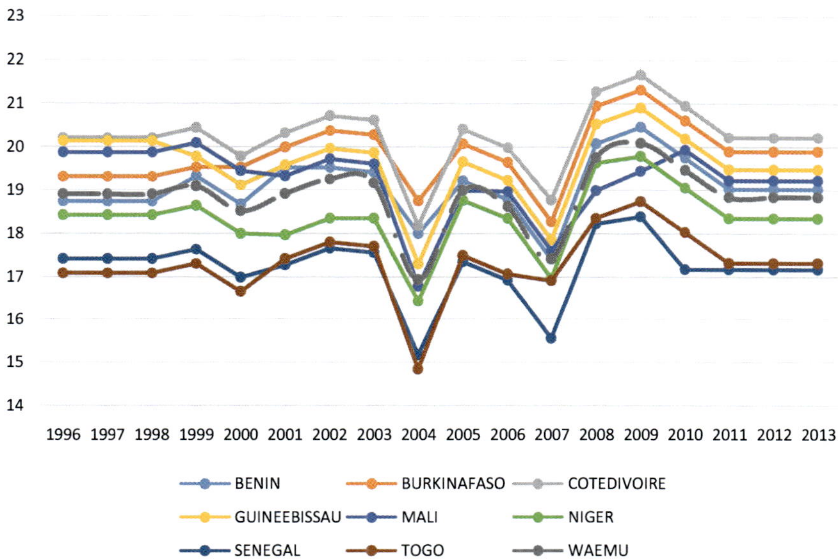

Source: World Development Indicators

References

Agbodji, A. E. (2007). Intégration et échanges commerciaux intra sous-régionaux: le cas de l'UEMOA. *Revue africaine de l'Intégration, 1*(1), 161–188.

Amr, S. H. (2013, May). Theories of economic integration: A survey of economic and political literature. *International Journal of Economy, Management and Social Sciences, 2*(5), 133–155.

Anderson, J. E., & Marcouiller, D. (2002). Insecurity and the pattern of trade: An empirical investigation. *The Review of Economics and Statistics, 84*(2), 342–352.

BAD. (2013a, Juillet). http://www.afdb.org/uploads/tx_llafdbpapers/Impact_des_Unions_Montaires_sur_les_changes_commerciaux._Le_cas_de_lUEMOA_V4.pdf. Récupéré sur http://www.afdb.org: http://www.afdb.org

BAD. (2013b). http://www.afdb.org/uploads/tx_llafdbpapers/Integration_regionale_et_echange_des_produits_agricoles_au_sein_de_l_UEMOA-une_analyse_par_le_modele_de_gravite.pdf. Récupéré sur http://www.afdb.org/uploads/tx_llafdbpapers/Integration_regionale_et_echange_des_produits_agricoles_au_sein_de_l_UEMOA-une_analyse_par_le_modele_de_gravite.pdf: http://www.afdb.org

Balasubramanyam, V. N., Salisu, M., & Sapsford, D. (1996). Foreign direct investment and growth in EP and IS countries. *The Econometrics Journal, 106*, 92–105.

Bhagwati, J. (1971). Trade-diverting customs unions and welfare-improvement: A clarification. *The Econometrics Journal, 81*(323), 580–587.

Cahérine, A. B., Stéphanie, B., & Celine, C. (2013). Impact de l'Intégration sur le Commerce. In D. G. Anne-Marie, G. Samuel, G. Patrick, & G. J. Sylviane (Eds.), *Intégration régionale pour le développement en zone franc* (pp. 212–249). Paris: Economica.

Coe, D. T., & Helpman, E. (1995). International R & D spillovers. *European Economic Review, 39*, 859–887.

Coe, D. T., Helpman, E., & Hoffmaister, A. W. (1997). North-South R & D spillovers. *The Econometrics Journal, 107*, 134–149.

Egger, P., & Pfaffermayr, M. (2004). Distance, trade and FDI: A Hausman-Taylor Sur approach. *Journal of Applied Econometrics, 19*(2), 227–246.

Francoisa, J., & Manchin, M. (2007). *Institutions, infrastructure, and trade*. Economics working paper no. 77.

Gbetnkom, D., & Avom, D. (2005). Intégration par le marché: le cas de l'UEMOA. *Region et développement, 22*, 86–103.

Hurlin, C., & Mignon, V. (2004). Une Synthèse des Tests de Racine Unitaire en sur Données de Panel. *Economie et Prévision, 169–171*, :251–295.

Im, K. S., Pesaran, M. H., & Shin, Y. (2003). Testing for unit roots in heterogeneous panels. *Journal of Econometrics, 115*(1), 53–74.

Levchenko, A. A. (2007). Institutional quality and international trade. *The Review of Economic Studies, 74*(3), 791–819.

Limão, N., & Venables, A. J. (2001). Infrastructure, geographical disadvantage, transport costs, and trade. *The World Bank Economic Review, 15*(3), 451–479.

Linders, G. J., Hl Slangen, A., De Groot, H. L., & Beugelsdijk, S. (2005). *Cultural and institutional determinants of bilateral trade flows*. Tinbergen Institute discussion paper, no. 05–074/3.

Longo, R., & Sekkat, K. (2004, August). Economic obstacles to expanding intra-african trade. *World Development, 32*(8), 1309–1321.

Maddala, G. S., & Wu, S. (1999). A comparative study of unit root tests with panel data and a new simple test. *Oxford Bulletin of Economics and Statistics, 61*(S1), 631–652.

Nayo, A., & Egoumé-Bossogo, P. (2011). *Feeling the elephant's weight: The impact of Côte d'Ivoire's crisis on WAEMU trade*. IMF working papers, pp. 1–32.

Norehan, A., Hussin, A., & Hadi, M. O. (2014). The determinants of trade and trade direction of Arab Maghreb union (AMU). *Journal of Empirical Economics, 2*(2), 46–62.

Rodrik, D. (1997). *Trade policy and economic performance in Sub-Saharan Africa*. NBER working paper, no. 6562. Cambridge, MA: NBER.

Santos-Silva, J., & Tenreyro, S. (2006). The log of gravity. *The Review of Economics and Statistics, 88*(4), 641–658.

Santos-Silva, J. S., & Tenreyro, S. (2011). Further simulation evidence on the performance of the Poisson pseudo-maximum likelihood estimator. *Economics Letters, 112*(2), 220–222.

Sekkat, K., & Varoudakis, A. (2000). Exchange rate management and manufactured exports in sub-Saharan Africa. *Journal of Development Economics, 61*(1), 237–253.

UNCTAD. (2016, Mai 10). http://unctad.org/en/Pages/Statistics.aspx. Récupéré sur http://unctad.org: http://unctad.org

Wang, C., Wei, Y., & Liu, X. (2010). Determinants of bilateral trade flows in OECD countries: Evidence from gravity panel data models. *World Economics, 33*(7), 894–915.

Part II
External Trade

Growing External Trade, Development and Structural Heterogeneity in West Africa: Examining the Evidence

Akpan H. Ekpo and Douglason G. Omotor

Contents

Abstract The paper sets out to determine the extent which West African economies are integrated, their take in the global value chains and some important parameters which could influence their trade flows given the perceived structural heterogeneity amongst them. The findings and results from the West African Enabling Trade Index, their participation in Global Value Chains and estimated simple gravity model among others suggest that trade performance of the subregion did not sufficiently improve. Second, access to trade finance and identifying potential markets and buyers were among the most problematic factors that inhibit export trade in the region. The implication is that reducing these barriers will enable trade contribute to prosperity and welfare. Rising depth of integration in the sub-region, though marginal, is associated with rising income over time. As such, if the sub-region were to pursue a strategy of development anchored on integration and laced with value chain creation, income levels could improve as they acquire new capabilities and diversification In addition there is evidence of economic size (GDP) and geographical nearness (proximity and infrastructure) of West African economies to be very significant in inter and intra-trading. The paper recommends that the West African region rather than be overwhelmed with observed limitations, the subregion should leverage on its enormous potential to integrate into the global value chains. This can be achieved through deliberate efforts to build developmental states, promote export diversification, enhance structural transformation and harness the

A. H. Ekpo (✉) · D. G. Omotor
West African Institute for Financial and Economic Management (WAIFEM), Lagos, Nigeria

D. Seck (ed.), *The External Sector of Africa's Economy*, Advances in African Economic, Social and Political Development,
https://doi.org/10.1007/978-3-319-97913-7_4

dividends of its demographic transition. It is only then, trade for inclusive development and equity can be achieved; else, the 'Africa is rising' paradigm would be a mere slogan associated only with its rising population as well as rising export commodity prices.

1 Introduction

The role external trade plays in the economic development of economies is well documented in the literature on international economics. A major finding from the comprehensive literature shows that internationally active countries tend to be more productive than countries which only produce for the domestic market (Sun and Heshmati 2010). This argument is built on the premise that the emergence and success of China as an economic power is woven on its adoption of an open door policy that is driven by guided liberalization and globalization. However, a competing line of thought in the literature as a result of change in the world economic order is the integration of economies as regional blocks; and this is forcing regions to have a rethink of their participation in international trade. As has been posited elsewhere, effective regional integration not only enhances trade within the region, it also attracts investments in manufacturing—a major source of job creation and economic growth (Njinkeu 2012). In addition, intraregional trade contributes largely to inclusive growth than extra regional trade, because it encompasses more manufactures, SMEs and jobs which also create equity. Third, deeper regional integration enhances competitiveness at the international level and facilitates relations with the emerging regional countries, where there are many opportunities (Bárcena et al. 2014).

In the projected regional contribution to world economic growth for 2011–2017 for instance, developing Asian countries are expected to be responsible for 50% of world economic growth. The contribution of Latin America and the Caribbean with a forecast of 8.3% almost doubled Africa's contribution (Bárcena et.al. 2014). Africa with a projected economic growth rate of 4.8% (recently revised downward to 4.3; IMF 2016) as a continent, lagged behind other continents except for Australia and New Zealand whose projected growth was put at 1.1% (see Fig. 1). Further contention that reinforces the regional integration trade in the case of Africa's regional integration is hinged on the 2005 highincome World Trade Organization (WTO) members agreement to provide least-developed countries (LDCs), most of which are in Africa access for at least 97% of their tariff lines (product categories). Citing the incapability of Africa to optimize such an offer, it was reasoned that northern or western-based trade preference schemes cannot but feature "hub and spoke" characteristics which are not in the best interest of the continent as they would rather constrain than enhance intra-African trade (Oyedije 2012).

This paper while noting the effects of international trade on economic growth to be of great significance in this globalized era, the highly fragmented nature of African economies and most copiously the West African sub-region, prevents

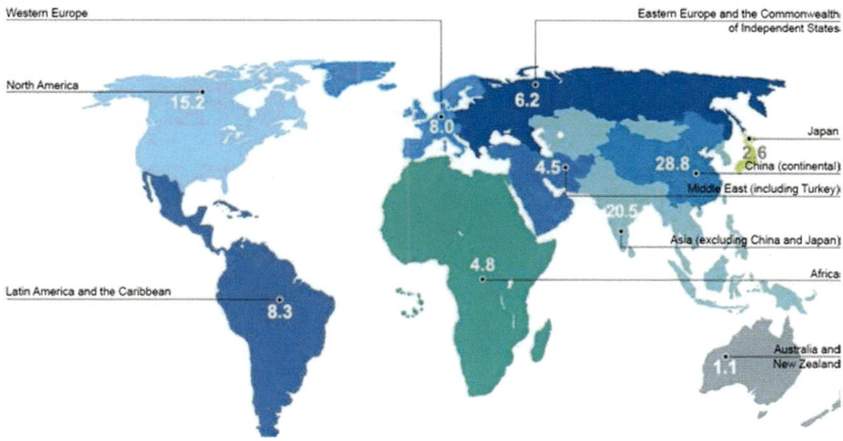

Fig. 1 Projected regional contributions to world economic growth, 2011–2017 (*Percentages*). *Source*: Economic Commission for Latin America and the Caribbean (ECLAC), on the basis of International Monetary Fund (IMF), *World Economic Outlook*, April 2012

development of efficient supply chains and value addition as they are not only mono-cultural primary exporters of natural resources and commodities, their growth patterns are divergent, unbalanced and structurally heterogeneous. Studying the West African sub-region from these perspectives would help policymakers map out appropriate policies aimed at promoting the sub-region's integration through trade and global value chains.

The rest of the paper is structured as follows: Following the introduction, Sect. 2 reviews trade and development literature; Sect. 3 highlights some stylized facts of the ECOWAS economies; while in Sect. 4 discusses the degree of West Africa's integration into the global value chains. Sect. 5 specifies and estimates the gravity model; while Sect. 6 concludes the paper. It is anticipated that discussions in the paper would provoke robust debate on the subject matter with the aim of influencing policy.

2 Trade and Development Literature

The literature on international trade and development is extensive, especially when related to inclusiveness and equitable development. In some instances, the interrelationships have been broken down into various streams. Without summarizing all of the discussions on these interrelationships, some references following Bárcena et al. (2014) are given below in relation to recent evidence. First, the Economic Commission for Latin America and the Caribbean (ECLAC) key arguments in the book; "Time for Equality: Closing gaps, Opening Trails (2010)"- that structural heterogeneity of Latin American and Caribbean economies as one of the main causes of the social inequality that exists in the region's economies, and which partly accounts for the region's low growth in recent times (Bárcena et al. 2014: 23).

Structural heterogeneity in this context relates to the fact that while big firms in developing and emerging countries of ECLAC on the same stratum with their counterparts in industrialized economies, behave the same way, small and medium enterprises (SMEs) in these economies do not share same characteristics with their peers in western countries. Rather, SMEs in ECLAC are marked by large asymmetries among segments of enterprises and workers, with bulk of their jobs concentrated in very low productive sectors. Further evidences on this can be found in Bannier and Zahn (2014), Mateev and Anastasov (2010), Beck et al. (2003) among others. The held view is that, while SMEs are important drivers of productivity-enhancing innovation particularly in developed economies, the low-productivity sectors they belong generally in developing economies make it very difficult for them to innovate, adopt technology and promote learning processes unlike their equals in industrialized economies. Such internal disparities exacerbate systemic competitiveness problems when compared with industrialized countries. This viciously creates external gap and structural heterogeneity which may be responsible for the deep social inequality in developing regions globally (Bárcena et al. 2014; Altenburg and Eckhardt 2006). To simultaneously address these internal and external structural gaps require achieving faster and more inclusive development.

The inclusive growth/development paradigm guides countries to make choices from a diverse spectrum of policy incentives and institutional mechanisms in order to widen social inclusion in the process and benefits of economic growth without dampening incentives to work, save, and invest (Samans et al. 2015). One sphere of thought that is apparent to fostering such inclusive sustainable growth which can promote productivity and employment for a broad group of workers and firms is trade. To further buttress this perspective, Bárcena et al. (2014) wrote:

> Trade contributes to this process when workers and firms are able to adjust to enter growing economic activities and adopt new technologies. Countries must change the way they relate to each other if they are to reduce global inequities and ensure improvements in human development. Boosting the potential of producers and consumers in favour of a more inclusive development will require the modificiation of forms of international trade unfavourable to developing countries, since the protectionism of industrialized countries and existing asymmetries are beyond their control. Governments must ensure access to knowledge and new technologies for the vast majority of society, promote training and access to international quality standards in SMEs, and invest in infrastructure, transport and logistics in order to reduce structural heterogeneity (p. 29).

In efforts to appreciate trade openness in reducing structural heterogeneity, related studies attempt to ascertain the degree to which economies are integrated into the global value chains and determine some important parameters which could influence trade flows. However, such studies on the West African region are scanty.

The OECD, WTO and World Bank Group Report prepared for the G20 Trade Ministers Meeting, Sydney, Australia, 19 July 2014 observed that the growth of global value chains (GVCs) in recent times contributed to increased interconnectedness of economies and estimated that over 70% of global trade was in intermediate goods and services and in capital goods. The Report further revealed that income created within GVCs has doubled, on average, over the last 15 years; and in China, income associated with GVCs grew sixfold. Some other studies on how GVCs enhanced exports are Aksoy et al. (2005), Rios and Jaffee (2008), Alfaro and Rodriguez-Clare (2004), Hou (2013). In a related study, Saliola and Zanfei (2009: 369), using data on 1385 firms active in Thailand in 2001–2003, applied a multinomial logit model to test how the nature and intensity of multinational presence and the competencies of local firms affect the organization of international knowledge transfer. Saliola and Zanfei reported that knowledge intensive relationships, which are characterized by a significant transmission of technical and organizational competencies along the value chains, are positively associated with the presence of global buyers in the local market.

In a Final Report submitted by SAANA Consulting to the UK aid of UK Government in 2014, it was noted that diversification and linking up with global value chains are essential to Southern Africa regional development. Also key, according to the Report is the importance of scaling up investment for agriculture development through support to SMEs, regional infrastructure finance and their integration to nascent regional value chains. The empirical findings of the Report provide some evidence-based guidance on the linkages between trade, growth and poverty reduction. On an aggregate level, it was found that openness to trade in Southern Africa region has a positive impact on poverty alleviation through its effect on economic growth. The study in its remarks noted particularly, the impactful effects of supporting women and trade. In a study Ekpo (2015) showed empirically that openness in West Africa did not contribute to growth and development during the period 1970–2014.

A recent paper by Amoako-Tuffour et al. (2016) opined that trade facilitation stimulates economic transformation by raising exports, supporting export diversification, reallocating resources to more productive activities, improving access to cheaper and better-quality imported inputs and enabling participation in value chains. These authors argued further that West Africa with an enlarged regional market of about 336 million people with 2014 average per capita income of $798 can enhance their opportunities for industrial growth, widen the scope of their enterprises and benefit from economies of scale.

In subsequent sections that follow, the paper discusses some basic issues which relate to West Africa's participation in the Global Value Chains and also attempt to estimate a simple Gravity model after a review of some stylized facts about the ECOWAS region.

3 The ECOWAS Economies: Some Stylized Facts

The causes of the abrupt end that underlined the 'Africa is rising' theorizing in the last decade were alluded to three key transitions: (a) the slowdown and restructuring of economic activity in China away from investment and manufacturing toward consumption and services, (b) declining commodity prices and strains in some large emerging market economies like India, Brazil, etc., and (c) ease of monetary policy of some major advanced economy central banks in reaction to tight monetary policy in the context of a resilient United States recovery (IMF 2016). These key transitions have exogenous impact on African economies and as such, the marked expansion that followed the external trade in the West Africa region particularly did not produce a balanced economic, social and territorial development; rather, it created a challenge.

This section describes some stylized facts about the economies of West African countries. These include geographical size and their population, human development index, output growth, real per capita, government deficits, among others. Table 1 provides some basic data about the 16 countries that makeup the region. The countries include 15 member countries of the Economic Community of West African States (ECOWAS) and Mauretania (opted out in January, 2000). ECOWAS was primarily created on May 28, 1975 to promote economic cooperation within the sub-region.

The sub region has a total surface area of 5.1 million km^2 accounting for 17% of Africa's total surface area. The current population of West Africa is 362,807,216 and constitutes 29.87% of Africa's total population as at June 17, 2016, based on the latest United Nations estimates. The West African population is dominated by Nigeria, Africa's largest economy and most populous country in the continent with an estimated population of 186,987,563 people. Nigeria accounts for approximately 51.54% of the entire region's population.

The 'Africa is Rising' theorizing since 2000s was anchored on many factors; first, though not the most important is the demographic dividend with the projection that Africa will account for 3.2 billion of the projected 4 billion increase in the global population by 2100. This alone is a market, and when coupled with the rising share of its working age population with productive potentials, the demographic transformation of the continent as thought, should have visible implications for the global economy (Drummond et al. 2014: 4). Second, two decades of strong and sustained growth in sub-Saharan Africa from the mid-1990s. This was occasioned by a combination of factors among them, implementation of sound macroeconomic policies, favorable external conditions, fiscal space created by the post–debt relief, and the strengthening of political and economic institutions until the global financial crisis. The worsening external conditions that followed the global financial crisis have now become less supportive (Bárcena et al. 2014) with attendant backlash effects on economies of primary exporting countries most of them in sub-Saharan.

The region's gross domestic product (GDP) per capita ranges from US$800 in Niger to USD 4400 in Cape Verde. Nigeria was projected to account for nearly 78%

Table 1 Summary statistic for West African countries

Countries	Surface area km^2	Population (17 June, 2016)	HDI 2015 estimates for 2014	Real per capita GDP (2014) %	Fiscal balance 2014 excldg. grants	Trade balance (% GDP)
Benin	112,622	11,170,385	0.480	2.8	−3.5	−11.7
Burkina Faso	274,200	18,640,594	0.402	1.1	−6.1	−1.9
Cape Verde	4033	527,077	0.646	−0.2	−11.7	−34.1
Cote d'Ivoire	322,463	23,261,353	0.462	4.8	−4.6	9.8
Gambia (The)	11,295	2,055,821	0.441	−2.9	−12.7	−22.8
Ghana	238,533	28,041,456	0.579	1.6	−10.5	−4.1
Guinea	245,857	12,951,521	0.411	−2.1	−11.4	−6.6
Guinea-Bissau	36,125	1,889,002	0.420	0.3	−11.6	−15.5
Liberia	111,369	4,616,674	0.430	−2.0	−10.5	−32.8
Mali	1,240,192	18,141,800	0.419	3.5	−9.4	−24.2
Mauritania[a]	1,030,700	4,167,747	0.506	n.a.	n.a.	n.a.
Niger	1,267,000	20,725,960	0.348	2.9	−11.2	−12.6
Nigeria	923,768	186,987,563	0.514	3.5	−2.3	6.1
Senegal	196,722	15,595,475	0.466	1.6	−7.9	−19.8
Sierra Leone	71,740	6,593,903	0.413	3.9	−7.0	5.2
Togo	56,785	7,499,331	0.484	2.5	−7.9	−18.6
ECOWAS	5.1 million km^2	362,807,216	0.464	3.2	−3.5	3.8

Sources: http://www.worldometers.info/world-population/africa-population/
http://inafrica24.com/modernity/ecowas-outlook-2015-gdp-growth-projected-7/#sthash.qII8TSrm.dpuf
https://en.wikipedia.org/wiki/List_of_African_countries_by_Human_Development_Index
Note: [a]Mauritania is no longer in ECOWAS

of ECOWAS' GDP in 2015, being the biggest economy on the continent. The sub regions' real Gross Domestic Product (GDP) growth was projected to hit 7.1% in 2015 as against 6.3% in 2014 (ECOWAS Outlook 2015). In January 2016, the IMF predicted a declining 2016 GDP growth of 4.1% for the West African sub-region and by April 2016, however, the fund cut that growth forecast to 2.3%, a 1.8 percentage point difference largely due to the slow growth in oil-exporting and other primary commodity exporting countries (Golubski 2016).

The member countries however, have similar levels of human development index (HDI), which stand at an average of 0.464 as only Cape Verde and Ghana crossed a threshold of 55%. The region also shares some similar social values and culture; although its populations are drawn from many different ethnic groups.

The overall fiscal balance for the ECOWAS countries in 2014 deteriorated generally. Under the baseline assumptions, fiscal balances are projected to deteriorate more for oil exporters and improve for other economies in 2015–2016 as a result of decline in oil prices. Most of the economies in the region are suffering from twin deficits—negative domestic fiscal balance as well as negative trade balance. The implication is that both the domestic and external sectors of the economies are performing below full potential and that the economies are indebted internally and externally. In addition, real per capita GDP for the region though relatively low in 2014 (averaging 3.2%), this may be due to the slowdown and restructuring of economic activity in China away from investment and manufacturing toward consumption and services, on the one hand, and declining commodity prices and strains in some large emerging market economies like India, Brazil, etc. It has also been speculated that the exit of the United Kingdom (BRIEXIT) may equally have a backlash effects on the sub-region. The trade balance for the region even in the midst of high demand for its primary commodities, it was in deficit for all the ECOWAS countries except for Cote d'Ivoire, Nigeria and Sierra Leone.

Using the Enabling Trade Index (ETI) on a scale of 1–7, developed within the context of the World Economic Forum's Enabling Trade program, ECOWAS countries share similar rating which averaged 3.2 point. Thus, differences across member countries are relatively small; ranging from 2.9 to 3.6 on a continuum of 1–7. As Table 1 further illustrates, of the 138 countries ranked, only The Gambia and Senegal were within the bracket of the first 100 countries. Precisely, they occupy 99th and 100th position; while Burkina Faso and Guinea are among the six lowest-ranked countries. Also very disturbing from the Report; 14 of the bottom 20 countries ranked have their share of mineral products in total exports above 70%. This also implied that commodity-rich countries performed, on the average, much worse than others within income shares (The Global Enabling Trade Report 2014). Consequently, the trade performance of the sub-region can be construed to imply that the liberalization efforts of the region in recent times are yet to sufficiently improve its trade performance. This is not surprising as Ekpo (2015) established that trade between countries in the sub-region and the rest of the world is unequal. Nigeria, the biggest economy in the region and the African continent, occupies a low 124 position; reminiscent of the challenges the country faces. As Fig. 2 discloses, Nigeria's market is very open; however, non-tariff barriers (mostly, foreign market access, operating environment and, availability and quality of transport infrastructure) hinder its trade development.

If the ETI scores of ECOWAS block is placed side by side with those of Association of South East Asian Nations (ASEAN) countries and the Organization for Economic Co-operation and Development (OECD) for the same period, 2014; their comparative average scores as related in Tables 2 and 3 are indicative that ECOWAS countries are lagging behind the other related trading blocks.

As a follow-up to the ETI, Table 4 discloses that in most ECOWAS countries, the most problematic factors that inhibit export trade in the region is access to trade finance and identifying potential markets and buyers; while for importation, burdensome import procedures, tariffs and corruption at the boarder rank highest. The implication is that reducing these barriers will enable trade contribute to prosperity

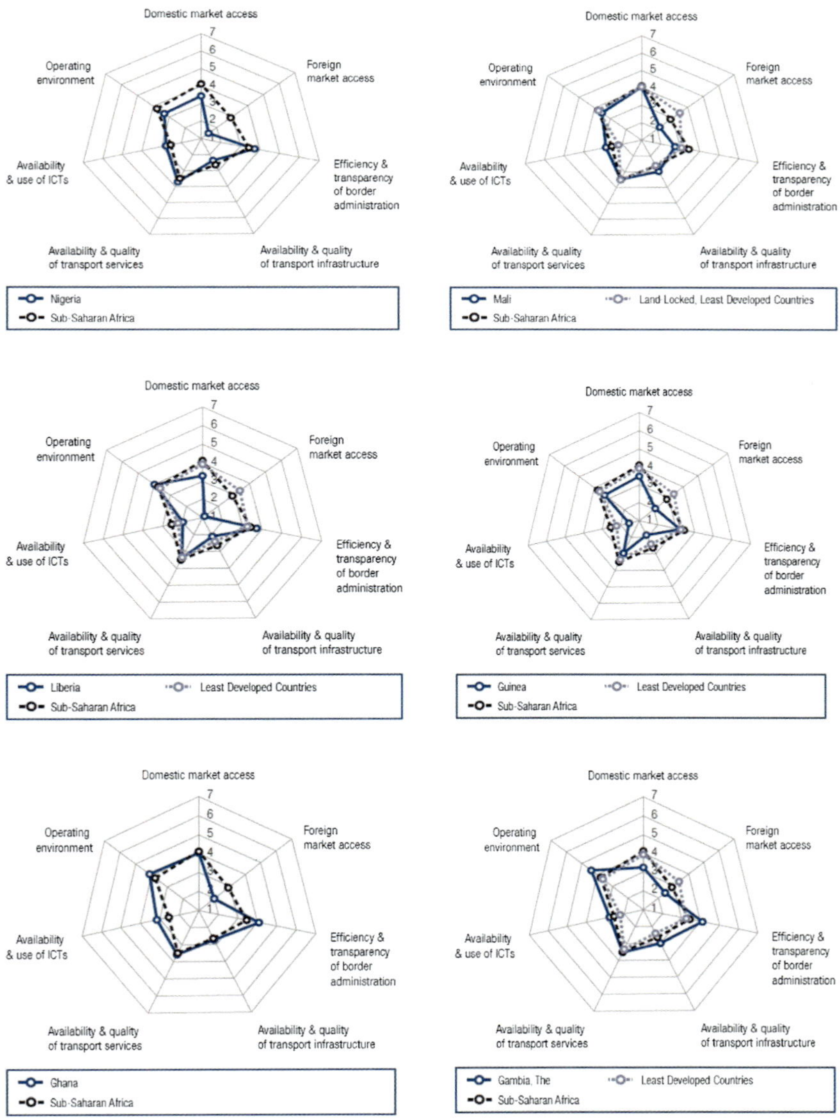

Fig. 2 Enabling trade index of selected West African countries 2014

and welfare. This has been established and is now widely accepted in trade empirics (Bhagwati 2013).The facts revealed by the data so far is indicative of lack of integration into global value chains and internal chains including the shallow linkages in the West African trade corridor. The region barely kept up with rapid

Table 2 Enabling trade index 2014

Country	Rank (out of 138)	Rank (ECOWAS)	Score (1–7)
Benin	127	8	3.1
Burkina Faso	133	9	2.9
Cote d'Ivoire	117	4	3.3
Gambia, The	99	1	3.6
Ghana	102	3	3.6
Guinea	135	10	2.9
Liberia	126	7	3.1
Mali	123	5	3.1
Nigeria	124	6	3.1
Senegal	100	2	3.6
Average			3.23

Source: The Global Enabling Trade Report (2014)

Table 3 Enabling trade index for selected ASEAN countries and OECD (2014)

ASEAN Countries				OECD	
Country	Score	Rank	Country	Score	Rank
Singapore	5.9	1	Netherland	5.3	3
Malaysia	4.8	25	New Zealand	5.2	4
Thailand	4.2	57	Finland	5.2	5
Indonesia	4.2	58	United Kingdom	5.2	6
Macedonia	4.1	63	Switzerland	5.2	7
Philippines	4.1	64	Sweden	5.1	9
Vietnam	4.0	72	Germany	5.1	10
Cambodia	3.7	93	Luxembourg	5.1	11
Average	4.38		Average	5.18	

Source: The Global Enabling Trade Report (2014)

expansion of global trade in the last decades which was majorly determined by addition of value to trade. The next section addresses this issue.

4 West African Integration into the Global Value Chains

Global trade in the last decades grew substantially with much impact on labour productivity, though not proportionately in sub-Saharan Africa. The trade gap in sub-Saharan Africa and its integration into the global value chain is well documented, especially in studies that have applied the 'gravity models' (Elson 2013; Regional Economic Outlook 2015); even though, unrecorded flows across the continent may be higher. In one of such recent studies, trade flows in sub-Saharan Africa region were recorded to be significantly lower than other regions of world;

Table 4 Most problematic factors for trade, 2013

	Most problematic factors for export		Most problematic factors for importing		
Country	Access to trade finance	Identifying potential markets and buyers	Burdensome import procedures	Corruption at the boarder	Tariffs
Benin	1st	2nd	1st	3rd	2nd
Burkina Faso	1st	2nd	1st	4th	3rd
Cote d'Ivoire	1st	2nd	2nd	4th	1st
Gambia, The	1st	2nd	3rd	2nd	1st
Ghana	1st	4th	1st	3rd	2nd
Guinea	1st	4th	1st	2nd	3rd
Liberia	5th	3rd	2nd	1st	3rd
Mali	2nd	1st	2nd	3rd	1st
Nigeria	1st	4th	2nd	1st	3rd
Senegal	2nd	1st	1st	4th	2nd

Source: The Global Enabling Trade Report (2014)

largely inhibited by low purchasing power, relative longer distances and a higher number of landlocked countries (Head and Mayer 2014). The study further reports that bilateral trade flows in sub-Saharan Africa are lower than the rest of the world by an average of 51%, and for Southeast Asia and Europe, sub-Saharan Africa bilateral trade flows were lower by 84% and 80% respectively (see Fig. 3). This is despite various intraregional and interregional trade agreements entered into by sub-Saharan African countries (Regional Economic Outlook 2015) as other regions of the world benefit more in the new wave of a global value trade space.

The global value chain is an additional dimension of globalization imploded by expansion in trade due to technological progress, cheaper communication cost, policy reforms, etc. As trade become more disperse globally, countries are able to exploit their comparative advantages, using the opportunity to add their quantum to the production chain without necessarily possessing all technical no-how and upstream capabilities. The global value chain is the "systems of supply chains in which value is added at each stage before crossing the border to be passed on to the next stage- global value chains" (Regional Economic Outlook 2015: 56). This section assesses to some extent, West African integration depth in the global value chain and where they stand in this landscape.

Some ways of assessing the depth of regional integration in the global value chain are; by estimating the group's shares of foreign value added of countries exports in percent to GDP per capita; second, by evaluating the level of participation of the sub-region in global value chains. The latter case concerns exports (in percent) of the sub-region to value chain addition in form of forward integration, domestic value added and backward integration. Third, but also related to the second, is by considering relatively, each country's (in the sub-region for which data is available) depth

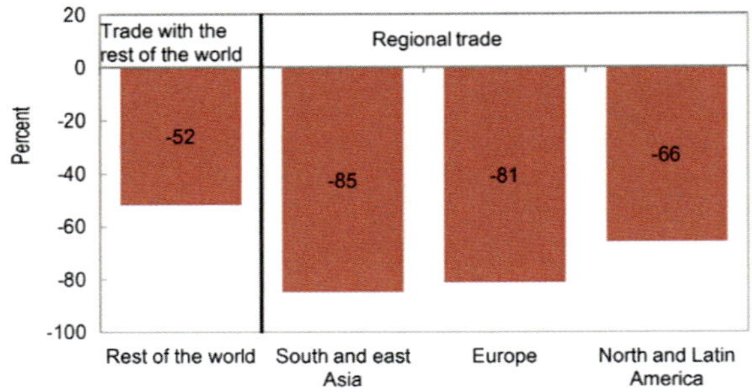

Fig. 3 Sub-saharan Africa: trade flows compared with other regions. *Source*: Regional Economic Outlook: Sub-Saharan Africa (2015: 54)

of integration into the global value chains in a comparative form. The fourth is to link the trading countries magnitude of bilateral trade flows (analyzing gravity model) to characteristics such as geographical nearness or proximity, cultural affiliation or relationship, language or past colonial ties. Other controlled variables are the size and level of development of the trading economies (Head and Mayer 2014). A primer analysis of the gravity model of ECOWAS countries as earlier mentioned is examined in Sect. 5.

Measuring the degree of integration into the global value chains at the global level is accompanied by increase in income levels (Regional Economic Outlook 2015) and as the literature has it, in this form of circumstance, rising depth of integration is associated with rising income over time, especially for developing economies. To accomplish this form of assessment, following the Regional Economic Outlook (2015) approach, the group's shares of foreign value added of countries exports in percent to GDP per capita for the period 1990–2012 (referred to traditionally as backward integration; see Fig. 2), for seven West African countries (Benin, Burkina Faso, The Gambia, Nigeria, Senegal, Sierra Leone and Togo) and Mauritania was estimated. From the estimated result (based on 2014 Eora Multiregional Input-Output database[1]) as reported in Eq. (1), the inference is that rising depth of integration has been associated with rising income over time for the West African economies, all things being equal. As such, if the sub-region were to pursue a strategy of development anchored on integration and laced with value chain creation, income levels could improve as they acquire new capabilities, benefit of knowledge spillover and better efforts of comparative advantage by providing them opportunity of diversifying and upgrading production (Regional Economic Outlook 2015).

[1]EORA Disaggregated into 189 countries, historical time series over 1990–2011. It includes tables of basic prices, as well as two margins (taxes on products and subsidies on products); Eora's MRIO tables were modelled based on existing sources—national accounts data, Comtrade import and export data, among others—when national input-output or supply-use tables were not available. Other limitations go beyond just Eora and affect all MRIO tables. E.g. they are not able to accurately assess the services. They are subject to two assumptions: all products (for export and domestic use) have the same import content (proportionality assumption and they assume uniform use of inputs among all firms in sector) Contribution of domestic value addition in gross exports (used by UNCTAD, World Bank and other users).

$$y = -1.12x^2 + 15.56x - 58.88 \qquad R^{-2} = 0.26 \qquad (1)$$

As further enunciated and established elsewhere, enhanced participation in global value chains is equally associated with more inclusive growth, especially when the sectors targeted are labor intensive and employ relatively lower-skilled workers (Regional Economic Outlook 2015; UNCTAD 2013; Maertens et al. 2011). However, to what extent do countries of the sub-region participate in the global value chains?

In order to assess the depth of integration further, the level of participation of the subregion in global value chains is evaluated. This concerns measuring exports (in percent) of the sub-region to value chain addition in form of ***backward integration*** (reflects the extent to which a country is integrated relatively downstream of the value chain, measured as the ***Foreign Value added***, ***FVA***), ***domestic value added, DVA*** (products consumed directly in the country where it is exported) and ***forward integration;*** reflects the extent to which a country is integrated relatively upstream of the value chain (Regional Economic Outlook 2015: 60). Figures 4, 5, 6 and 7 reflect these scenarios.

In Fig. 4, participation in global value chains averaged for the periods, 1991–1995 and 2008–2012 is reported. Relatively compared, Sub-Saharan African countries are still at the start of their integration process into global value chains. At 15% of exports, the share of foreign value added embedded in the production of exports of sub-Saharan African countries is very low even when compared with average observed in other developing and emerging market economies (Regional Economic Outlook 2015: 57).

The depth of integration into global value chains for the period 1990–2012 for selected West African countries is reported in Fig. 5. For all the countries for which data was available, none crossed a threshold of one percent depth. More worrisome is Nigeria reported to be the biggest economy not only in the sub-region but also in

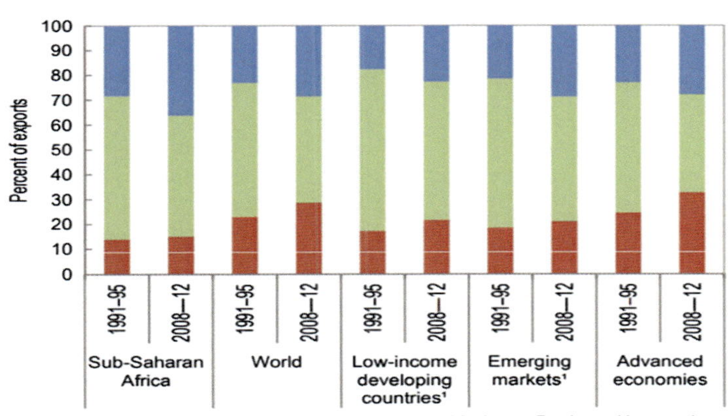

Fig. 4 Participation in global value chains, average 1991–1995 and 2008–2012. *Source*: Regional Economic Outlook (2015)

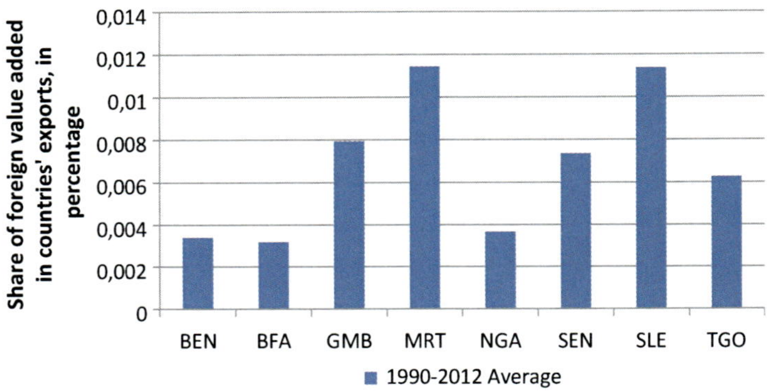

Fig. 5 West Africa: Depth of integration into global value chains, average 1990–2012. *Source*: Authors' based on Eora Database, 2014

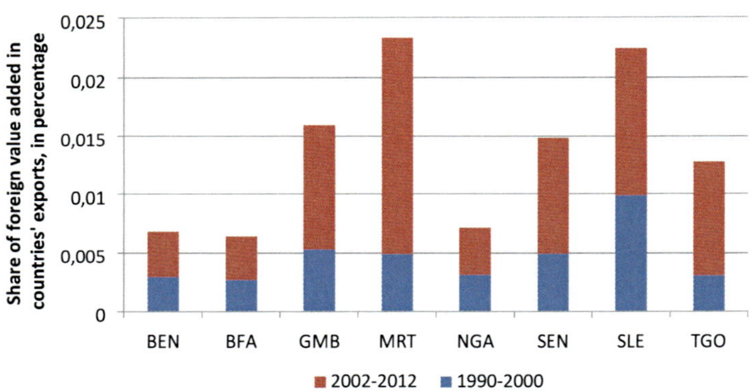

Fig. 6 West Africa: Depth of integration into global value chains, average 1990–2000 versus 2002–12. *Source*: Authors' based on Eora Database, 2014

sub-Saharan Africa, ranked relatively lower than countries like The Gambia. This may not be surprising for three reasons; first, re-export trade alone earns The Gambia more than Three billion dalasis per annum, equivalent to one third of the National budget, second, as established elsewhere (Regional Economic Outlook 2015), oil exporting nations are the least integrated into global value chains in terms of FVA content of their exports; suggesting lack of diversification away from natural resources; and third, the fact that informal trade in the sub-region is not well documented (Njie 2014). In addition, to answer the question as to which country could serve as an anchor for West Africa's integration into the global value chain, the response may be none given their performance. As Fig. 6 also reveals, the depth of West Africa's integration into the global value chains has barely increased since the mid-1990s. A signal that the sub-region like the sub-Saharan region is yet to join this global momentum and take advantage of lifting its productivity and create jobs—often associated with participation in global value chains. A notorious impediment to

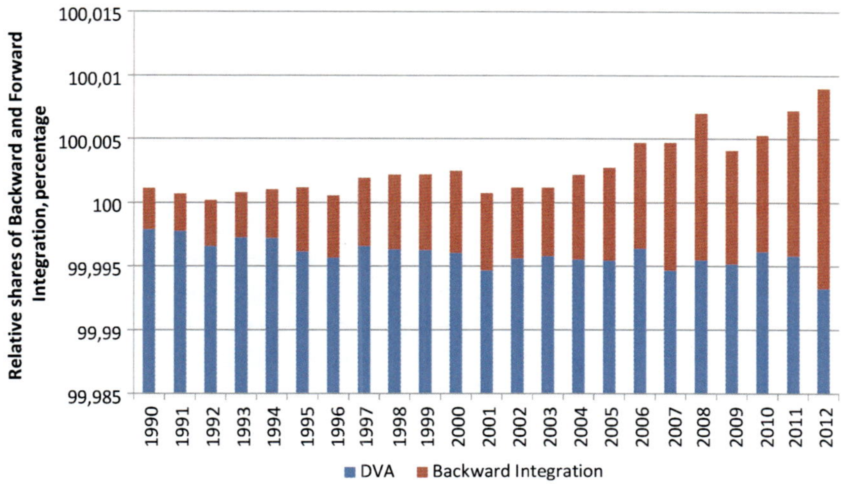

Fig. 7 West Africa: Participation in global value chains, average 1990–2012. *Source*: Authors' based on Eora Database, 2014

the value creation chains is insufficient infrastructure and this has made upstream value addition of the sub-region insignificant. A turn to Fig. 7 tells the story better.

As Fig. 7 displays, forward Integration is near zero. Using a threshold of 100%, DVA which is Domestic value added of products consumed directly in the country was over 99.99%, implying that forward integration which reflects the extent to which a country is integrated relatively upstream of the value chain is near zero.

Rather than perceive the performance of the sub-region as abysmally poor and forsaken, one upshot is that the sub-region still has an enormous potential to integrate into global value chains. To leverage on this potential, policies and actions in the sub-region would require deliberate efforts to build developmental state, enhance structural transformation, harness the dividends of its demographic transition, promote export diversification, and encourage domestic markets and readiness to absorb technology and skills from abroad. It is only then, else; the so call 'Africa is rising' is a mere slogan associated only with its rising population and the then export rising commodity prices.

5 Model Specification and Empirical Estimates of the Gravity Model

In this section, we intend to modestly estimate an augmented basic gravity model based on a balanced panel dataset of fifteen countries mainly of the ECOWAS block for the period, 2006–2013 using the United Nations Conference on Trade and Development (UNCTAD) Statistics database, World Bank World Development Indicators (WDI) and Centre d' Etudes Prospectives et d' Informations

Internationales (CEPII). Our empirical specification of the gravity model is a modified extract form from the West African Economic Outlook (2015) equation:

$$x_{ijt} = a_{Ex}M_{itEx} + a_{Im}M_{jtIm} + \theta D_{ijt} + a_t + u_{ijt} \quad (2)$$

Where, x_{ijt} the exports from exporting country i to importing country j in year t, are conditioned on M_{it}^{Ex} and M_{jt}^{Im} vectors of the attributes of exporting country i and importing country j and a_t, the year fixed effect. In addition, other important parameters which influence trade flows or trade costs factors between I and j are denoted by D_{ijt}; while u_{ijt} denotes unobserved determinants of bilateral trade costs. All variables, with the exception of index variables, are in logs. To handle the issue of the heterogeneity of unknown form, we opted for the estimation of Random Estimate (RE).

The results of the estimation in Table 5 report evidence of economic size (GDP) and distance (proximity and infrastructure) of West African economies to be significant. In other words a higher GDP increases trade while a longer distance inhibits trade. This partially reflects importance of intra-trade flows to the economies of the region and could imply relative high levels of income as the economies grow and become more integrated; all things being equal. Though not surprising, a fascinating finding in the analysis is that, having past colonial ties does increase trade significantly unlike sharing a common language and common border. Conclusively, the two most important factors of the gravity estimation in explaining bilateral trade flows in West Africa, particularly in the ECOWAS bloc are the geographical distance (with an inverse relationship, as the theory explains) among the countries, and their economic size (GDP). Exports of landlocked countries are 17.2% lower compared to non-landlocked countries. However, this variable is statistically insignificant; while imports of landlocked importing countries are 60% lower compared to non-landlocked countries. The importer landlocked variable is weakly significant statistically at 10%. Generally, the results are in line with those found in other gravity model studies, suggesting that the results are consistent.

Table 5 Gravity model estimate

	Robust random estimate (In trade)
Constant	2.94*(1.74)
Exporter ln (GDP per capita)	0.60***(0.08)
Importer ln (GDP per capita)	0.25***(0.08)
Log of distance	−0.79***(0.22)
Common official language	0.20(0.59)
Common border	−0.11(0.36)
Exporter landlocked	−0.17(0.28)
Importer landlocked	−0.60*(0.32)
Common colonizer	1.24**(0.62)
Observations	1481

Robust standard errors in parentheses
*indicate significance at 10%, **at 5%, and ***at 1%

6 Summary and Conclusion

In early 2000, the concept of 'Africa is Rising' theorizing was added to the Continent's lexicon largely due to first, a market related demographic dividend with the projection that Africa will account for 3.2 billion of the projected 4 billion increase in the global population by 2100. Second, the almost two decades of strong and sustained growth in sub-Saharan Africa from the mid-1990s; occasioned by a combination of factors among them, favorable external conditions, rising export commodity prices and fiscal space created by the post–debt relief before the global financial crisis. Unfortunately, worsening external conditions which followed the global financial crisis that was believed to have begun in July 2007, have now had its toile of backlash effects on economies of primary exporting countries most of them in sub-Saharan. To overcome these challenges, contemporary antidotes have been sought not only in improved trade among integrating and geographical nearness of economies, increased global value chains addition have been prescribed.

The paper sets out to determine the extent which West African economies are integrated, their take in the global value chains and some important parameters which could influence their trade flows given the perceived structural heterogeneity amongst them.

The findings and results from the West African Enabling Trade Index, their participation in Global Value Chains and estimated simple gravity model suggest the following: first, the trade performance of the sub-region can be construed to imply that the liberalization efforts of the region in recent times did not sufficiently improve its trade performance. Second, the most problematic factors that inhibit export trade in the region is access to trade finance and identifying potential markets and buyers; while for importation, burdensome import procedures, tariffs and corruption at the boarder rank highest. The implication is that reducing these barriers will enable trade contribute to prosperity and welfare. Third, rising depth of integration in the sub-region, though marginal, has been associated with rising income over time, all things being equal. As such, if the sub-region were to pursue a strategy of development anchored on integration and laced with value chain creation, income levels could improve as they acquire new capabilities, knowledge spillover and opportunity of diversifying and upgrading production. Fifth, the sub-region marred by insufficient infrastructure that has made upstream value addition of the sub-region insignificant like the sub-Saharan region is yet to take advantage of lifting its productivity and job creation; often associated with participation in global value chains. Sixth, there is evidence of economic size (GDP) and geographical nearness (proximity and infrastructure) of West African economies to be very significant in inter and intra-trading.

It is our observation that rather than perceive the performance of the sub-region as too abysmally poor and forsaken, there is an enormous potential for the West African economies to integrate into global value chains. To leverage on this potential, policies and actions in the subregion would require deliberate efforts to build developmental states, enhance structural transformation, harness the dividends of its demographic transition, promote export diversification, and encourage domestic markets. It is only then, the benefits associated with trade for inclusive development and equity can be achieved; else, the so called 'Africa is rising' paradigm would be a mere slogan associated only with its rising population.

References

Aksoy, M., et al. (2005). *Global agricultural trade and developing countries, World Bank.* Washington, DC: World Bank Publications.

Alfaro, L., & Rodriguez-Clare, A. (2004). Multinationals and linkages: An empirical investigation. *Economica, 4*(2), 113–169.

Altenburg, T., & Eckhardt, U. (2006). *Productivity enhancement and equitable development: Challenges for SME development.* Vienna: United Nations Industrial Development Organization.

Amoako-Tuffour, J., Balchin, N, Calabrese, L., & Mendez-Parra, M. (2016). Trade facilitation and economic transformation in Africa. In Paper prepared jointly by *ACET and ODI's Supporting Economic Transformation Programme for the 2016 African Transformation Forum* in Kigali, March, 14–15, 2016.

Bannier, C. E., & Zahn, S. (2014). SMEs' growth heterogeneity - evidence from regional developments. *International Journal of Business Administration, 5*(2), 23.

Bárcena, A., Prado, A., Rosales, O., & Pérez, R. (2014). *International trade and inclusive development building synergies.* United Nations publication, LC/G.2562, September 2014, United Nations, Santiago, Chile.

Beck, Th., Demirgüç-Kunt, A., & Levine, R. (2003). *Small and medium enterprises, growth, and poverty: Cross-country evidence.* World Bank policy research working paper 3178, December. Washington, DC: World Bank.

Bhagwati, J. (2013). Dawn of a new system. *Finance and Development, 50*(4), 8–13.

Drummond, P., Thakoor, V., & Yu, S. (2014). *Africa rising: Harnessing the demographic dividend.* IMF working paper, WP/14/143.

Elson, A. (2013). *Globalization and development: Why East Asia surged ahead and Latin America fell behind.* New York: Palgrave Macmillan.

Ekpo, A. (2015). Public investment and competitiveness in ECOWAS: An empirical investigation. In Paper presented at the 6th *Annual Conference on Regional Integration in Africa* (ACRIA 6), Lagos, July 1–3, 2015

Golubski, C. (2016). *Africa in the news: Growth forecasts for Africa largely cut, Djibouti, Chad, Comoros, and Sudan vote, and UNICEF highlights Boko Haram atrocities.* http://www.brookings.edu/blogs/africa-in-focus/posts/2016/04/15-growth-forecasts-africaunicef-boko-haram-golubski

Head, K., & Mayer, T. (2014). Gravity equations: Workhorse, toolkit, and cookbook. In E. Helpman, K. Rogoff, & G. Gopinath (Eds.), *Handbook of international economics.* Amsterdam: Elsevier.

Hou, M. A. (2013). *Export supply chain organization and food safety and quality standards: A case study of the Moroccan fruit and vegetable sector.* Dottorato Di Ricerca in Economia E PoliticaAgraria Ed Alimentari, Università di Bologna.

International Monetary Fund. (2015, October). *World economic outlook: Adjusting to lower commodity prices.* Washington, DC.

International Monetary Fund (IMF). (2016, January). *World economic outlook update.* Washington, DC: IMF.

Mateev, M., & Anastasov, Y. (2010). Determinants of small and medium sized fast growingenterprises in central and eastern Europe: A panel data analysis. *Finance Theory & Practice, 34*(3), 269–295.

Maertens, M., Colen, L., & Swinnen, J. (2011). Globalization and poverty in Senegal: A worst case scenario? *European Review of Agricultural Economics, 38*(1), 31–54.

Njie, O. (2014). *Gambia: Open the border to save the re-export trade*. FOROYAA Newspaper (Serrekunda), FOROYAA Newspaper (Serrekunda).

Njinkeu, D. (2012). *Boosting Intra-African trade: What role for external trade regime?* http://blogs.worldbank.org/africacan/boosting-intra-african-trade-what-role-for-externaltrade-regime

OECD, WTO, and World Bank Group. (2014). *Global value chains: Challenges, opportunities, and implications for policy*. Report prepared for the G20 trade ministers meeting Sydney, 19 July 2014.

Oyedije, A. (2012). *Submitted by Shanta Devarajan on Fri, 01/13/2012*. http://www.bing.com/search?q=enhance+intra-African+trade+Oyejide%2C+2012&qs=n&form=QBRE&pq=enhance+intraafrican+trade+oyejide%2C+2012&sc=0-41&sp=-1&sk=&cvid=2A1CFF9230EF442C849BBBF6085D50B1

Rios, L. B. D., & Jaffee, S. (2008). *Barrier, catalyst, or distraction? Standards, competitiveness, and Africa's groundnut export to Europe*. Agriculture and rural development discussion paper 39, the World Bank.

SAANA Consulting. (2014). *Advancing regional integration in Southern Africa: An evidence based, forward looking study on regional trade and integration in the tripartite region, focusing primarily on Southern Africa*. Final report submitted to the UK Government.

Saliola, F., & Zanfei, A. (2009). Multinational firms, global value chains and the organization of knowledge transfer. *Research Policy, 38*(2), 369–381.

Samans, R., Blanke, J., Corrigan, G., & Drzeniek, M. (2015). *The inclusive growthand development report*. Geneva: World Economic Forum.

Sun, P., & Heshmati, A. (2010). *International trade and its effects on economic growth in China*. IZA discussion paper no. 5151, August 2010

World Economic Forum. (2014). *The global enabling trade report 2014*. Geneva: WEF.

UNCTAD. (2013). *Global value chains: Investment and trade for development*. World investment report, United Nations conference on trade and development. New York and Geneva: United Nations Publishing.

Driving Factors of Intra-regional Trade in Agricultural Goods: The Case of West African Economic and Monetary Union

Toussaint Houeninvo and Philippe Sèdédji

Contents

T. Houeninvo (✉)
African Development Bank, Regional Office for East Africa, Nairobi, Kenya
e-mail: t.houeninvo@afdb.org

P. Sèdédji
Ministry of Development, Economic Analysis and Prospects, Cotonou, Republic of Benin

D. Seck (ed.), *The External Sector of Africa's Economy*, Advances in African Economic, Social and Political Development,
https://doi.org/10.1007/978-3-319-97913-7_5

Abstract Since the 2008 financial crisis and the 2010 European debt crisis, and their impact on African exports, strengthening regional integration appears to be an alternative to building resilience to shocks and promoting economic development in West Africa. Experience shows that the debt crisis in Europe has negatively affected exports of several African countries. Similar effects have been observed during the recent decline in commodity prices. Given that countries of the Economic and Monetary Union of West Africa (UEMOA) are agriculture dominant countries with the share of agricultural value added to GDP representing between 20% and 46% of countries, boosting intra-region trade, specifically intra-WAEMU agricultural exports, can serve as a key factor for inclusive development in West Africa.

The inclusiveness of the development is strengthened by the fact that most of the population in West Africa lives in rural area and does not benefit directly from the broad economic growth at macro level. Intra-regional trade in agricultural products in such a condition could contribute to reducing inequality and poverty.

One of the constraints to trade in West Africa is the quality of transport and the related cost of transportation and logistics including non-tariff barriers that jeopardize competitiveness of West African products as compared to imported goods from outside WAEMU. Several goods imported from out of the continent, especially from Asia, Europe and America have been more competitive than the intra WAEMU products.

The main research question is the impact of distance (transport/logistical cost) and the level of development on intra-WAEMU agricultural exports. The paper analyzes the determinants of intra-WAEMU trade in agricultural products and therefore the variables on which policymakers could act to promote intra-regional trade. The analysis uses panel data in a gravity model over the period 1996–2013 covering seven (7) West African Countries with yearly data. The results indicate that the two gravity factors meaning the level of development measured by GDP as well as the distance are highly significant at 1% with the expected signs.

Regarding the four control variables namely population (pop), foreign direct investment (FDI), Political stability and the Common External Tariff, all of them have the expected signs but only FDI with 2 lags is significant. Similar to the core variables of the model, FDI is strongly significant at 1%.

Overall, the results indicate that 1% increase in GDP leads to 0.9% increase in intra-regional export of agricultural goods. This calls for actions to deepen the Common agricultural policy of WAEMU for agricultural transformation in WAEMU zone in order to improve the wellbeing of the poor. On that result, the agricultural transformation strategy for Africa recently adopted by African Development Bank is timely.

As for the distance, a 1% increase in the distance leads to 0.8% decrease in intra-regional agricultural exports. This call for deeper actions at WAEMU level to modernize the corridors and reduce red tape and roads harassment.

As for FDI, 1% increase in FDI leads to 0.25% increase in intra-regional exports. This call for actions at WAEMU level to attract FDI in the agricultural sector for the exploitation of the abundant available arable land in WAEMU member countries.

1 Introduction

West African Economic and Monetary union (WAEMU), established by the Treaty of 10 January 1994 involves eight (08) countries in West Africa.[1] For the economic integration of its eight member States, WAEMU, set in the establishing treaty, five major objectives that reflect the desire of the Member States to create a genuine economic and competitive area among them. These objectives are the followings: (i) strengthening the competitiveness of economic and financial activities of Member States; (ii) convergence of economic performance and policies of the Member States, by the institution of a multilateral surveillance mechanism; (iii) the creation of a common market based on the free movement of persons, goods, services, capital and the right of establishment, a common external tariff and a common commercial policy; (iv) the coordination of national sectoral policies, the implementation of joint actions and eventually common policies in key areas of economic activity; (v) the harmonization of legislation of Member States to facilitate the proper functioning of the common market.

All WAEMU member countries are agriculture dominated ones. Indeed, the share of agricultural value added in GDP varies between 20% and 46% and the sector's contribution to economic growth is around 50% for some of them.[2] Consequently, Common Agricultural Policy, that was the first sector policy adopted by WAEMU, appears crucial to the achievement of the objectives set by the Founding Member Countries. Therefore, it is expected that an increased intra agricultural WAEMU exports would have a positive impact on the quality of growth by making it more inclusive and hence contribute to more poverty reduction.

The main thrusts of the Common Agricultural Policy of WAEMU (CAP) as they appear in article 13 of the Additional Protocol No. 11 of WAEMU Treaty cover matters such as: (i) Achieving food security and adequate self-sufficiency within the Union, taking into account the complementarities between the Member States and their respective comparative advantages; (ii) Improving conditions of the markets in agricultural livestock and fishery goods for both producers and consumers.

[1]Benin, Burkina Faso, Côte d'Ivoire, Guinea Bissau, Mali, Niger, Senegal and Togo.

[2]Houeninvo T. (2002), WAEMU Common Agricultural Policy: Challenges for Benin, Economic Policy Analysis Unit, Benin.

The specific objectives are:

- Regaining the regional food market by promoting crude agricultural products (raw materials) as well as improving their storage condition, processing and marketing.
- Provide adequate protection for local food products in face of imports.
- Improve quality control and standards for agricultural product and particularly for those intended to be exported.

Several priorities arise from these thrusts namely the promotion of agricultural marketing, animal husbandry and fisheries. Therefore, one might expect an intensification of intra-community trade in agricultural products as a result of the adoption of those pillars of the Common Agricultural Policy of WAEMU.

2 Overview of Trade Liberalization Since the 1990s in the WAEMU and Observed Intra WAEMU Trade

The structure of WAEMU tariff applied on external trade includes the Custom rate and two community tax namely Community Solidarity Levy (1%) and the Statistical Tax (1%). Trade liberalization initiated in early 1990s with the structural adjustment programs in different WAEMU Countries has been strengthened since 1996 by the Additional Act 96/04 of 16 May 1996 that has led today to the removal of quotas and other quantitative restrictions. It also led to 0% of tariff on crude products originating from WAEMU countries including agricultural non processed goods. Moreover, since January 2003, there is the lifting of the certificate of origin requirement for raw products including agricultural intra-WAEMU exports except seafood. Nevertheless non harmonized tariff rates charged by different member countries before 2000, could not promote the development of intra-Community trade as shown in Table 1 below.

Table 1 Minimum and maximum rate of tariff rate in WAEMU countries on 1 January 1998

	Types of tariff	
Countries	Minimal rate	Maximal rate excluding community solidarity tax (1%) and statistical tax (1%)
Benin	2%	20%
Burkina Faso	9%	33%
Côte d'Ivoire	7.6%	35%
Guinea-Bissau	10%	105%
Mali	8%	30%
Niger	10%	30%
Senegal	25%	60%
Togo	6%	20%

Source: WAEMU Commission

The introduction of the CET since January 1st, 2000, which aims at promoting intra-regional production and trade distinguished four categories of goods (0, 1, 2, 3) and four related tariff structures respectively of 0%, 5%, 10% and 20%.

Category 0 goods which has a 0% tariff consists of a list of product with high social and cultural value. They are drugs, condoms, books, newspapers, health rehabilitation devices.

Category 1 goods that has 5% tariff consists of basic need goods, basic raw materials, capital goods, specific inputs.

Category 2 goods that has 10% tariff consists of intermediate product inputs.

Category 3 goods levied at 20% consists of final consumer goods and all other products non-listed in other categories.

Since 1st january 2015, there is the entry to force of the CET of ECOWAS which is mainly the CET of WAEMU plus a fifth category of tariff at 35%. This new category is to support the development of key promising ECOWAS sectors such as agro-industry, breeding, textile.

Table 2 shows that the implementation of a common external tariff has not only harmonized tariff rates in Member countries, but reduced them except for Benin which has the lowest tariff level before the CET.

In addition to those taxes that are applied on a permanent basis there are temporary taxes among which we can mention the Cyclical Import Tax (CIP) and the Depgressive Protection Tax (DPT).

- The Cyclical Import Tax (CIP) is a mechanism that aims at cushioning the effects of changes in international prices on community production and is used to counteract unfair trade practices including dumping. Agricultural goods are qualified for this treatment. Its implementation is linked to a trigger price calculated from a comparison of international prices for products considered at their Cost Insurance Freight (CIF) import values. A flat rate of 10% was used.
- There has been also from 1999 to 2005 The "Degressive Protection Tax" (DPT). A product of WAEMU is eligible for the TDP if the implementation of the CET causes significant reduction in the Effective Protection Rate (EPR) for this product. If the EPR drop is between 25% and 50%, the product benefits from a low TDP of 10%. But if the decline is greater than or equal to 50%, the product is

Table 2 Overall rate of CET into force since 2000 and 2015

	Tariff			
Categories	Tariff rate (%)	Statistical tax (ST) (%)	Community solidarity tax (CST) (%)	Overall tariff (%)
Category 0	0	1	1	2
Category 1	5	1	1	7
Category 2	10	1	1	12
Category 3	20	1	1	22
Category 5 (ECOWAS CET since 2015)	35	1	1	37

Source: WAEMU and ECOWAS Commissions

granted a high TDP of 20%. As its name indicates, it is a regressive tax designed to enable industries heavily affected by the implementation of the CET in order to face the increased competition generated by the tariff disarmament brought by the CET. The products affected by the DPT are those within the industry and agribusiness

In spite of all these measures one can notice that several years after the creation of the UEMOA in 1994 and the adoption of a Common External Tariff in 2000 (Customs Union), the intra-WAEMU trade is still low estimated at 12% between 1994 and 2014. As compared to the expectations, at the time of the establishment of the CET, WAEMU Commission was expecting to reach 25% of intra-WAEMU trade at the end of 2005 (Coulibaly et al. 2015). Hence despite the different measures undertaken to promote intra-WAEMU trade, actual intra-regional trade level is way below the expected one. In terms of comparison to the other Regional integration zone, Intra-trade is about 64% for European Union, 60% pour North American Free Trade Area (NAFTA), 35% for ASEAN and 30% for MERCOSUR. WAEMU intra-regional trade is even lower for agricultural goods especially agricultural exports. While intra-WAEMU trade is estimated at 12% of total WAEMU, intraWAEMU agricultural exports represent only 4% of total WAEMU[3] exports. In terms of share of intra-WAEMU agricultural exports in intra-WAEMU exports, they are estimated at 29.20% in 1996 and 32.3% in 2015, hardly 3% points increase over 21 years since the signing of the agreement establishing the WAEMU zone.

According to a recent statement by the President of the WAEMU this low level of intraWAEMU trade is due to lack of competitiveness due to cost factors, the supply, the structural weakness of the physical infrastructure, lack of complementarity between the economies and obstacles to the free movement of goods in the countries.[4]

For example, the 17th report of the Observatory of Abnormal Practices (OAP) of WAEMU based on a 2011 survey, indicates that of the six WAEMU corridors[5] followed by the OAP, there is a clear improvement but with some country disparities. Thus very high unlawful levies persist on corridors that lead to Abidjan[6] even if those illegal levies are decreasing. The corridors linking Ouagadougou and Bamako are considered the most expensive with an average illegal collection of CFAF 6000 per 100 km. In terms of country discrepancies Benin is the Country where there is the highest unlawful levy estimated at CFAF 34,749 while Senegal has the lowest illegal collection of WAEMU estimated at CFAF 5322.

Alongside these road harassment (NTBs) in the Zone, the low degree of processing including that of agricultural products is also an obstacle that reduces

[3]In 2012, Intra-WAEMU agricultural export value is CFAF 459.7billion for total WAEMU export of CFAF 11223.3 billion.

[4]http://news.adakar.com/h/8790.html dated 22 March 2014.

[5]Tema (Ghana)-Ouagadougou (Burkina Faso), Ouagadougou-Bamako, Lome-Ouagadougou, Bamako-Dakar Abidjan-Ouagadougou and Abidjan-Bamako.

[6]This is probably due to the conflict situation where the rebels levy their own tax and non-tax collection over which the Central State based in Abidjan has no control.

the opportunities for trade between countries of the UEMOA zone. This is also why the trade of manufactured goods increased in world trade while the one from unprocessed goods declined. As it has been established in empirical studies, the more the level of processing is high, the more there are several types of products that are traded.[7] In contrary, when it is a raw material, it can only be exported to Europe or Asia that has the processing capacity and less in WAEMU countries which have a similar level of development and industrialization. Also, the longer the distance is, it increases the probability of ransoming on the road from the police and other security agents which increases transportation costs and discourage trade.[8]

Given the importance of agriculture (share of agricultural value added in GDP varying between 20% and 46% and the sector's share to GDP that could reach 50% for some of WAEMU countries),[9] it is expected that an increase in intra-WAEMU agricultural exports would have a positive impact on the quality of growth by making it more inclusive and hence contribute to a more poverty reduction. Moreover, at a time where there is a decline in commodity price at international level in addition to the debt crisis in Europe which both have a negative impact on African agricultural export, questioning the driving factors of intraregional agricultural exports and identifying the barriers to them in order to promote resilience and an effective and dynamic integration in WAEMU is timely.

3 Theoretical and Empirical Foundations of the Gravity Model in the Analysis of Trade in Regional Integration Area

The gravity model, which is adapted from the universal law of gravitation, has been very successful in the field of bilateral trade studies. The underlining assumption is that the GDP, that is the economic mass, acts as the attractor of trade between two trading partners and therefore exert a positive effect on trade. In contrast, distance, a measure of the cost of transport used by most studies, serves as resistance factor and plays a negative role in trade.

From an empirical point of view, Tinbergen (1962) applied this law to international trade flows. In the gravity model, Tinbergen used GDP to express the economic weight of each country. Also, to test the validity of the gravity model, Xubei (2001) has applied it in the case of trade between the Chinese provinces and

[7]This is the case of the automotive industry in Europe, America and Asia.

[8]It is the case of the complaints of trucks owners of Niger, about harassment in the transport of their cargo from the Port of Cotonou to Niamey, that led Benin Chamber of Commerce Managers to go to Niger for public awareness campaigns on new measures taken by Benin to reduce road harassment and smooth road traffics for Niger stakeholder.

[9]Houeninvo T. (2002), WAEMU Common Agricultural Policy: Challenges for Benin, Economic Policy Analysis Unit, Benin.

Japan from 1988 to 1997. He used at the same time the panel estimates and cross section estimates. The Panel method has taken into account the individual effects but in the fixed effects models, the distance disappears into the equations of estimates because of its non-variability over time, which did not allow to measure it influence on trade. In contrary the "cross-sectional method" suffers from the disadvantages of the reduced number of samples, but it allowed him to study the evolution of the impacts of different measures of distance on trade. Using those two methods has enabled Xubei to get complementary results.

Many studies using gravity models techniques were carried out on the potential of international trade flows. In particular the model of Linnemann (1966) has been widely used and is known for its empirical success. The factors underlying trade flows are the export supply of a country i, the import demand of country j and a resistance factor to trade flows between these countries. The author obtained his model by replacing in its gravity equation those three factors by variables such as national income, population, geographical distance and the existence of a preferential trade agreement. For their part, Jakab et al. (2001) looked at the level of trade balance of the Czech Republic, Hungary and Poland from a specification of the Linnemann (1966) equation. Estimating that equation with the error terms, allowed them to reach an accurate assessment of the potential trade. Gbetnkom and Avom (2005) used a gravity model to analyse the determinants of intra-WAEMU trade over 1990–2000 with two sub-periods 1990–1994 and 1996–2000 and a special focus on the role of economic reforms. They found that regional integration increases substantially trade after economic reforms have been implemented. Coulibaly et al. (2015) used a gravity model to assess the impact of the CET of ECOWAS that entered into force on January 2015 and to be applied by WAEMU member countries. They found that intra-WAEMU trade will improve while intra ECOWAS trade will remain low after the entry to force the CET of ECOWAS unless capacity building programme has been put into place in ECIOWAS to support the implementation of ECOWAS CET.

The major problem of the gravity model remains the measure of the resistance factor. Obviously, there are many other factors than the distance that influence the cost of transport but the main assumption in the gravity model is that the distance is the main resistance one. This seems to be likely in a region where road connectivity and networks are of poor quality. Traditionally "distance as the crow flies" is considered as gross proxy of the resistance factor. But in fact there is a risk of losing valuable information on the quality of road, the existence of road barriers and other Non-Tariff Barriers that can amplified the negative effect on trade. Therefore some authors like Hummels (1999) replaced the bird's distance by the actual distance. Moreover, Limao and Venables (1999) attempted to take into account the influence of the quality of infrastructure in the transport cost. In his article, to better approximate the resistance factor, Luo (2001) constructed a new measure of distance taking into account the influence of the ease of transport and tried to group the determinants of transport costs in one variable, called the "actual distance adjusted." By demonstrating the respective impacts of different measures of distance, she could decide between them according to their performance as resistance factor in the gravity equation.

4 Presentation of the Model and the Variables

The main objective is to test the extent to which intra-WAEMU agricultural exports are driven by the distance (transport/logistical cost) and the level of development (measured by the GDP). This is done using a gravity model.

4.1 The Gravity Model

From economic point of view, the use of gravity models in the analysis of international trade is based on the logic according to which the flows of trade between two countries depend positively on their "economic weight" measured by their Gross Domestic Products (GDP) and inversely on the distance separating these two countries. In other words, the potential of a country to provide (export) products requested by its economic partners depends on its own economic size measured by GDP, while demand in partner countries (importers) depends on the income or GDP of these countries. The role of distance becomes evident when we are in presence of two trading partner countries with the same pair of GDP (same economic size). Thus, the basic gravity model is as follows: $EXPA_{ij}=BY_i^{a1}Y_j^{a2}DIST_{ij}^{a3}$

$$EXPA_{ij} = BDIST\underline{Y}^{ia1}\underline{Y}^{aj\ 2}_{ija_3} \tag{1}$$

with a1, a2 > 0 and a3 < 0, where $EXPA_{ij}$ is the value of Exports from country i to country j

B is an intercept;
t is the period;
Y_i is the GDP of Country i during the period considered;
Y_j is the GDP of Country j during the period considered;
$DIST_{ij}$ is the distance between country i and country j ($i \neq j$). In practice it is the distance between the major capitals and ports of the two countries.[10]

[10]The idea of taking the distance between the two capitals or major ports is consistent with the basic logic of Newton because according to it, the masses of the two particles can be treated as concentrated at their centers so that the distance between the two objects is measured by the distance between their centers.

Taking the logarithm of Eq. (1) gives:

$$\log\left(EXPA_{ij}\right) = \log[B) + a1\log(Y_i) + a2\log\left(Y_j\right) + a3\log\left(DIST_{ij}\right) \qquad (2)$$

where a1 and a2 are >0 and a3 < 0.

The success of the simple gravity model, (with only GDP and distance as explanatory variables), is remarkable in empirical studies. But external trade is not influenced only by these two factors. Some other factors include the characteristics of partner countries. We add consequently other potential determinants as control variables in the extension of the model. This extension which follows the models used by Luo Xubei (2001), Gbetnkom and Avom (2005), Coulibaly et al. (2015) has the advantage to improve the gravity model by limiting the risk of bias in the coefficient estimates that comes from the omission of relevant variables. Thus the extended model with partner's country features can be written as follows:

$$\left(EXPA_{ij}\right) = \log(B) + \sum_{k1}^{ki} a_{1k}\log(X_{ki}) + \sum_{k1}^{kj} a_{2k}\log\left(X_{kj}\right) + a_3\log\log\left(DIST_{ij}\right)\cdot \qquad (3)$$

where X_{ki} and X_{kj} represent respectively the features of trade partner countries.

In the case of our paper, we consider the WAEMU (j) as a single block. Thus we assume that the characteristics of the WAEMU (j) are identical for the various countries (i). This allows us to consider the WAEMU as a more or less homogeneous entity. This assumption is consistent with data available at WAEMU Commission which compiles rather intra agricultural exports by WAEMU country and not the flow of agricultural exports from one WAEMU country to the other.

4.2 The Variables

To better capture the influence of specific characteristics of trade partner countries in this case, the expansion of the classic gravity model includes in addition to GDP and the distance variables such as Foreign Direct Investment, population of each member country, a dummy variable that captures the degree of integration among trading countries. This variable is set to one (1) for the years after the implementation of the Common External Tariff (CET) and zero (0) for the years before. In order to capture the security challenges West African Countries are facing including boko haram and jihadist movements and recent attacks in Mali, Burkina et Côte d'Ivoire, an institutional variable meaning political stability or absence of terrorism has been included to measure the quality of governance.

Therefore the expanded version of Eq. (3) taking into account the period considered can be written as follow:

$$\log(EXPA_{it}) = \log(B) + a_1\log(GDP_{it}) + a_2\log\left(DIST_{ij}\right) + a_3\log(POP_{it}) \\ + a_4\log(FDI_{it-2}) + a_5Z_{it} + a_6PS_{it} + \varepsilon_{it} \tag{4}$$

where $EXPA_{ij}$ is the total agricultural exports from country i to other member countries of WAEMU during year t

GDP_{it} is the GDP of country i in the year t
$DIST_{ij}$ is the distance from country i to the other member countries of WAEMU (block j)
POP_{it} is the population of country I in the year t
FDI_{it-2} is the Foreign Direct Investment of year t − 2. This is to take into account the time lag between the investment and its effects on agricultural exports
Z_{it} is a dummy variable for the Common External Tariff during the period t
PS_{it} stands for political stability/absence of terrorism
ε_{it} is the error term

4.3 Hypothesis and Expected Signs of the Coefficients

4.3.1 Gross Domestic Product

The GDP is expected to have a positive effect according to the theory of gravitation. In fact, according to the law of gravity, the attractive force is positively related to the mass of materials. Here GDP represents this mass In other words $a1$ is expected to be positive. Therefore ∂(EXPA)/∂(GDP) > 0.

4.3.2 Distance

According to the basic theory of the gravity model, the distance has a negative impact on trade including agricultural intra WAEMU exports. Here we use road distance. This is justified by the fact that transactions of goods are made mainly by road within WAEMU. To be consistent with the data we have so far from WAEMU on agricultural exports which is on the total agricultural goods exports by each member country to all other WAEMU countries, WAEMU being seen as an entity, the distance considered here is rather the distance between the exporting countries and the other WAEMU countries. This is the total distance between the Capitalcity/main port of country i to the WAEMU (block j). Indeed, capital cities are considered the transaction distribution centers to the other countries. Therefore, the distances used here are not necessarily the shortest paths but critical paths meaning the way to reach more easily the capitals when transporting a good. Therefore $a2$ is expected to be negative meaning ∂(EXPA)/∂(Dist) < 0.

4.3.3 Population

The population can either have a positive or negative sign depending on the assumption made. If we suppose Hechscher-Ohlin theorem that applies, this will mean that countries trade level is determined by their intensity of their factor endowments and the ability to exploiting their comparative advantages. In these conditions assuming that countries rather export labor intensive products then the expected sign for population variable will be positive. This means that the sign *a*3 is expected to be negative. ∂(EXPA)/∂(POP) > 0. In other words this means that countries trade with partners if their development levels are different. In contrary, according to some authors such as Lindert, countries trade more if their levels of development are closer. Therefore in the case Lindert assumptions applies, the sign of the population variable will be negative. Considering that WAEMU countries are grossly at the same development level, we assume Lindert hypothesis applies meaning that ∂(XPA)/∂(POP) < 0.

4.3.4 Foreign Direct Investment

Since part of international trade is usually intra-firm trade and within the UEMOA policies are designed to attract foreign investors, we assume that FDI influences positively exports of agricultural goods including those processed. The ideal situation would be to have specific FDI data on agriculture but since this is not available we assume that FDI act whether directly (where they are investment in agriculture) or indirectly including through the logistics to support trade. The 2 years delayed value of FDI is justified by the fact that there is always a time lag between the period of the introduction of a foreign direct investment and the period the exported products can benefit from such an investment. Therefore the expected sign of the coefficient *a*4 is expected to have a positive sign. Therefore ∂(EXP)/∂(FDIt-2) > 0.

4.3.5 Level of Integration

We introduce a dummy variable that measure the entry to force of the WAEMU Common External Tariff to capture the degree of integration of the countries of the Union. It will take the value 0 before 2000 and 1afterwards. Hence the expected sign of this variable is positive as CET is a step to Common Trade Policy and Custom Union that are both meant to accelerate regional integration and trade including hose of agricultural goods. Thus *a*5 is expected to have a positive sign.

Table 3 Recap of the expected signs of the variables of the model

Variables	Intercept	GDPit	DISTij	POPit	FDIit	Zit	PSit
Coefficients	b0	al	a2	a3	a4	a5	a6
Expected signs	+	+	−	−	+	+	+

4.3.6 Political Stability and Absence of Terrorism

Terrorist attacks as they appear recently in the region can be a serious impediment to exports including those of agricultural goods. In an areas invaded by some rebel groups and terrorists farmers usually have been chased from their land and became refugees elsewhere. Political instability and lack security in general is a threat to trade while political stability and absence of terrorism has a positive effect on trade comprising agricultural exports. Thus it is expected that political stability and lack of terrorism in West Africa would have a positive impact on export. Thus *a*6 is expected to be positive as indicated in Table 3.

5 Data Sources and Sampling

Gross Domestic Product (GDPit), Population (POPit) come from World Development Indicators and Foreign Direct Investment (FDI) come from UNCTAD. Exports of agricultural of a member country (EXPA) to other WAEMU countries, Common External Tariff (Z) come from WAEMU Commission. Distance data are from http://www.levoyageur.net/distances/distance.html and Political Stability or absence of terrorism data come from World Governance Indicators (www.govindicators.org). The sample on which our analysis is composed consist of seven WAEMU member countries over 1996–2013 leading to 126 observations of panel data. Guinea Bissau has been excluded from the sample mainly because of missing data on variables such as FDI.

6 Model Specification (Fixed-Effects, Random-Effects or Mixed Effects Model) and Results

Since the use of fixed-effect or random-effect model in panel data estimation depends on whether the hypothesis according to which individual country effect are correlated with the explanatory variables applies or not, there is a need to perform some model specification tests. Several types of test have been considered to that end including Fischer test and Hausman test. Breusch and Pagan Lagrangian Multiplier test for random-effects. While the Fischer global test measures the global significance of individual effects (fixed-effects), Breusch Pagan Lagrangian Multiplier, the Hausman test the presence of random-effects.

In the Fischer test using STATA software with which we regressed exports on the other explanatory variables the R^2 "within" coefficient of determination which gives the explanatory power of the fixed-effects model has a very weak value of 0.19. This suggests that the assumption of the presence of fixed-effects is not corroborated. The random-effects has been tested and the R^2 "between" coefficient of determination which gives the explanatory power of the random-effects model has a value of 0.69 corroborating the randomeffects assumptions. Moreover in order to deepen the specification process we run the Hausman test for which the probability is 54%. Since the probability is greater than 10%, the Hausman test corroborates the choice in favor of a random-effects model. This is consistent with the fact that the within estimator is unable to estimate the marginal impact of variables that are invariant over time (e.g. distance in our case).

Estimating the model under the above assumption and after performing the required econometric testing (Wooldgride autocorrelation test, Breusch-Pagan heteroscedasticity)[11] gives the following results as shown in Table 4.

The non-significance of Political Stability (PS) may be explained by the fact that security issues appears very recently with terrorist attacks in Mali (March 2012 and November 2015), Burkina Faso (January 2016) and Côte d'Ivoire (2002 crisis and terrorist attack March 2016). Thus the marginal occurring of terrorist attacks during the period may explain the nonsignificance of PS. As for variable Z its

Table 4 Recapitulation of the results

	(1)	(2)
	Log (EXPA)	Log (EXPA)
Intercept	2.56 (0.31)	–
Log (GDP)	1.01* (3.13)	0.92** (7.01)
Log (DIST)	−0.97* (−3.02)	−0.80** (−12.18)
Log (FDI-2)	0.27* (2.80)	0.24** (3.34)
Log (POP)	−0.13 (−0.27)	–
PS	0.11 (1.13)	–
Z	0.15 (0.94)	–
Observations	111	111
Wald chi2 (6)	349.86	6196.70
Prob > chi2	0.0000	0.0000

t student statistics are in parenthesis
**Coefficient significant at 1%
*Coefficient significant at the 5%

[11]See details in annex.

non-significance may be related to the fact that all the countries considered belong to WAEMU and apply the CET which may make its effect nonsignificant. As for population the non-significance may be related to the fact that taking into account the effects of the main variables (GDP, Distance and Foreign Direct Investment), that are strongly significant, the population effect is negligible.

7 Economic Analysis of the Results

As shown in Table 2, in the panel random effects models, all the key variables are significant and have the expected signs. The basic variables (the two factors of gravity) are significant at 1% level with the expected signs. Regarding the four control variables meaning population (pop), foreign direct investment (FDI-2), Political stability and the Common External Tariff, all of them have the expected signs but only the FDI with 2 lag years is significant. Similar to the core variables of the model the FDI is strongly significant at 1%.

Thus, the level of development as measured by GDP plays a positive role on agricultural (exports, in our case) within WAEMU. The results indicate that 1% increase of GDP leads to 0.9% increase in intra-WAEMU agricultural exports. This calls for actions to deepen the Common agricultural policy of WAEMU for an agricultural transformation in WAEMU zone. The level of intra WAEMU agricultural exports will probably be even higher if the degree of transformation of the country where high as it will create new lines of products for potential intra trade. Given the strong share of agriculture in the GDP and employment in member countries, actions and reforms taken to that end will contribute to promote inclusive growth.

Distance has a negative and significant sign. 1% increase in distance will lead to 0.8% in intra-WAEMU agricultural exports. This means that the longer the distance is, it discriminates against trade especially agricultural ones because they reach the destination country at a very expensive cost and thus are less competitive. Indeed, although the regional regulatory framework enshrines the free movement of agricultural products, in practice, the development of trade and the competitiveness of these products in West Africa are hampered by road harassments and other NTBs. They appear as a result of administrative officials (police, customs officers, Gendarmes, unions, etc.) that are supposed to ensure the proper implementation of guidelines and measures set out in the development of regional trade. Such a result indicates that greater efforts are needed to be made at WAEMU level to continue to modernize the corridors and making them friendlier and more attractive at economic point of view (reducing red tape and developing economic activities along the WAEMU corridors). For the moment the WAEMU roads and corridors are not easily practicable for stakeholders.

As for foreign direct investment (FDI), 1% in the FDI (with 2 lag years) will yield 0.25% increase in intra WAEMU agricultural exports. This means that foreign direct investment and foreign agricultural intra-regional trade are complementary. In particular, it seems that this relationship is consistent with the life-cycle theory of the products: in the period when the production of goods becomes standardized, developed countries invest in developing countries to exploit labor comparative advantages. This calls for more reforms in business environment to attract more FDI in agricultural sector in WAEMU zone including to support agricultural transformation.

8 Concluding Remarks and Policy Recommendations

Overall, a 1% increase in GDP leads to 0.9% increase in intra-regional export of agricultural goods while a 1% increase in the distance leads to 0.8% decrease in intra-regional agricultural exports. As for FDI, a 1% increase in FDI leads to 0.25 increase in intra-regional export.

These results call for the political and economic authorities of the WAEMU to undertake or deepen actions that can lead to modernize WAEMU corridors in order to make them economically friendly, attract FDI in the agricultural sector to exploit the available land and natural endowment of member countries. Such actions will boost trade in agricultural products and thus intra-regional trade as a whole for more inclusive growth. Given the negative effect of European debt crisis (since 2010) combined with the current decline trend in commodity price, and their negative impact on African country exports, stimulating intraWAEMU agricultural exports appears as an alternative to build resilience to shocks and promote economic development in West Africa.

These results call for some policy recommendations including the following:

- Macroeconomic and structural reforms that can lead to an overall increase of GDP and the level of development of WAEMU which will in turn favor intra-WAEMU agricultural exports
- Construction/modernization of West African Corridors to facilitate connection among West African Countries
- Reforms in agricultural sector including attracting FDI to modernize the sector and promote agricultural transformation as it appears in an agricultural transformation strategy for Africa under preparation at African Development Bank.

Acknowledgements We would like to thank Makhtar Gueye for excellent Research Assistance but all errors remain ours.

Annex

Econometric Tests

Test of Fixed-Effect

```
. xtreg lnexpa lndist lnpop l(2).lnfdi lngdp ps z,fe
note: lndist omitted because of collinearity

Fixed-effects (within) regression               Number of obs      =       111
Group variable: pays                            Number of groups   =         7

R-sq:  within  = 0.1949                         Obs per group: min =        15
between = 0.2912                                        avg =      15.9

       overall = 0.2542                                        max =        16

                                                F(5,99)            =      4.79
                                                                            corr(u
                                                                            _i,
                                                                            Xb)  =
      lnexpa       Coef.    Std. Err.      t    P>|t|     [95% Conf. Interval] -
                                                                            0.1588
                                                                            Prob >
lndist                                                        0  (omitted)  F
       lnpop    2.071363    2.071387    1.00   0.320    -2.038718   6.181445  =
                                                                            0.0006

lnfdi
         L2.
                 .035519    .1199692    0.30   0.768     -.202526   .2735639

       lngdp     .023461    .8100645    0.03   0.977    -1.583883   1.630805

          ps    .3162668    .1563709    2.02   0.046      .005993   .6265406
           z    .0732268    .2449747    0.30   0.766    -.4128561   .5593097
       _cons   -31.20199      27.364   -1.14   0.257     -85.4981   23.09411

sigma_u                                                             .89954219
     sigma_e   .65441462
         rho   .65391425   (fraction of variance due to u_i)


F test that all u_i=0:     F(6, 99) =     17.68            Prob > F = 0.0000
```

.

R-square within is low (0.19) rejecting the assumption of presence of fixed-effects.

Test of Random-Effects

```
. xtreg lnexpa lndist lnpop l(2).lnfdi lngdp ps z,re

Random-effects GLS regression                Number of obs      =        111
Group variable: pays                         Number of groups   =          7

R-sq:  within  = 0.1248                      Obs per group: min =         15         between =
0.6939                                     avg =        15.9

       overall = 0.4697                                        max =         16

                                             Wald chi2(6)       =      92.12 corr(u_i, X)    = 0
(assumed)                       Prob > chi2        =     0.0000

      lnexpa |      Coef.   Std. Err.      z    P>|z|     [95% Conf. Interval]

                                                                              -.9364451
lndist       | .4085023     -2.29    0.022     -1.737095    -.1357954
       lnpop |  -.1966828   .4783984    -0.41   0.681    -1.134326    .7409609

lnfdi
         L2. |
                .1490457   .1058094     1.41   0.159     -.058337    .3564284

       lngdp |   1.121183   .3104734     3.61   0.000     .5126668      1.7297
          ps |  -.0485505   .1732258    -0.28   0.779    -.3880668    .2909658
           z |   -.056838   .2656214    -0.21   0.831    -.5774464    .4637705
       _cons |   3.927192   8.395503     0.47   0.640    -12.52769    20.38208
                                                                                        0
sigma_u
     sigma_e |  .65441462
         rho |          0   (fraction of variance due to u_i)
```

The R-square between is comfortable (0.69) corroborating the presence of random-effects.

Hausman Fixed-Effects vs. Random-Effects Specification Test

```
. hausman fixed random

                    —— Coefficients
               (b)              (B)                  (b-B)
             sqrt(diag(V_b-V_B))                      fixed
             random        Difference           S.E.
-------------+------------------------------------------------
lnpop        |     2.716332      1.229896           1.486435
             |                                      1.411541
             |    -.0344987     -.0104635          -.0240352
L2.lnfdi     |.0307014
             |    -.2236286      .3578782          -.5815068
lngdp        |.533601
--------------------------------------------------------------

b = consistent under Ho and Ha; obtained from xtreg

B = inconsistent under Ha, efficient under Ho;

obtained from xtreg     Test:  Ho:  difference in

coefficients not systematic

                  chi2(3) = (b-B)'[(V_b-V_B)^(-
1)](b-B)
                          =        2.17
                Prob>chi2 =      0.5379
```

The probability of 53.8% >10% this corroborates the choice in favor of random-effects.

Test of Breusch and Pagan Lagrangian Multiplier Test for Random-Effects

This helps between random regression and a simple OLS. The null Hypothesis is that variances across entities is zero meaning no difference across units (better to use OLS). But if the null hypothesis is rejected that OLS cannot generate efficient estimators

```
. xttest0

Breusch and Pagan Lagrangian multiplier test

for random effects         lnexpa[pays,t] =

Xb + u[pays] + e[pays,t]

        Estimated results:
                 |          Var
                 |sd = sqrt(Var)
         --------+----------------
         lnexpa  |   1.433141
         e       |1.197138
         --      |   .4373365
                 |.6613142
                 |   .9652731
                 |.9824831
        Test:    Var(u) = 0
                              chibar2(01) =    105.17
                           Prob > chibar2 =    0.0000
```

With the Chi2 value of 105 with a zero probability the null hypothesis is rejected (presence of heteroscedasticity). Therefore GLS will be used to run the random-effects model.

Woodridge 2002 Test of Non-autocorrelation of First Order Residue

The H0 hypothesis tests the non-autocorrelation of first order residue.

```
. xtserial lnexpa lngdp lndis lnfdi

Wooldridge test for autocorrelation in panel data
H0: no first-order autocorrelation
    F(1,       6) =      0.698
           Prob > F =      0.4356
```

The probability value of 0.43 indicates the non-rejection of H0.

The Extended Model

```
. xtgls lnexpa lngdp lndis l(2).lnfdi lnpop ps z,
panel(hetero)

Cross-sectional time-series FGLS regression

Coefficients:  generalized least squares
Panels:        heteroskedastic
Correlation:   no autocorrelation

Estimated covariances      =         7          Number of obs
=       111
Estimated autocorrelations =         0          Number of
groups    =          7 Estimated coefficients     =         7
Obs per group: min =         15
avg =  15.85714
max =         16
Wald chi2(6)        =     349.86
Prob > chi2         =     0.0000

------------------------------------------------------------
            |       Coef.    Std. Err.       z     P>|z|      [95%
lnexpa      |Conf. Interval]
------------------------------------------------------------

lngdp       |
            |     1.01123     .3232602           3.13      0.002
            |.377652    1.644809
            |    -.9685454     .3205064      -3.02      0.003      -
lndis       |1.596726    -.3403643

lnfdi       |
L2.         |
            |    .2731904     .0975606           2.80      0.005
            |.0819751     .4644056
            |    -.1328034     .4953704      -0.27      0.789      -
lnpop       |1.103712     .8381047
            |    .1117178     .0989324       1.13      0.259      -
ps          |.0821862     .3056218
            |    .1523556     .1620583       0.94      0.347      -
z           |.1652729     .469984
            |    2.565751      8.30442       0.31      0.757      -
_cons       |13.71061     18.84212
```

The Final Model After Eliminating Progressively the Non-significant Variables

```
. xtgls lnexpa lngdp lndis l(2).lnfdi    ,nocons
panel(hetero)

Cross-sectional time-series FGLS regression

Coefficients:   generalized least squares
Panels:         heteroskedastic
Correlation:    no autocorrelation

Estimated covariances      =         7
Number of obs      =        111
Estimated autocorrelations =         0
Number of groups   =         7 Estimated
coefficients      =         3          Obs per
group: min =          15
avg =  15.85714
max =          16
Wald chi2(3)         =    6196.70
Prob > chi2          =     0.0000
```

lnexpa	Coef. Std. Err. [95% Conf. Interval]	z	P>|z|
lngdp	.9196049 .1312278 .6624031 1.176807	7.01	0.000
lndis	-.7982803 .0655204 -.9266979 -.6698626	-12.18	0.000
lnfdi			
L2.	.2459153 .0737341 .1013991 .3904315	3.34	0.001

References

Coulibaly, A. D., Traoré, M., & Diarra, S. (2015). UEMOA versus CEDEAO: Analyse par le modèle de gravité des créations des flux de commerce intra-communautaire, Document de réflexion, Commission de l'UEMOA, Janvier.

Gbetnkom, D., & Avom, D. (2005). Intégration par le marché: Le Cas de l'UEMOA. *Région et développement, 22*, 86–103.

Houeninvo, T. (2002). La politique agricole commune de l'UEMOA: enjeux pour le Bénin. CAPE.

Hummels, D. (1999). Toward and geography of trade costs. Retrieved from http://gsbwww.uchicago.edu/fac/david.hummels/research/vs/

Jakab, Z.-M., Kovacs, M.-A., & Oszlay, A. (2001). How far has trade integration advanced?: An analysis of actual and potential trade of three Central and Eastern European countries. *Journal of Comparative Economics, 29*, 276–292.

Limao, N., & Venables, A. J. (1999, December). *Infrastructure, geographical disadvantage, and transport costs*. Policy research Working Paper No 2257. The World Bank.

Linnemann, H. (1966). *An econometric study of international trade flows*. Amsterdam: North-Holland.

Tinbergen, J. (1962). *Shaping the world economy: Suggestions for an international world economic policy*. New York: Twientieth Century Fund.

Xubei, L. (2001). La mesure de la distance dans le modèle de gravité: une application au commerce des provinces chinoises avec le Japon. *Revue Région et Développement, 13*, 163–180.

Trade Openness and Food Security in Africa: A Comparative Study of CEMAC and WAEMU Countries

Giscard Assoumou-Ella and Ismaelline Eba-Nguema

Contents

Abstract The paper conducted comparative analysis of the effect of trade liberalization on food security in CEMAC and WAEMU Countries with data spanning the period 1987–2014. Overall the findings lead to the conclusion of a negative effect in general. The beneficial effect of trade on the food situation is most visible in terms of availability. Also, it leads to lower prices. However, adverse terms of trade appeared to wipe off the positive effects and lead to food insecurity. This outcome is robust for both the CEMAC and WAEMU samples. With regard to policy, these countries should implement trade policies to facilitate of openness, while supporting and diversifying domestic food production.

G. Assoumou-Ella
CIREGED, Université Omar Bongo, Libreville, Gabon

I. Eba-Nguema (✉)
Faculty of Legal Economic and Social Sciences-Souissi, Rabat, Morocco

D. Seck (ed.), *The External Sector of Africa's Economy*, Advances in African Economic, Social and Political Development,
https://doi.org/10.1007/978-3-319-97913-7_6

1 Introduction

To better understand the link between trade and food security in Africa, it is necessary to take an historical approach. Indeed, production structures were essentially alien to African economies and the predominance of export cultures over self-sufficiency had its origins in the colonial economy. Production in the periphery was essentially oriented for providing both agricultural and non-agricultural commodities to the metropolis. Under this arrangement, food self-sufficiency declined in the colonies as a result of exports to Europe on one hand and food imports rose substantially on the other hand (Rodney 1987).

Thus, in the early years of independence, many African countries continued with the colonial economic structures by adopting a development model based on commodity production for export to industrialized countries. However, almost 20 years later, the results were far from satisfactory. This is why African leaders adopted the Lagos Plan of Action in April 1980. This framework was to lead the continent towards more regional and pan-African integration. The ultimate goal was to achieve self-sufficiency at both national and collective levels. In essence, the plan was to strengthen inter-African trade. However, in the mid-80s, many African countries facing economic difficulties had to adopt far-reaching reforms under the auspices of the Structural Adjustment Programs (SAPs). The embrace of reforms was a precondition to obtain loans especially from the World Bank and the International Monetary Fund. One key goal of the SAP was to liberalize African economies and thereby improve their international openness (Oyejide 2005). Based on this paradigm, food security could be achieved by increasing the capacity of African countries to generate enough exports earnings to finance their food imports. African countries have strengthened their food policy by joining in 1995 to the World Trade Organization (WTO).

Given the foregoing context, we probe into two major research questions namely; what is the effect of trade liberalization on food security in Africa? Does trade openness promote food security in Africa?

We have chosen to conduct the study in the countries of the Economic and Monetary Community of Central Africa (CEMAC) and the West African Economic and Monetary Union (WAEMU) because of their similarity regarding their insertion in international trade inspired to Heckscher-Ohlin-Samuelson model (HOS) of international trade. Also, both groups have track records of continuous policy of trade liberalization and face common challenges in their efforts at achieving food security objectives (see Sects. 2 and 3 provide more details).

The link between food security and trade liberalization in these two regions is further analyzed by integrating the four dimensions of food security that are internationally recognized. These dimensions are: the availability, access, stability and utilization. To our knowledge, no previous study has integrated all these dimensions to evaluate the effect of trade liberalization on food security.

This work will be organized as following: the summary of the liberalization process in Africa is subject of Sect. 1. In Sects. 2 and 3, we examine the plausible factors that lead to the observed persistence of food insecurity in the countries of the sample. The literature review is in Sect. 4. Data description, analysis and the choice of the empirical models are the subjects of Sect. 5. Finally, in Sect. 6 the results of econometric estimates and the interpretations are presented.

2 Summary of the Liberalization Process in CEMAC and WAEMU Regions

The food strategies in Africa, particularly in CEMAC and WAEMU, were initially implemented in terms of self-sufficiency just after the 1973/1974 crisis before being oriented towards exports in the early 80s. The debt crisis and the adoption of the SAPs officially marked the liberalization of the agricultural sector in both regions (Padilla 1997). While Europe and the United States have historically implementing policies that strengthen their agriculture and seek new opportunities, most Central and West African countries have rather reduced agricultural subsidies. Further to this, marketing agencies for domestic food products have equally been privatized (Charvet 1987). Despite the recommendations of the Bretton Woods institutions, many countries retain the subsidy policies for consumption on necessity products (mainly consisting of imported products: cereals, sugar, gas, oil, etc.). These policies had a significant impact on African rural areas that were the mainstay of many economies in the continent. The rural areas have become increasingly abandoned resulting in acceleration of the migration process to the cities (De Schutter 2014).

In 1994, African countries in general, those of CEMAC and WAEMU in particular, intensified their agricultural liberal policies by accession to the World Trade Organization. The agreements on agriculture, the sanitary and phyto-sanitary rules, are in principle supposed to offer new market opportunities for the exports of African economies. However, the opening of the food industry to international competition would also enable these countries to disengage from the agricultural sector. In other words, it offers the possibility to import the food needed to feed their populations through export earnings (De Shutter 2014). Thus, these countries adopted the HOS model of international trade by specializing in the exports of raw materials and the imports of finished products including foods.

In sum, the adoption of the SAPs and the accession of the CEMAC and West Africa countries to the WTO officially laid the groundwork for the liberalization of agriculture. But, what were the results of this food security policy in both regions?

3 Persistence of Food Insecurity in CEMAC and WAEMU Regions

The liberalization initiated in the CEMAC and WAEMU regions in the 80s failed to eradicate food insecurity. Indeed, the recent food crisis (2007–2011) has hit African populations the hardest. As highlighted by Eba Nguema and Ella Assoumou (2014), "a reality that has been forgotten in the 90s is namely that the apparent improvement of food data in Africa is mainly due to food imports".

One of the consequences of agricultural liberalization in these two regions is the withdrawal of their Governments in terms of agrarian policies. This neglect has also introduced two problems namely: dependence and impoverishment of rural regions. The level of food availability is therefore sustained by imports in both regions. For instance, in 2011, the food dependency ratio in the CEMAC was 46.56%, while that of WAEMU was 27.36% (FAO 2016). Although the level of food imports in the CEMAC is relatively smaller than that of the WAEMU, the two regions saw their imports increase significantly. Moreover, food imports have weighed increasingly on the export earnings of these two regions. Indeed in 2011, the share of food imports in total merchandise exports was 11.66% in CEMAC and 28.62% in WAEMU (FAO 2016).

Despite some differences, the food situations of CEMAC and WAEMU are relatively similar. It appears that both regions have made progress in terms of availability, but this has not been followed by a substantial improvement in food utilization. Indeed, the scale of the food deficit remains relatively large. In 2013, the food deficit in the CEMAC was estimated at 172.4%. Over the same period it was recorded as 106.62% in WAEMU (FAO 2016). A high level of food deficit means that these commodities which people must access are not used optimally. This state of affairs may be due in part to the inability of the populations of the CEMAC and WAEMU to have the financial means to ensure the preservation and processing of purchased food.

Given the persistence of food insecurity on the continent, the African authorities and the international community have inserted the issue of food security into their political agendas. Along this line, the ECOWAP project that aims to establish a common agricultural policy in West Africa was presented in 2008 at the Paris meeting on the initiative of the European Union and the ECOWAS Commission (ECOWAS Commission 2008).

Similarly, following the food crisis of 2007–2011, the Board of CEMAC Ministers reaffirmed its commitment to the implementation of the common agricultural policy as set out in 2003 (CEMAC 2009). Without denouncing trade as a pillar of food security, African leaders, however, seem decided on protecting their populations from the deleterious consequences of excessive dependence on food imports.

4 Literature Review

At the World Food Summit in Rome in 1996, the various States and participating organizations concluded that food security exists when "at all times, all human beings have physical and economic access to safe and nutritious food for satisfying their dietary needs and food preferences necessary for an active and healthy life." Despite the fact that this definition had been recognized internationally, there are numerous studies that do not include all food security dimensions which are: availability, access, stability and utilization for analyzing the effect of trade liberalization on food security in developing countries in general and African countries in particular.

The first dimension we discuss in this literature review is availability. This implies the proportion of stored food or the supply present on the national market. For this purpose, Dorosh (2001) notes that following a poor harvest in 1997 and a flood in 1998 in Bangladesh; the private merchants imported several million tons of rice from India. Thus, trade liberalization between India and Bangladesh in the early 1990s helped to increase domestic supplies and to stabilize the prices in this country. Imports from alternative sources also enhance food availability in the country if another production deficit takes place. But they would face higher transport costs; implying less importing companies, given the economies of scale of the shipments by sea. However, this positive contribution of trade liberalization to short-term food security in Bangladesh does not minimize the importance of increasing domestic agricultural productivity and rural economic growth to enable poor rural households purchase food. Nevertheless, the experience of Bangladesh shows that trade liberalization has potential benefits for national food security by allowing a rapid increase in food supply particularly when there is deficit in national production. Regarding Nepal, Pyakuryal et al. (2010) show that among the South Asian countries, this country was a more liberalized economy in the 1980s and 1990s. The country took several measures to reduce the size of its public food distribution system and removed a multitude of agricultural subsidies. To measure the effects of these policies on food security, the authors' focused specifically on the evolution of availability per capita in Nepal. Due to the increased availability in the country, the authors' conclude on an improvement in the food situation in Nepal since the engagement of the liberalization process.

In focusing solely on availability, these studies lead to questionable results regarding the wider effects of openness on food security. Indeed, the increased availability is certainly a necessary condition for achieving food security, but it is not sufficient. The increased availability can result not in an increase in domestic production, but in food imports. Very large increases in imports may exacerbate to some extent, the risk of food imports addiction. When the food dependency ratio exceeds 50%, people are exposed to potential external shocks in the event of sudden price increases for key consumption commodities. The poorest people see in these conditions, their food expenditures increase alarmingly. This is basically what happened during the recent food crisis (2007–2011) in African countries.

Similarly, the increased availability does not mean that people have access to food. There may be surplus in terms of production or in terms of food imports. However, it is also vital that the populations have the financial means to procure them. For all these reasons, we conclude that the results of previous studies do not actually reflect the effect of trade liberalization on food security in general.

The accessibility signifies the ability to access healthy and nutritious food in the country. For this purpose, Bowdler and Malik (2006) find a negative effect of openness on inflation volatility using a dynamic panel model in a sample of developed and developing countries. Indeed, the results show that openness increases the volatility of growth of currency reserves and terms of trade. In other words, trade liberalization was not accompanied by an increase in the propensity of the State to finance food imports. On the contrary, due to the rise in inflation, the countries of the sample saw their import capacity deteriorate. This does not mean, however, that there is a decline in imports, but simply that the State must increase its debt to procure them or rely on food aid in order to increase the supply available in the country.

Moreover, such a situation can affect the populations of these countries who bear the brunt, in many cases, of the increase in food prices in the country in times of high inflation growth. Rising food prices inevitably reduces real household income (purchasing power) and the affordability of food. On this same perspective, Dorosh et al. (2009) reach similar conclusions. However, studies of these authors appear fragile in some respects. In excluding the availability, the authors face a size limit in their reasoning.

In principle, trade liberalization should, in accordance with our prior discussion, increase availability. However, increased availability should, through free competition, result in lower prices. This may, in some measure, adjust the import prices at the level of import capacity of States or the actual income of the inhabitants. Thus, by excluding availability, the authors are not able to indicate whether the negative effect of openness on accessibility could, in this context, be annihilated by higher availability.

Concerning stability (the stability of food prices), Ambagna et al. (2012), show that openness increases the volatility of grain prices in the markets of Yaoundé and Douala (Cameroon). Indeed, they found the elasticities of transmission of international price volatilities on the national prices to be 94.71% and 70% respectively for the two markets. Gerard et al. (2008) found the same results by using a wider range of domestic products. Brooks et al. (2013) analyzed the effect of trade on food security by calculating an indicator of "bilateral imports' penetration" which measures the dependence of a country on imports of food from its trading partners. The results suggested that measures aimed at diversifying the supply sources reduced the vulnerability to partners' food shocks, and therefore improved food security. However, these results do not seem robust enough, because of the narrow focus on stability alone. It is true that volatility remains a concern for the most dependent on the imports of food, because of its potential impact on food prices, therefore the accessibility to food in times of crisis. However, the effect of trade liberalization on food security should also be assessed in terms of other dimensions of food security.

It would have been more relevant had the authors analyzed how price volatility may negatively impact food availability in the country, as well as household income. Furthermore, the authors do not consider that utilization remains an important dimension in the assessment of food security status. The utilization is the ability of households to use nutritious foods without interruption. To evaluate the effect of openness on food security, it would be important to view whether the openness is accompanied by an improvement of living population conditions and decrease in existing inequalities. In fact, access to a decent income allows people to obtain a richer and more varied diet.

Thus, Abdullateef and Ijaiya (2010) find a negative impact of agricultural liberalization on food security in Nigeria. They noted that the number of under-nourished people, and therefore vulnerable, has sharply increased despite the liberalization policies initiated since the 80s.

Despite the fact that all studies that have been cited in this literature review have relevant results, they can be easily challenged especially on the grounds of their arbitrary choice of a food security dimension and deliberate exclusion of others. To avoid such bias, we chose to introduce as part of our comparative study, all four dimensions of food security to yield more robust findings on the impact of trade liberalization on food security.

5 Empirical Modeling

5.1 Variables

In this context, we have chosen for availability, the average value of food production (***vmpa***) and the share of cereals, roots and tubers in the food energy intake (***pcrtaea***). For accessibility, we have the national food prices index (***inpa***), the extent of the food shortage (***ada***) and the household final consumption expenditure (***hfce***). It should be noted here that FAO retains GDP per capita as a measure the household purchasing power. However, the countries of our sample are characterized by inequalities in the distribution of national income. Thus, we think that the best indicator is the household consumption expenditure. For stability, we retain the value of food imports to total merchandise exports (***viaetm***), the dependency rate to cereal imports (***tdeic***) and the volatility of the food prices at national level (***ipdann***). Finally for utilization, we selected the variability in food availability per capita (***vdah***), the prevalence of anemia among children under5-years old (***paem5***) and the number of under-nourished people (***npsa***).

The empirical study examines the effect of openness on food security, comparing the situations of CEMAC and WAEMU, during the period 1987–2014. The data used come from the databases of the FAO and World Bank; online data catalogs. The effect of trade on food security indices used is measured by analyzing the impact of the trade openness index (exports + imports)/GDP (***index***) and the terms of trade (***tot***) on these explanatory variables. We also have the control variables that are most often used in the studies on food security: rural population (***rpop***) and urban population (***upop***). Their inclusion puts into perspective the link between agriculture, food security and population movement in developing countries. The infantile mortality (***mort***) variable permits us to approximate the state of health system. We also have private and public investment (***inv***) and the household final consumption expenditure (except if they are the dependent variable) (***hfce***).

5.2 Theoretical Framework and Econometric Models

The theoretical framework is the Heckscher-Ohlin-Samuelson (HOS) model of international trade. The countries of the CEMAC and WAEMU have a comparative advantage in the production of raw materials. This is why the implementation of the HOS theory of international trade in these countries led to their specialization in the exports of raw materials and the imports of food products through export earnings. Thus, we make the assumption that this specialization has a significant effect on food security in these countries. In this context, the purpose of this empirical study is to see whether this effect is positive, negative or zero.

The first step is to choose the model adapted to our data. To this end, we conduct a test of presence of the individual effects using the modified version of the Lagrange multiplier test of Breusch and Pagan (1980) developed by Moulton and Randolph (1989). The result led to reject the assumption of no individual specific effects. Thus, we formalize the individual effects in fixed and random effects.

In the Error Component Models, the specific individual and temporal effects are random. In this study, we use the simplified modeling where it is supposed that the disruption of the model is only composed of α_i, an individual specific effect, and $e_{i,t}$, a random disruption. According to Pirotte (2011), this presentation is often used in empirical works that use panel data with individual dimension. Also, the sample is often incomplete regarding the population studied (this is the case of this study). We use the logarithm for interpreting the results in terms of elasticities. In this context, we have:

$$\begin{aligned}\log(vmpa)_{i,t} &= a + b_1\log(index)_{i,t} + b_2\log(tot)_{i,t} + b_3\log(rpop)_{i,t}\\ &\quad + b_4\log(upop)_{i,t} + b_5\log(mort)_{i,t} + b_6\log(inv)_{i,t}\\ &\quad + b_7\log(hfce)_{i,t} + \varepsilon_{i,t} \qquad (1)\end{aligned}$$

With $i = 1,\ldots,N$, $t = 1,\ldots,T$ and $\varepsilon_{i,t} = \alpha_i + e_{i,t}$. $\varepsilon_{i,t}$ is composed by α_i, individuals factors that are not taking into account in the model, and $e_{i,t}$, a random perturbation. They are independently and identically distributed: $\alpha_i \sim i.i.d.(0,\ \sigma_\alpha^2)$ and $e_{i,t} \sim i.i.d.(0,\ \sigma_e^2)$.

Note that we have 11 explanatory variables. Thus, we estimate 11 different models. However, to simplify the presentation, we represent only the equations involving ***vmpa***.

Contrary to Eq. (1), we now assume that the effects are not random, but certain. In this context, the disturbance of the model is a classic disruption $e_{i,t}$. The individual and temporal characteristics are represented by constants that take into account some unobserved characteristics of individuals and/or periods. In this study, we use a fixed effects model assuming that the relationship between the dependent variable and the explanatory variables are the same for all individuals:

$$\begin{aligned}\log(vmpa)_{i,t} &= a + b_1\log(index)_{i,t} + b_2\log(tot)_{i,t} + b_3\log(rpop)_{i,t} \\ &\quad + b_4\log(upop)_{i,t} + b_5\log(mort)_{i,t} + b_6\log(inv)_{i,t} \\ &\quad + b_7\log(hfce)_{i,t} + e_{i,t} \qquad (2)\end{aligned}$$

With $e_{i,t}$, the error, i, individual and t, le time.

In the previous two specifications, questions concerning the existence of the rolling gap (because we have incomplete panels), correlation and heteroscedasticity are discussed. In the case of rolling gap, we use the method of Nijman and Verbeek (1992). The idea is to compare the results of estimates of cylindered and incomplete samples. If there is a significant difference, one concludes that there is a rolling gap and retains the result of incomplete panel; which we did in our study. Concerning the assumption of homoscedasticity we check if the error variance of each individual is constant. Do we have $\sigma_{it}^2 = \sigma_i^2$ ou $\sigma_i^2 = \sigma^2$ for all individual i ? According to the Breusch-Pagan test, there is heteroscedasticity in most cases. According to the Wald test, heteroscedasticity is interindividual. In addition, the same error variance for every individual leads to conclude on the existence of intra-individual homoskedasticity. Finally in these cases, data have the following structure: homoskedasticity intra-individual ($\sigma_{it}^2 = \sigma_i^2 \forall t$) and inter heteroscedasticity ($\sigma_i^2 \neq \sigma^2$ $\forall i = 1, \ldots, N$).

Also, we treat problems of correlation of residuals between individuals and the autocorrelation of residuals. Also, according to the Breusch-Pagan test, the results suggest that there is no autocorrelation of the errors. So we correct the heteroscedasticity and the possible unobserved heterogeneity using robust estimation. In addition, to correct a potential endogeneity gap, we instrument the investment variable by real GDP. Finally, the choice between models with fixed or random effects is ascertained based on the Hausman (1978) test. We observe that the "p-values" are >5% in most estimates. In this context, the random effects models are not biased (Table 1).

Table 1 Openness and food security (availability)

	WAEMU		CEMAC		WAEMU		CEMAC	
	log (***vmpa***)		log (***vmpa***)		log (***pcrtaea***)		log (***pcrtaea***)	
	RE	***FE***	***RE***	***FE***	***RE***	***FE***	***RE***	***FE***
log (***index***)	−0.003* (−1.65)	−0.028*** (−2.96)	−0.35*** (−3.33)	−0.349*** (−3.49)	0.007*** (2.41)	0.006*** (2.49)	0.029* (1.63)	0.028** (2)
log (***tot***)	−5.74* (−1.63)	−5.74* (−1.63)	−1.1* (−1.75)	−1.1* (−1.69)	−8.69* (−1.85)	−8.7* (−1.91)	−2.86 (−1.53)	−7.41 (−0.67)
log (***rpop***)	3.18*** (2.52)	3.18*** (2.52)	6.01* (1.83)	6.05* (1.91)	−8.56*** (−5.29)	−8.57*** (−5.46)	−1.35** (−2.08)	−4.3*** (−7.54)
log (***upop***)	−0.001*** (−4.07)	−0.001*** (−4.07)	−0.001*** (−4.67)	−0.001*** (−4.87)	−2.3*** (−3.28)	−6.76*** (−4.91)	−2.5*** (−4.57)	−1.76*** (−4.11)
log (***mort***)	−0.741*** (−5.03)	−0.741*** (−5.03)	−1.459*** (−4.76)	−1.3*** (−4.98)	0.056*** (2.97)	0.056*** (3.07)	0.334*** (4.17)	0.259*** (3.42)
log (***inv***)	−2.35** (−2.1)	−1.42*** (−2.48)	−1.32*** (−2.83)	−1.32*** (−2.96)	−4.19*** (−2.75)	−4.19*** (−2.84)	−1.16* (−1.93)	−1.3* (−1.94)
log (***hfce***)	1.28 (0.33)	7.24 (0.00)	1.3*** (5.63)	1.34*** (5.92)	1.89*** (3.48)	1.89*** (3.6)	6.28* (1.65)	5.94** (2.36)
const	7.169 (0.44)	8.155*** (12.44)	9.315*** (12.77)	8*** (13.32)	7.852*** (34.01)	8.261*** (17.7)	9.99*** (4.72)	9.091*** (12.63)
R^2	0.72	0.77	0.95	0.9	0.76	0.8	0.92	0.95

Radom effect models (***RE***) and fixed effect models (***FE***), period studied: 1987–2014. Dependent variables: ***vmpa*** and ***pcrtaea***

*, ** and ***: significant result at 1%, 5% and 10% of error margin

6 Results and Conclusion

6.1 Results

The openness index (***index***) and the terms of trade (***tot***) negatively affected the average value of food production (***vmpa***) in WAEMU and CEMAC countries. However, the impact is by far more important in CEMAC with an elasticity of −0.35 for openness index, compared to WAEMU where it is −0003. But the evolution of the terms of trade is more detrimental to food production in WAEMU (−5.74) compared to that of CEMAC (−1.1). In both regions, the increase of the rural population (***rpop***) had a positive effect on food production, while that of the urban population (***upop***) had negative impact. Mortality (***mort***) also had a negative effect on production. Thus, countries need to place special emphasis on health, because a sick person cannot work on the farm. Investment (***inv***) had a negative sign. This means that investment is oriented to other activity sectors other than agriculture. The countries of the sample should therefore encourage firms to invest in agricultural production. Finally, household consumption expenditure (***hfce***) positively influenced agricultural production. Food consumption both increased demand and positively influenced investment.

Regarding the share of cereals, roots and tubers in food energy intake (***pcrtaea***), the openness index (***index***) has a positive effect on this variable. So food imports increased food supplies in the countries of the sample in respect of cereals, roots and tubers. This result is consistent with the literature findings on the effect of openness on food availability (See, for example, Dorosh 2001; Korinek and Melatos 2009; Pyakuryal et al. 2010). However, changes in the terms of trade had a detrimental effect on this indicator. The exports of the countries of the sample are mainly the agricultural and non-agricultural commodities and the imports are the finished products. The cost of finished products is superior to that of unprocessed products. This translates into a shortfall for Africa that does not have enough income to pay for food imports rich in energy intake (Tables 2, 3, and 4).

The opening index (***index***) decreased food prices (***inpa***) in WAEMU and CEMAC. But the elasticity is low (−0.001 and −0.008 for the WAEMU and CEMAC respectively). This result is in conformity with the pioneering work of Romer (1993) and others that were conducted afterwards (Calderon 2004; Bowdler and Malik 2006). However, changing terms of trade (***tot***) drove these prices upwards, because the value of finished products is higher than that of commodities that constitute the bulk of exports of the countries of the sample. Therefore, although statistically the opening leads to lower prices, countries do not have enough currency to pay for imports due to the adverse terms of trade.

Regarding the extent of food shortages (***ada***), we see that openness (***index***) helped to mitigate this phenomenon in both zones. But this effect is canceled out by the unfavorable terms of trade (***tot***) that widened the deficit. Thus, the elasticities for openness are −0123 and −0523 in WAEMU and CEMAC, while those of terms of trade are 2.65 and 3.12.

Table 2 Openness and food security (accessibility)

	WAEMU		CEMAC		WAEMU		CEMAC		WAEMU		CEMAC	
	log (***inpa***)		log (***inpa***)		log (***ada***)		log (***ada***)		log (***hfce***)		log (***hfce***)	
	RE	***FE***	***RE***	***FE***	***RE***	***FE***	***RE***	***FE***	***RE***	***FE***	***RE***	***FE***
log (***index***)	−0.001* (−1.74)	−0.001*** (−3.28)	−0.008* (−1.65)	−0.008* (−1.68)	−0.123*** (−2.65)	−0.146*** (−6.05)	−0.523* (−1.79)	−0.5* (−1.9)	−1.636*** (−3.52)	−2.183*** (−6.08)	−1.33*** (−2.91)	−1.02** (−2)
log (***tot***)	2.24* (1.83)	2.45*** (2.24)	3.22* (1.68)	1.34* (1.82)	2.65*** (4.72)	7.56*** (2.63)	3.12* (1.65)	3.12* (1.72)	−0.005*** (−6.62)	−0.001** (−2)	−0.001*** (−2.84)	−0.001* (−1.65)
log (***rpop***)	−1.52** (−2.14)	−1.52** (−2.14)	−1.98*** (−6.94)	−3.45** (−2)	−0.91* (−1.65)	−0.001*** (−2.98)	−0.001*** (−4.1)	−0.001*** (−4.35)	−1.387*** (−6.62)	−2.981** (−2.34)	−3.759*** (−2.6)	−8.879*** (−3.87)
log (***upop***)	9.68 (0.37)	5.56 (0.78)	8.06* (1.68)	7** (2.27)	0.001* (1.84)	0.001*** (5.38)	0.001*** (4.8)	0.001*** (5.1)	1.149*** (16.08)	1.184*** (3.3)	6.594*** (4.69)	11.675*** (8.55)
log (***mort***)	0.003*** (3.03)	0.003*** (3.03)	0.033*** (4.45)	0.514*** (2.97)	1.284*** (4.79)	6.05*** (11.1)	10.877*** (6.63)	10.877*** (7.04)	−8.533** (−2)	−7* (−1.84)	−3.58*** (−2.67)	−1.87*** (−7.22)
log (***inv***)	−7.06* (−1.62)	−7.06* (−1.62)	−3.81* (−1.93)	−4* (−1.74)	−5.15*** (−3.05)	−5.15*** (−3.05)	−1.38 (−0.63)	−1.36 (−0.67)	1.942*** (11.41)	2.179*** (17.77)	1.279*** (7.73)	2.2* (1.8)
log (***hfce***)	1.68 (1.1)	3.99 (0.19)	1.87*** (2.83)	2** (2)	1.14* (1.89)	1.87*** (3.6)	4.23 (0.63)	4.35 (0.67)				
const	2.344*** (29.36)	1.603*** (2.94)	−8.378*** (−4.46)	−8.963*** (−2.84)	10*** (12.81)	6.515*** (9.23)	−9.95*** (−4.84)	−10*** (−5.14)	1.97** (2)	2.88*** (3.2)	2.6*** (2.76)	1.75*** (6.99)
R^2	0.88	0.82	0.95	0.9	0.85	0.81	0.98	0.9	0.99	0.97	0.99	0.9

Radom effect models (***RE***) and fixed effect models (***FE***), period studied: 1987–2014. Dependent variables: ***inpa, ada*** *and* ***hfce***
*, ** and ***: significant result at 1%, 5% and 10% of error margin

Table 3 Openness and food security (stability)

	WAEMU		CEMAC		WAEMU		CEMAC		WAEMU		CEMAC	
	log (***viaetm***)		log (***viaetm***)		log (***tdeic***)		log (***tdeic***)		log (***ipdann***)		log (***ipdann***)	
	RE	***FE***	***RE***	***FE***	***RE***	***FE***	***RE***	***FE***	***RE***	***FE***	***RE***	***FE***
log (***index***)	−0.091*** (−7.23)	−0.09*** (−7.47)	−0.037*** (−2.56)	−0.023* (−1.68)	0.029*** (4.58)	0.029*** (4.73)	0.148*** (4.17)	0.15*** (4.37)	0.006* (1.84)	0.05*** (2.91)	0.086** (2.19)	0.087** (2.42)
log (***tot***)	2.54* (1.76)	5.96* (1.8)	4.43** (2.16)	4.29*** (3.53)	−3.64*** (−3.36)	−3*** (−3.47)	−1.11*** (−3.33)	−1.112*** (−3.49)	7.81* (1.79)	6.28* (1.69)	4.98** (2.14)	4.99** (2.36)
log (***rpop***)	−1.02* (−1.69)	−0.000* (−1.9)	−6.89** (−2.53)	−4.51*** (−6.73)	−4.27*** (−11.45)	−4.27*** (−11.82)	−8.58*** (−7.46)	−8.59*** (−7.82)	−4.61 (−0.93)	−3.44 (−1.05)	−2.66*** (−2.76)	−2.67*** (−3.04)
log (***upop***)	9.05*** (2.84)	9.06*** (2.93)	2.47* (1.83)	2.31*** (3.94)	0.001*** (6.31)	0.001*** (6.52)	9.68*** (10.16)	9.88*** (10.65)	5.43*** (2.96)	5.43*** (3.14)	1.89 (0.24)	1.9 (0.27)
log (***mort***)	−0.36*** (−4.19)	−0.564* (−1.78)	−0.324* (1.86)	−0.302*** (−2.91)	−0.271*** (−6.24)	−0.271*** (−6.45)	−0.561*** (−3.95)	−0.651*** (−4.13)	0.089 (1.19)	0.277 (0.8)	0.255** (2.34)	0.258*** (2.58)
log (***inv***)	1.67*** (2.4)	3.49*** (3.6)	1.62*** (2.54)	1.76** (2.27)	1.55*** (4.4)	1.38*** (3.05)	2.96 (1.34)	2.98 (1.41)	−1.09*** (−3.59)	−1.26*** (−2.72)	−8.68 (−0.75)	−8.69 (−86)
log (***hfce***)	8.41*** (3.41)	9.37*** (2.59)	3.6 (1.21)	3.05 (0.91)	−4.53*** (−3.63)	−3.71** (−2.2)	−4.23*** (−5.68)	−4.236*** (−5.95)	4.31*** (4.08)	4.61*** (2.65)	1.55*** (2.8)	1.58*** (3.08)
const	9.083*** (9.4)	12.43*** (4.04)	9.155*** (3.12)	9.608*** (4.33)	9.477*** (11.41)	9.06* (1.7)	10.944*** (9.24)	10.384*** (10.732)	9.866*** (6.64)	10*** (7.53)	9.631*** (6)	10.631*** (4.06)
R^2	0.66	0.7	0.95	0.91	0.98	0.87	0.99	0.98	0.9	0.85	0.98	0.9

Radom effect models (***RE***) and fixed effect models (***FE***), period studied: 1987–2014. Dependents variables: ***viaetm***, ***tdeic*** *and* ***ipdann***

*, ** and ***: significant result at 1%, 5% and 10% of error margin

Table 4 Openness and food security (utilization)

	WAEMU		CEMAC		WAEMU		CEMAC		WAEMU		CEMAC	
	log (***vdah***)		log (***vdah***)		log (***paem5***)		log (***paem5***)		log (***npsa***)		log (***npsa***)	
	RE	***FE***	***RE***	***FE***	***RE***	***FE***	***RE***	***FE***	***RE***	***FE***	***RE***	***FE***
log (***index***)	−0.12*** (−8.27)	−0.172*** (−8.73)	−0.171* (−1.64)	−0.191* (−1.66)	0.011*** (3.48)	0.01*** (3.61)	0.042*** (4.36)	0.054*** (5.14)	−0.001** (−2.16)	−0.001*** (−2.47)	−0.008*** (−2.96)	−0.004* (−1.98)
log (***tot***)	8.51*** (3.58)	4* (1.62)	6.18* (1.68)	3.9* (1.63)	−1.84*** (−3.39)	−1.83*** (−3.52)	−1.53* (−1.65)	−3* (−1.7)	2.77*** (3.77)	5.96* (1.65)	3.01*** (3.02)	4** (2)
log (***rpop***)	6.23*** (7.2)	3.43* (1.8)	9.66*** (2.63)	10*** (2.87)	4.79*** (2.44)	4.8*** (2.54)	9.4*** (2.64)	8*** (3.5)	−1.65*** (−5.85)	−4.82*** (−4.31)	−2.13** (−2.13)	−3.57*** (−3.66)
log (***upop***)	−6.15* (1.63)	−5.83* (1.65)	2.63 (0.97)	3.3 (0.43)	−1.44* (−1.74)	−1.4* (−1.8)	−2.41*** (−9.12)	−4.75*** (−13.71)	2.57** (2.2)	7.75*** (3.93)	3.68*** (4.54)	1.77** (2.72)
log (***mort***)	−0.92* (−1.85)	−1.046*** (−2.5)	−1.713*** (−2.8)	−1.132** (−2)	−0.067*** (−2.83)	−0.066*** (−2.93)	−0.212*** (−4.48)	−0.185*** (−2.95)	0.016*** (4.57)	0.047*** (6.89)	0.044*** (2.86)	0.063*** (4.22)
log (***inv***)	1.16* (1.62)	1.08* (1.96)	5.64 (0.55)	7.35 (0.61)	1.81 (1.03)	1.81 (1.07)	2.11 (0.3)	4.17 (0.79)	−6.04*** (−2.74)	−3.72** (−2.23)	−3.85* (−1.9)	−3.14*** (−3.04)
log (***hfce***)	1.95 (0.75)	4.04 (0.92)	2.78 (0.84)	3 (0.1)	−1.52*** (−2.44)	−1.53*** (−2.54)	−4.26** (−2.04)	−4* (−1.75)	−1.09* (−1.67)	−1.27* (−1.93)	−2.61*** (−4.98)	−3*** (−2.55)
const	11.431*** (9.96)	9.873*** (7.49)	−7 (−0.84)	−9 (−0.6)	7.707*** (30.63)	8*** (31.79)	9.446*** (16.97)	10*** (11.03)	2.462*** (6.74)	6.4*** (7.19)	−2.012* (−1.62)	−3* (−1.95)
R^2	0.81	0.79	0.99	0.9	0.72	0.78	0.9	0.95	0.62	0.63	0.99	0.9

Radom effect models (***RE***) and fixed effect models (***FE***), period studied: 1987–2014. Dependents variables: ***vdah***, ***paem5*** and ***npsa***
*, ** and ***: significant result at 1%, 5% and 10% of error margin

Finally, as regards expenditure on household consumption (***hfce***), the openness index (***index***) and the terms of trade (***tot***) had negative effects on the former in both zones. Thus, even if the openness causes decline in food prices, the destruction of domestic production and unfavorable terms of trade cancel this beneficial effect on household purchasing power out. Thus, the effect of openness on household consumption is found to be generally negative.

The value of food imports to total merchandise exports (***viaetm***) declined when the openness index (***index***) increased in both areas. Thus, the increase in the volume of food imports leading to lower prices, this normally results in a relative decrease of their value relative to exports. However, the general evolution of terms of trade (***tot***), taking into account all goods imported and exported, destroys this apparent improvement of the purchasing power of the exports compared to that of the food imports. These elasticities ranged from 2.54 to 4.43 in WAEMU and CEMAC.

The openness index (***index***) lead to the increase in the dependency ratio in respect of cereal imports (***tdeic***) in both areas, CEMAC being more affected than WAEMU (0.148 and 0.029 respectively). This result goes in the same direction as the conclusions of Brooks et al. (2013). Thus, openness has a negative impact on local production and it naturally leads to greater dependence on food imports. However, the raw materials exported by the countries of the sample lose their purchasing power compared to the imported finished products. In this context, the adverse terms of trade decrease the dependency, because even if imports exist, people do not have enough income to purchase them.

The openness index (***index***) and the terms of trade (***tot***) increased the instability of food prices at national level (***ipdann***). Indeed, countries are not only exposed to fluctuations in world prices, but also to changes in domestic production. The unfavorable terms of trade decreased the purchasing power of the households and impacted the price level. This result goes in the same direction with the extant empirical literature (for example Gerard et al. 2008; Ambagna et al. 2012).

Finally for utilization, the opening index (***index***) had a negative effect on the variability of per capita food availability (***vdah***), because openness had a negative effect on domestic food production (see Table 1), and most of the agricultural products on the domestic market are imported. This does not promote diversity of available food and leads to behavioral change in household consumption. Unlike the openness index, the terms of trade (***tot***) had a positive effect on the diversity of food supplies. These opposite effects are also noticeable in terms of the index of the prevalence of anemia among children under 5 years (***paem5***) and the number of undernourished people (***npsa***). Indeed, openness reinforced the prevalence and fight against malnutrition, but this result is curbed by the unfavorable terms of trade.

6.2 Conclusion

In conclusion, trade liberalization had a negative effect on food security in general. Despite the fact that it lead to lower prices, it had a negative impact on household consumer spending. The decrease in household income had implications for their purchasing power. Under these conditions, households cannot buy food items even at low prices. The beneficial effect of trade on the food situation is most visible in terms of availability of cereals, roots and tubers in the food energy intake, the scale of the food shortage, the value of food imports to total exports goods, the index of the prevalence of anemia among children under 5 years and the number of undernourished people. However, these positive results are annihilated by the unfavorable evolution of the terms of trade in the countries of the sample thus precipitating food insecurity. Therefore, with regard to policy, these countries should implement trade policies to facilitate of openness, while supporting and diversifying domestic food production.

References

Abdullateef, U., & Ijaiya, A. T. (2010). Agricultural trade liberalization and food security in Nigeria. *Journal of Economics and International Finance, 2*(12), 299–307.

Ambagna, J. J., Sikod, F., & Kane, G. Q. (2012). La transmission de l'instabilité des prix mondiaux des céréales aux marchés camerounais: cas des marchés de Yaoundé et Douala. *5*[emes] *Journées de recherche en Sciences sociales INRA-SFER-CIRAD.*

Bowdler, C. & Malik, A. (2006). *Openness and inflation volatility: Panel data evidence*. 20th Annual Congress of the European Economic Association, Amsterdam.

Breusch, T. S., & Pagan, A. R. (1980). The Lagrange multiplier test and its applications to model specification in econometrics. *Review of Economics Studies, 47*, 239–253.

Brooks, D., Ferrarini, B., & Go, E. (2013). *Bilateral trade and food security*. ADB Economics Working Paper Series No. 367.

Calderon, C. (2004). *Trade openness and real exchange rate volatility: Panel data evidence*. Central Bank of Chile Working Papers N°294.

Charvet, J. P. (1987). *Le désordre alimentaire mondial, surplus et pénuries: le scandale*. Hatier, collection J. Breton.

ECOWAS Commission. (2008). *La politique agricole régionale de l'Afrique de l'Ouest: de l'agriculture le levier de l'intégration régionale*. ECOWAP. Retrieved from http://www.diplomatie.gouv.fr/fr/IMG/pdf/01_ComCEDEAO.pdf

Communauté Economique et Monétaire de l'Afrique Centrale. (2009). *Stratégie agricole commune des Etats membres de la CEMAC*. Document de travail. Retrieved from http://www.coton-acp.org/docs/politiques/Strategie_Agricole_Commune_CEMAC.pdf

De Schutter, O. (2014). *Commerce international et souveraineté alimentaire: pourquoi la libéralisation accrue du commerce international des produits agricoles n'est pas la solution à la question de la faim*. Université catholique de Louvain Working Paper.

Dorosh, P. (2001). Trade liberalization and national food security: Rice trade between Bangladesh and India. *World Development, 29*(4), 673–689.

Dorosh, P., Dradri, S., & Haggblade, S. (2009). Regional trade, government policy and food security: Recent evidence from Zambia. *Food Policy, 34*, 350–366.

Eba Nguema, I., & Assoumou Ella, G. (2014). Trade liberalization and food security: For a New Green Revolution in Africa. *Journal of Food Security, 2*(2), 42–50.

FAO. (2006, 2008, 2013, 2014, 2016). *Etat de l'insécurité alimentaire dans le monde*. Rome.

Gerard, F., Dorin, B., Beliere, J. F., Diarra, A., Keita, S. M., & Dury, S. (2008). *Flambée des prix alimentaires internationaux: opportunité ou désastre pour les populations les plus pauvres?* Working Paper Moisa N°8.

Hausman, J. A. (1978). Specification tests in econometrics. *Econometrica, 46*(6), 1251–1271.

Korinek, J., & Melatos, M. (2009) *Effets de certains accords commerciaux régionaux sur les échanges agricoles*. Editions OCDE.

Moulton, B. R., & Randolph, W. C. (1989). Alternative tests of the error component model. *Econometrica, 57*, 685–693.

Nijman, T. E., & Verbeek, M. (1992). Nonresponse in panel data: The impact on estimates of a life cycle consumption function. *Journal of Applied Econometrics, 7*, 243–257.

Oyejide, T. A. (2005). *Trade liberalization, regional integration and African development in the context of structural adjustment*. IDRC/CRDI.

Padilla, P. (1997). *La sécurité alimentaire des villes africaines: le rôle des SADA*. Communication présentée au séminaire sous régional FAO-ISRA, Approvisionnement et distribution alimentaires des villes de l'Afrique francophone, Dakar, 14–17 avril 1997.

Pirotte, A. (2011). *Econométrie des données de panel: Théorie et applications*. Economica.

Pyakuryal, B., Roy, D., & Thapa, Y. B. (2010). Trade liberalization and food security in Nepal. *Food Policy, 25*, 20–31.

Rodney, W. (1987). Histoire générale de l'Afrique. In UNESCO (Ed.), *VII l'Afrique sous domination coloniale, 1880–1935* (pp. 361–380).

Romer, D. (1993). Openness and inflation: Theory and evidences. *Quarterly Journal of Economics, 108*, 869–903.

Trade in Services for Growth and Structural Transformation in West Africa

Françoise Okah Efogo

Contents

Abstract The objective of this paper is to identify the categories of services likely to foster structural transformation and economic growth in ECOWAS. This paper seeks to move beyond theoretical exercise by offering policy solutions which could streamline services trade in ECOWAS, thereby allowing it to take advantage of expansion in this sector. For this, we rely on data from ECOWAS countries between 1995 and 2015 from the UNCTAD database and WDI (2016) database. Results from a dynamic panel model show that for each ECOWAS countries there is at least one category of services that promotes structural transformation and/or economic growth. Services trade (imports and/or exports) could be a powerful tool for economic growth, structural transformation and integration if the various countries rely on the appropriate service for this purpose.

F. Okah Efogo (✉)
Faculty of Economics and Management, University of Yaounde II, Soa, Cameroon

D. Seck (ed.), *The External Sector of Africa's Economy*, Advances in African Economic, Social and Political Development,
https://doi.org/10.1007/978-3-319-97913-7_7

1 Introduction

Trade in services has become a major subject of interest in Africa and developing countries. Indeed, the current WTO round of negotiation centered on the trade of services as a means for development. The recent Nairobi package drawn from the tenth WTO ministerial conference indicates that preferential treatment will be given to service providers from LDCs. Similarly, the 2015's UNCTAD report on Africa focused on the ways to unlock the potential of African trade in services as a driver of inclusive growth and structural transformation. This report states that African countries should shift away from subsistence and non-tradable services to services which engender greater value added and economic growth (UNCTAD 2015). This view is echoed by Gelb et al. (2016) and Ghani and O'Connell (2016) who suggest that services can and should play a role as engines of growth and structural transformation in Sub-Saharan Africa (Cadot and de Melo 2016). Therefore, it seems important to delineate which services African countries in general, should focus their efforts to improve economic growth and foster structural transformation. This, of course, is particularly relevant for LDCs in Africa. For this purpose, this paper addresses the issue of category of services that are capable of inspiring growth and encouraging structural transformation.

There are at least eight categories of services (AFRISTAT, UNCTADStat) and different sub-categories which are delivered in four modes as defined in General Agreement on Trade in Services (GATS). Mode 1, called cross-border supply, refers to the movement of services without relocation of either the consumer or the producer; Mode 2, called consumption abroad, refers to the movement of consumers to the foreign country providing the service; Mode 3, called commercial presence, involves the physical establishment of foreign enterprises in the country; Mode 4 concerns migration or movement of people, namely when the supplier and the consumer interact in a third-part foreign country. The four modes have disparate effects on economic growth because of the different transmission channels. Some services ease transactions (Hoekman and Mattoo 2011; Han et al. 2010) through space and time (transport, telecommunication, financial services); others improve factors productivity like work (R&D, health services and education) or capital (Triplett and Bosworth 2004; Inklaar et al. 2008; Ypma 2007 ...). Research has consistently demonstrated that efficient services decrease production costs (Wilson et al. 2003; Fink et al. 2002). It also notes that trade in services improve competitiveness, reinforce regional integration and diversification and help in solving infrastructural problems... (Nyunt 2009).

Nonetheless, given the technical, financial and human mean needed to develop all the sectors in all the modes, African countries should choose those which can create value and encourage development across other sectors. Given that maximum efficiency requires some services to be imported and others exported, this can be a daunting task. We thus seek to contribute to this task and to try to assess the different effects of some services and the specific flow (import, export) on which West African countries may rely. Therefore, this paper answers the following question:

which services are most conducive for growth and structural transformation in West African countries?

The question makes this article a continuation of the works of Cuyvers and Viviers who demonstrated that it is possible to streamline export promotion by determining the most efficient product-partner pairs for the promotion of economic growth (Cuyvers et al. 1995; Cuyvers 1997, 2004; Viviers and Pearson 2007; Viviers et al. 2009, 2010; Cuyvers and Viviers 2012). They apply their model, among other countries, in Belgium and South Africa. This work does not claim to identify such pairs in services, but has rather a more modest aspiration of identifying the categories of services which foster structural transformation and economic growth in ECOWAS. Nevertheless, it has the merit to fit the agenda proposed by Cuyvers and Viviers (2012) who state that *"future researches on the export opportunities of other exporting countries will lead to more insight in the patterns of international trade that shape economic development of countries and regions"* (p. 255).

Structural transformation is the reallocation of economic activities from low productivity to high productivity activities. It can take different paths, but generally it describes shifts of output and labor first from agriculture to manufacturing, then from manufacturing to services at later stages of development (Dabla-Norris et al. 2013). However, the last step of development is not always characterized by a shift from manufacturing to services since the two are seen as complements (Gadrey 2003; Gallouj and Djellal 2007).[1] An illustration of this can be easily found in Sub-Saharan Africa. The primary driver of the recent high growth episode is a declining share of agriculture and an increase in the share of services, while manufacturing remains broadly at the same level.

Following the words of UNCTAD (2015), African countries have the challenge to rely on services which generate greater value added and growth. This paper attempts to explore this challenge while assessing the effects of tradable services on growth and structural transformation. To the best of our knowledge, it is the first paper to do such a study in West African countries. Furthermore, the originality of the paper is derived from three unique sources. First, using the panel mean-group estimation, it allows a comparison of trade in services effects among West African countries. Secondly, it assesses the more efficient flow (export versus imports) in driving growth and structural transformation. Thirdly, it compares the effects of different categories of services in driving growth and structural transformation.

Results yield four notable findings: first, the most efficient traded service differ from one country to the other; second, the most efficient flow is different from one country to the other; third, the delay of impact differs between countries and fourth, trade in services is a key driver of economic growth and structural transformation. The second result proposes paths to reinforce ECOWAS regional integration in services.

---

[1]Gadrey J. (2003) *Socio-économie des Services.* La Découverte. Collection Repères; Gallouj C. et Djellal F. (2007), *Introduction à L'économie des Services.* Presses Universitaires de Grenoble. Collection « Economie en + ». France.

2 Stylized Facts

This section is dedicated to a description of the main feature of trade in services, growth and structural transformation in West Africa region. In this paper we use the wide definition of West African countries relying on countries belonging to ECOWAS. Thus, we examine the eight countries of WAEMU (Benin, Burkina Faso, Côte d'Ivoire, Guinea Bissau, Mali, Niger, Senegal, Togo) as well as Cape Verde, Gambia, Ghana, Guinea, Liberia, Nigeria and Sierra Leone. Data to be discussed come from both *UNCTADstat* and World Development Indicators (WDI 2016) databases.

2.1 Trade in Services in West African Countries Between 1995 and 2015

Trade in services in ECOWAS amounts to less than 2% of world trade in services. It is, nevertheless, noted that trade in services increased throughout the studied period in this part of Africa. However, this growth of trade in services is marked by fluctuations of greater or lesser magnitude. Figure 1 shows the evolution of total trade in services in each country of ECOWAS. It appears that, between 1995 and 2015, total trade in services accounts for less than 25% of GDP, except in Cabo

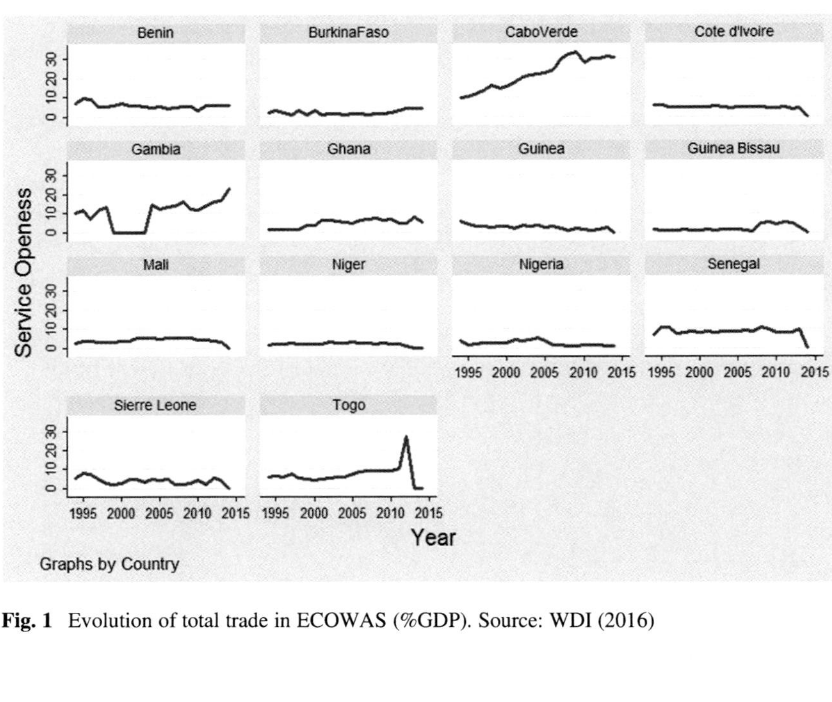

Fig. 1 Evolution of total trade in ECOWAS (%GDP). Source: WDI (2016)

Verde and Togo. Further, service trade balance sheet is in a deficit during the analyzed period. Nonetheless, in term of value added, services are about 40% and 45% of GDP respectively, making it the most important contributor sector to ECOWAS global value added.

Given the above observations, it appears that the service sector could become an engine of ECOWAS economic growth and structural transformation. In this regard, the African Center for Economic Transformation report (ACET 2014) identified the ways and means for African countries to turn potential opportunities into effective opportunities in the service sector. First, this report identifies two promising service sectors for African countries—tourism and teleservices. Tourism holds promise due to attractions of the varied cultures, wildlife, landscapes, and sunny beaches. Teleservices embody business process outsourcing based on fairly wages and medium skills. Cape Verde was ranked the 6th African country on 10 African countries most likely to benefit from the opportunities offered by tourism (UNWTO 2015). The travel and tourism sector represents between 16% and 20% of total trade in services during the studied period in ECOWAS, making it the second largest sector behind transportation services.

Yet these general observations obscure some of the more specific details which provide a holistic picture of the phenomena. For example, looking at Fig. 2, we can see that in some countries, services have always been the most important sector in

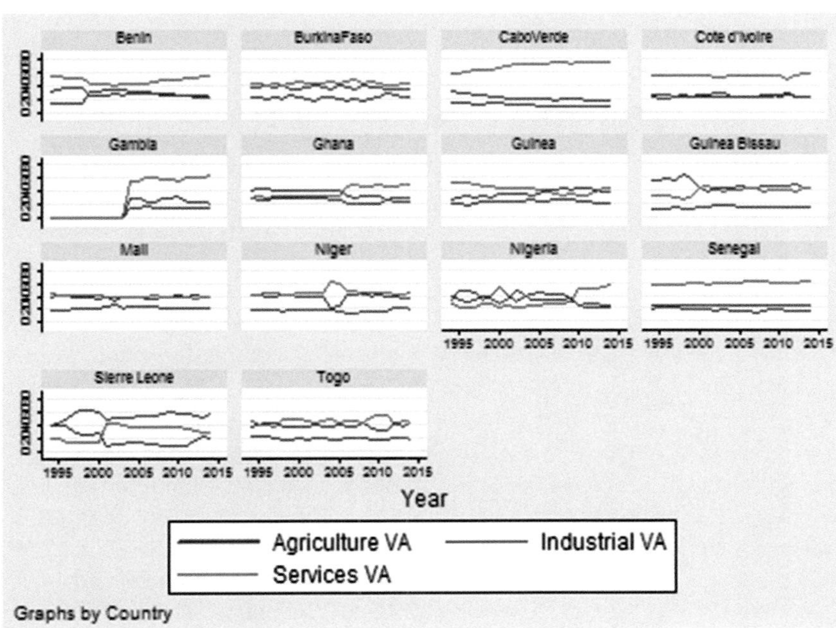

Fig. 2 By country economic sector value added (million $). Source: WDI (2016)

terms of value added shares (Benin, Burkina Faso, ...) while in others it only became the most important in the 2000s (Ghana, Nigeria).

In the same vein, the importance of some categories of services has diminished. For example, business services accounted for over 60% of trade in services in Cape Verde until 1998. Now it has gradually given way to services that were not part of the portfolio of exchanged services. This finding is in line with the second recommendation of the report on the structural transformation of Africa (ACET 2014). This particular recommendation concerns the diversification of trade and business partners. Diversification can be accomplished through the development of new markets and relies on the creation of high quality human capital. According to this report, "*economic transformation demands a healthy workforce equipped with the knowledge and skills to be highly productive on farms, in firms, and in government offices—and to generate innovations in technologies, processes, products, and services.*" (p. 14)

Finally, all categories of services can work for West African structural transformation. It is therefore prudent to diversify the portfolio of traded services, but to focus primarily on the services for which ECOWAS countries have a comparative advantage (technology, qualified personnel ...) as well as on services that can pull other sectors and on essential public services (infrastructure, education, health, port authority ...). Before delving into discussion on services and structural transformation, it is necessary to evaluate the evolution of structural transformation in ECOWAS.

2.2 Structural Transformation and Economic Growth in West Africa Between 1995 and 2015

On average GDP growth rates in ECOWAS (excluding Liberia) were 4.5% between 1995 and 2015 with a 7.62% rate of inflation. These macroeconomic results fail to meet either the optimal growth objectives or the convergence criteria in the WAEMU. During that period, exports of services increased by 24.37% while imports increased by 9.82%.With regards to the structural transformation, several indicators may be used for analysis. We begin with the least complex measure, the ratio ${}^{VA_{agriculture}}/_{VA_{industry}}$. Structural change results in a lower ratio. Figure 3 shows the evolution of this ratio for each country between 1995 and 2015. It appears that this ratio is unstable in most countries of ECOWAS (sawtooth evolution). Nevertheless we observe that there was a decrease in this ratio in Benin from 2000 to 2014; in Cape Verde from 2002 to 2014; in Côte d'Ivoire from 2002 to 2010; in Ghana from 2010 to 2014; in Guinea from 2005 to 2014; in Guinea Bissau from 2000 to 2014; in Niger from 2008 to 2014; in Nigeria from 2005 to 2015 and in Senegal in 2002. In other countries, we observe an increasing trend (Burkina Faso, Gambia, Mali, Sierra Leone, and Togo).

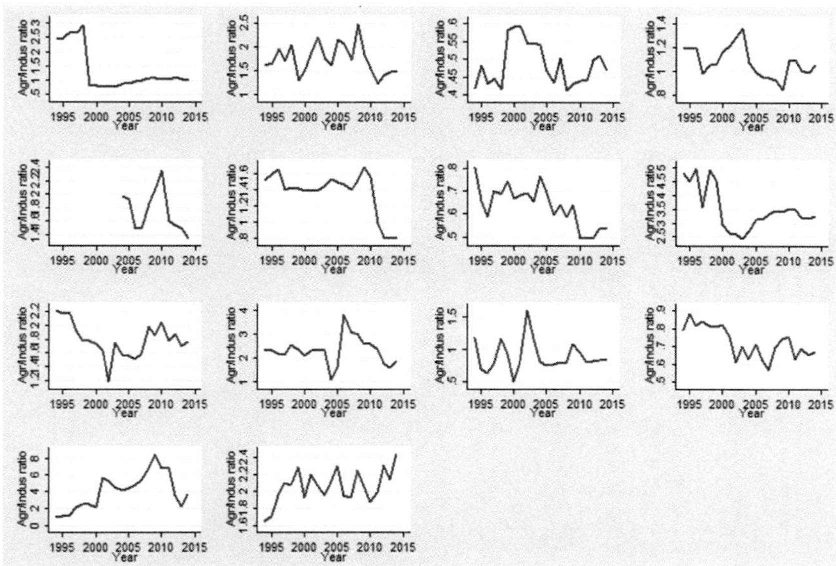

Fig. 3 Ratio agriculture/industry in ECOWAS countries. Source WDI (2016)

Another indicator is employment intensity in different sectors. Unfortunately there is not sufficient information relating to this indicator for the time period we examined. However, relying on available data (WDI 2016), it appears that between 2000 and 2010 the agriculture sector has been the most important employment provider (about 50%) followed by the service sector (about 35%). The secondary sector provides less than 20% of employment, whatever the considered country in ECOWAS. So according to this criterion, there is not yet structural transformation in ECOWAS countries.

Figure 3 offers a more nuanced account since in Cape Verde, for example, the value added share of industrial sector has always been higher than agriculture value added share. Moreover, structural transformation involves many more things than just a declining ratio. It is the reason why ACET report on African structural transformation provides an indicator (African Transformation Index) which is based on five criteria, namely the diversification of goods and services, export competitiveness, productivity, technology and human economic well-being.

This indicator is then applied and used to classify 21 African countries in ascending order. Six ECOWAS countries are among the 21 countries included in this report. They are classified as follows: Ivory Coast occupies the third place, followed by Senegal (4th), Benin (13th), Ghana (16th), Nigeria (19th) and Burkina Faso (21st). More, the report compares evolution of each country in relation to the classification of 2000 (1999–2001). It appears that Burkina Faso, Ghana and Senegal have declined; Nigeria has stagnated although it is now ranked before Burkina Faso;

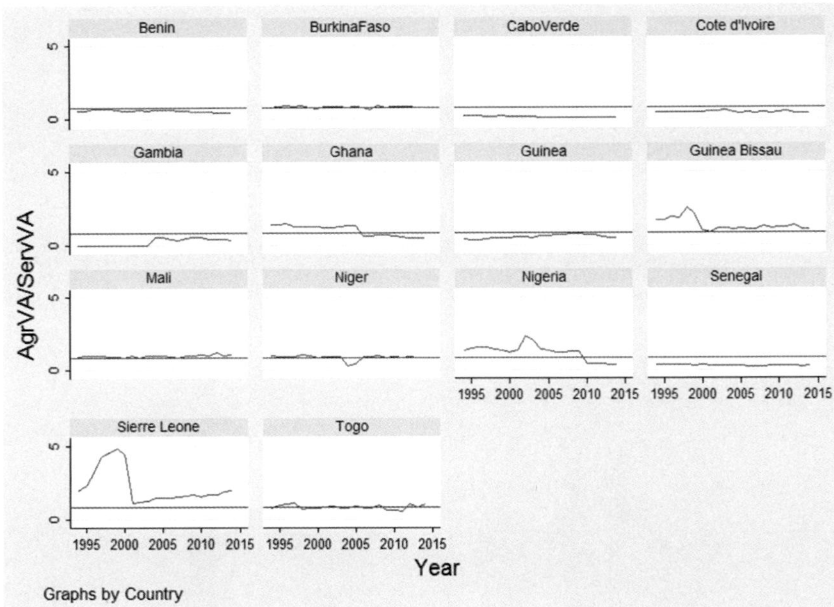

Fig. 4 Ratio agriculture/services in ECOWAS countries. Source WDI (2016)

Ivory Coast has progressed. Finally, even if the index considered here is more complex than the ratio, the implications seem to corroborate the results of the analysis of Fig. 3.

Figure 4 allows finalizing the review of structural transformation by making use of the $^{VA_{agriculture}}/_{VA_{services}}$ ratio. The red line is the mean value. It appears that in most ECOWAS countries, service sectors represent more weight than the agricultural sector in terms of value added (ratio < 1). This sudden change does not meet the pattern of structural transformation, nor is it anchored on a strong manufacturing sector. It then raises a number of questions. Specifically, it raises the question of whether the services sector is able to support sustainable growth and structural transformation.

In sum, structural transformation happens slowly in ECOWAS countries, but it is not based on an industrial sector that could ensure its sustainability. Moreover, the substitution between the services sector and agricultural sector is more pronounced than the substitution between the agricultural sector and the industrial sector (in terms of value added shares). All of which emphasize the importance of implementing strategies to take advantage of this service sector by identifying services with high potential. This is the purpose of the empirical section of this work.

3 Method and Model

3.1 Theoretical Rationality of the Model

How can trade in services (hence after TS) be included in a growth model? How can it be inserted in a structural transformation model? Many approaches can be used to answer this question. TS is linked to the well-established literature which notes trade's relationship with growth. Based on this literature, three main results can be noted: trade induced a significant increase in GDP growth rate (Alcalá and Ciccone 2004; Kose et al. 2006); trade reduces GDP growth rate (Rigobon and Rodrik 2005) or finally the relationship is not significant (Rodriguez and Rodrik 2001). Proponents of a non-significant relationship justify it by adding variables such as geography or institutional quality. When dealing with the inverse relationship, it comes that growth could have several positive effects. Growth encourages diversification and improvement of production through technological innovation. Growth conditions create a suitable environment for productive investment. Growth could also discourage brain drain.

The second approach is to emphasize the role of TS in growth. According to Hoekman and Mattoo (2011), services are inputs into the production process. Indeed, they help transactions through space (transport and telecommunication) or time (financial services). They are also determinants of the productivity of other production factors such as labor or capital (Triplett and Bosworth 2004; Inklaar et al. 2006; Ypma 2007; …). They enhance human capital (research-development and health services). Many authors like Hoekman and Saggi, Wilson et al. (2003), Fink et al. (2002) demonstrate that efficient services lower productivity costs and then strengthen growth. Finally, in the case of productivity hypothesis, it is imported services that may be use as inputs in production.

When we turn to exports, we find that they ameliorate balance of payments (BOP), leading to an increase in government revenues and, by this way, to an increase in GDP growth (see for example Nyunt 2009). Finally, there's a theoretical basis for the inclusion of TS in a growth model. It is then possible to build the model.

3.2 The Model

The basic model to be used relies on the hypothesis that services are inputs in production.

$$dy_{it} = \varphi y_{it-1} + \beta X_{it} + dy_{it-1}a_1 + y_{it-p}a_p + dX_{it}B_1 + \ldots + dX_{it-q}B_q + e_{it}$$

where y_{it} is either economic growth measured by GDP or structural transformation, φ is the error correction speed of adjustment, β is a Kx1 vector of parameters, $a_1 \ldots a_p$

are p parameters to be estimated, X_{it} is a 1xK vector of covariates, $B_1 \ldots B_q$ are vectors of parameters to be estimated, e_{it} is the error term. The covariates in the model are, price changes measured by the annual change in the index of consumer prices, capital measured by Gross Capital Formation, technology approximated by institutions, trade diversification, global trade openness and TS which is included category by category (see Table 1) in a first step as exportations and in a second step as importations. i is country's indicator and t represent the time span (1995–2015). Measurement of structural transformation is discussed in the following paragraph.

3.3 Measuring Trade in Services (TS)

TS measurement relies on data from *UNCTADStat* database. The choice of this set of data is based on its disaggregation. Indeed, *UNCTADstat* database records information on several categories of services described in the following table (Table 1). The content of each category is useful for discussion and understanding of empirical results. Each service can be delivered in four modes as described in the introduction. The twelfth category (FDI) describe trade in mode 3 (commercial presence) whatever the considered service. In the database, the inflows and outflows of FDI include the capital provided by the direct investor (either directly or through other companies with which it is linked) to a company. FDI outflows are exports in mode 3 while FDI inflows are imports. For mode 1 (cross border supply), mode 2 (consumption abroad) and mode 4 (movement of natural persons) unfortunately, *UNCTADstat* does not provide detailed data. This database records total trade in all modes (1, 2 and 4). Our discussion of the results is thus unable to put emphasis on the modes of supply, but rather on service category and flow (imports vs exports).

3.4 Measuring Structural Transformation

There are numerous studies dealing with measurement of structural changes (Kuznets 1966; Zoltan 1969; Duarte and Restuccia 2010; Herrendorf et al. 2013, 2014 …). Generally, in literature, structural transformation is a matter of change in sectoral productivity either at the industry level or at the global level. But it is also a wide concept embodying different major changes. These changes include a systematic fall over time in the share of labor allocated to agriculture, a steady increase in the share of labor in services, a hump-shaped pattern for the share of labor in manufacturing, a rising share of urban economic activity in industry and modern services, migration of rural workers to urban settings, and a demographic transition in birth and death rates that always leads to a spurt in population growth before a new equilibrium is reached. The three most common measures of economic activity at the

Table 1 Details of each category of services

Variable	Detailed description
1. Public services	Residual category covering transactions in goods and services carried out by government (embassies, consulates, military units, etc.) and not included in other categories. Transactions made by international organizations are also included there
2. Personal and cultural services	1. Audiovisual and related services attached to the production of movies, radio and television programs, musical recordings (and similar). 2. Fees paid to the personnel involved and the limited rights distributions, as well as payments related to sporting events, theatrical and variety shows. 3. Services associated with museums, libraries, archives and other cultural and sports activities. 4. Services of education and health with the exception of expenses related to education or health incurred by travelers (and listed under the category 'travel').
3. Other services to enterprises	Merchanting and other trade-related services, operational leasing services and miscellaneous business, professional and technical services (legal, accounting, consulting, advertising, R&D, etc.).
4. Royalties and licenses	Covers franchise fees and royalties paid for the use of trademarks and other royalties; and license fees related to the authorized use of intangible non-produced non-financial and property rights. Limited distribution rights of audiovisual products are not included in this category.
5. Informatics and information services	1. Services related to computer hardware and software and data processing services. 2. Services of the information communication, photographs, and feature articles to the media. 3. Other services that cover services for databases: design, storage and dissemination of data, are direct, subscriptions to periodicals.
6. Financial services	Financial intermediation services and auxiliary services, except those directly related to life insurance or pension funds (already included in insurance services).
7. Insurance services	Various forms of insurance, reinsurance and ancillary services. These services are measured or estimated the amount of service charges included in total premiums collected, not the actual total amount of premiums.
8. Building/construction services	Covers the construction and installation work for a company outside of the economy in which the company is resident.
9. Communication	Includes postal services (including messaging) and telecommunication services between residents and non-residents.
10. Travel and tourism services	Includes goods and services acquired from an economy by non-resident travelers during a stay of less than one year.
11. Transport services	All passenger services, the movement of goods (freight), rental of means of transport with crew, and related services except the freight insurance which is part of insurance services and purchases in ports by non-resident carriers and repairs of transportation equipment that are considered property.

(continued)

Table 1 (continued)

Variable	Detailed description
12. Foreign direct investment	FDI is composed of three categories: social capital, reinvested earnings and intra-company loans. 1. The share capital includes the purchase of shares of a company located abroad by the direct investor resident in the reporting economy. 2. Reinvested earnings in the share due to the direct investor (in proportion to its direct equity participation) of earnings not distributed as dividends by affiliated enterprises and branch profits that are not paid to the direct investor. These retained earnings by affiliates are reinvested. 3. Intra-company loans or intra-company transactions concerning debts or claims referring to loans and loans to short- or long-term funds between the direct investor (parent company) and related companies (affiliates).

Source: UNCTADstat (2016)

sectoral level are employment shares,[2] value added shares[3] and final consumption expenditure shares. The two first measures concern production while the last measure refers to consumption (Herrendorf et al. 2014). Given the above paragraph on theoretical rationality of our econometric model, we focus in this paper on structural changes in the production side of ECOWAS economies. Employment shares are calculated either by using workers or hours worked by sector, depending on data availability. Value added shares are typically expressed in current prices ("nominal shares"), but they may be expressed in constant prices also ("real shares").

Since available data on ECOWAS countries are not sufficient enough to analyze structural transformation in employment shares, which is a long term and continuous process, we rely here on value added shares. In this vein, we use a simple measure of structural transformation and a relative measure of structural transformation. According to the simple measure, there is structural transformation if we observe a decrease in the ratio $^{VA_{agriculture}}/_{VA_{industry}}$. Following the relative measure inspired from Zoltan (1969) there is structural transformation if there is an increase in the following ratio

$$s_t = \left[\frac{1 + (r_{it}/100)}{1 + (\bar{r}_t/100)} \right] * 100 - 100$$

where r_{it} is the annual growth rate of $VA_{industry}$ and $\bar{r}_t$ is the average annual growth rate of value added shares of all the sectors:

[2]Employment shares are calculated using either workers number or hours worked by sector.

[3]Typically expressed in current prices ("nominal shares"), they may also be expressed in constant prices ("real shares").

$$\left(\bar{r}_t = \frac{r_{it} + r_{at} + r_{st}}{3}\right)$$

3.5 Basic Statistics and First Insights in Data

The following table (Table 2) gives average descriptive statistics for variables included in the model, apart from detailed categorical TS. We observe that global trade in services, whatever the flow, is highly unstable (high standard deviation). Global imports are more volatile than global exports. Concerning structural transformation in ECOWAS, two observations can be made. First of all structural transformation is weak in ECOWAS whatever the considered indicator. In the same way, since 1995, even if there is a positive gap from the average evolution, structural transformation is slow in ECOWAS countries. Secondly, ECOWAS countries seem to be similar since the standard deviation of structural transformation indicators between countries is weak.

The first step of the analysis is to proceed to the stationary tests on the variables included in the model. The Im, Pesaran and Shin stationary test reveals that some variables are stationary while others are not. This gives a presumption of cointegration between these variables and the structural transformation indicator on the one hand, and a presumption of cointegration with economic growth in the other hand. Table 3 summarizes the results of the stationary test, including the decision (stationary or not) and the number of lags to consider. It appears that one can hypothesize a long-term relationship between technology (institutions) and structural transformation. It is also observed that imports of a number of services can have long-term effects, including communication services, transport services and travel/tourism services. Similarly, trade openness and trade in services openness could have a long term effect.

These first findings on the persistent effect of a shock on trade in certain services in ECOWAS must be refined using the econometric model presented in this section. The model is estimated with the three different estimators, namely the fixed effects estimator (fe), the mean group estimator (mg) which assigns each country a specific long-term relationship and a specific short-term relationship, the panel mean group estimator (pmg) which assigns to all of ECOWAS a common long-term equation and specific short-term relationships. The Hausman test and the AIC and BIC information criteria are then used to retain only the most relevant estimator whose details are presented in the following section.

4 Results and Discussion

Three sets of results are presented here. The first set focuses on service exports impact on structural transformation. The second set is about service imports effects on structural transformation. The last set concerns the link with economic growth.

Table 2 Summary statistics of variables

Variable		Mean	Std. Dev.	Min	Max	Observations
Diversification	Overall	0.7367013	0.1646358	0	0.8927317	N = 294
	Between		0.0490674	0.6626051	0.8115908	n = 14
	Within		0.1576759	−0.0748895	0.9186344	T = 21
GDP (%)	Overall	4.500691	4.747994	−28.09998	33.73578	N = 294
	Between		1.548167	1.735305	7.692839	n = 14
	Within		4.506687	−25.33459	32.06546	T = 21
Price (%)	Overall	7.628278	11.29586	−35.83668	72.8355	N = 294
	Between		5.397084	3.117031	20.29814	n = 14
	Within		10.02278	−39.99879	63.32542	T = 21
Service exports	Overall	395.5857	627.7245	0	3473.18	N = 294
	Between		506.5723	13.84393	1830.828	n = 14
	Within		393.6228	−1435.242	2635.695	T = 21
Service imports	Overall	1233.999	3528.302	0	24,573.3	N = 294
	Between		2758.644	43.51287	10,647.4	n = 14
	Within		2314.791	−9413.403	15,159.9	T = 21
$ratio\left(\frac{Agriculture}{Industry}\right)$	Overall	1.637418	1.246255	0	8.440368	N = 294
	Between		1.063277	0.4861853	4.045158	n = 14
	Within		0.7069398	−1.43283	6.032627	T = 21
s_{it}	Overall	0.001756	0.1441967	−1.147555	1.193806	N = 270
	Between		0.0168858	−0.0284323	0.043621	n = 14
	Within		0.1432437	−1.117366	1.151941	T = 21
Political stability	Overall	−0.233589	0.7394331	−2.375094	1.115535	N = 294
	Between		0.5507793	−1.034948	0.8751491	n = 14
	Within		0.5139168	−2.032161	0.8013596	T = 21
Global openness	Overall	58.72657	24.16715	0	151.4438	N = 294
	Between		15.80695	36.63139	86.18699	n = 14
	Within		18.74158	−20.93727	130.5065	T = 21

Source: WDI (2016)

Table 3 Stationarity analysis of variables

Variable		Stationarity decision
Regulatory quality	RegQual	Non Stationary
Political stability	PolStab	Non Stationary
Agriculture/industry	Agri/Indus	Stationary
S_{it}	S_t	Stationary
Prices	CPI	Stationary
Economic growth	GDP	Stationary
Diversification	Diversif	Stationary
Service openness	ServOpen	Non Stationary
Global trade openness	GlOpen	Stationary
Total services exports	ServExp	Non Stationary
Total services imports	ServImp	Non Stationary
Public services exports	ServPubE	Stationary
Public services imports	ServPubM	Stationary
Insurance services exports	InsurServE	Stationary
Insurance services imports	InsurServM	Stationary
Transport services exports	TransE	Non Stationary
Transport services imports	TransM	Non Stationary
Personal and cultural services exports	PersServE	Stationary
Personal and cultural services imports	PersServM	Stationary
Other services to enterprises exports	OthServE	Stationary
Other services to enterprises imports	OthServE	Stationary
Travel and tourism services exports	TravE	Stationary
Travel and tourism services imports	TravM	Non Stationary
Foreign direct investment outflow	FDI_E	Stationary
Foreign direct investment intflow	FDI_M	Non Stationary

Source: WDI (2016) and UNCTADstat (2016)

Globally, all the results validate the hypothesis of common long run relationships in ECOWAS. Indeed, Hausman test proves that the panel mean-group estimator gives better results than other estimators. This estimator enforces long run elasticities to be equal across all panels. Moreover, there is a long run relationship between political and regulatory framework and structural transformation. The following expand on those findings further. Due to incompleteness of data for communication services, building services, financial services, informatics and information services and royalties, they have been removed from the analysis as shown in Table 3. Some of the dropped categories are identified as great value added services, namely communication, informatics/information and financial services. Thus our first recommendation is to improve data collection in ECOWAS countries for these categories. Caution is often rightly given against results which rely on insufficient data to emphasize services supply modes. However, our results are important in several ways which are clarified in the following subsections.

4.1 The Case of Services Exportations and Structural Transformation in ECOWAS

Results presented in Tables 4 and 5, show a mixed and diverse picture of ECOWAS regarding the role of trade in services exports in the structural transformation in terms of sectoral weight (Table 4) as well as in terms of relative sectoral growth (Table 5). Considering the ratio $^{VA_{agriculture}}/_{VA_{industry}}$ we observe that service exports do not affect the structural transformation in most countries of ECOWAS except in Côte d'Ivoire and in Gambia, where there is a two lagged positive impact (decrease in the ratio). A more detailed analysis (by service category) allows qualifying of the previous point. Indeed, with the exception of Benin, Guinea, Guinea Bissau and Nigeria, there are in each country at least one category of exported services which significantly promotes structural transformation. The reason why there is no category for those countries is certainly the lack of data about categories that may be useful for those countries, like communication, informatics and information, financial services and royalties.

In other countries, Table 4 point out potential exports to promote structural transformation. In Burkina Faso and Ghana emphasis may be on public services. In Niger and Gambia, apart from public administrative services, other categories should be inserted in the portfolio, namely tourism (Niger and Gambia), insurance

Table 4 Impact of services exportations on structural transformation in ECOWAS

	Total exports	FDI	Travel	Transport	Other services	Public services	Cultural services	Insurance services
Benin								
Burkina Faso						•*		
Cape Verde							•	
Cote d'Ivoire	•*							•*
Gambia	•*		•*		•*	•*		•*
Ghana						•		
Guinea								
Guinea Bissau								
Mali		•*				•	•	
Niger			•			•*		
Nigeria								
Senegal			•		•			•*
Sierra Leone				•				
Togo			•*		•			

Note: A star is added near the point to indicate a two lagged effect
Source: WDI (2016) and UNCTADstat (2016)

Table 5 Impact of services exportations on structural transformation (s_t) in ECOWAS

	Total exports	FDI	Travel	Transport	Other services	Public services	Cultural services	Insurance services
Benin						•		
Burkina Faso					•	•		
Cape Verde				•				
Cote d'Ivoire	•							•
Gambia	•*		•*	•*				•
Ghana	•*							
Guinea		•*	•*				•	
Guinea Bissau	•							•
Mali					•*			
Niger	•*		•*					
Nigeria			•*					
Senegal			•*		•*		•*	
Sierra Leone			•	•*	•*	•*		
Togo					•*		•*	

Note: A star is added near the point to indicate a two lagged effect
Source: WDI (2016) and UNCTADstat (2016)

services and services to enterprises (Gambia). Senegal and Togo may also focus on tourism and services to enterprises. Senegal, like Côte d'Ivoire, may also export insurance services to promote structural transformation. In Sierra Leone the most important service is transportation. In Mali, FDI, public administrative services and personal services (health, education, culture . . .) are those on which government may concentrate their export strategies. Personal and cultural services are also of great interest in Cape-Verde. Beyond the first reading of Table 4, something important to note is the difference in the delay of the impact. Generally, exports' effects are observed after 2 years. Sometimes (in detailed results available on request) the immediate effect is an increase in the ratio. This increase, which is an increase in value added share of agriculture, confirms that the anchor of structural transformation in Africa is agricultural sector which may be further developed and modernized to support the industrial sector.

Considering the alternative measure of structural transformation, namely the relative growth rate of the industrial sector (s_{it}), results in Table 5 tends to confirm some results from Table 4. However, it brings new results that corroborate the idea of Herrendorf et al. (2014) who states that results on structural transformation may be conditional to the metric used. Fifty per cent of results in Table 4 match results in Table 5 (in red). For example, in Côte d'Ivoire and Gambia insurance services improve industrial sector relative growth rate (Table 5) as well as the ratio of relative value added shares. The same observation can be made on public services in Burkina Faso; on services to enterprises in Senegal and Togo; on transport services in Sierra Leonne. Nonetheless, Table 5 brings new results relative to the effects of services exportations on industrial sector relative growth rate (in black). From this perspective, total exports in services improve the relative growth rate of industrial sector in Côte d'Ivoire, in Gambia, in Ghana, in Guinea Bissau and in Niger.

The second set of results presented in Table 5 gives two pieces of information. First, services exportations could accelerate wealth creation in industrial sector relatively to the average speed among the three sectors. Second, contrary to Table 4, all countries are concerned by this effect. Finally, there is at least one category of services which contribute to structural transformation in ECOWAS. Governments may, therefore, study strategies to improve exports of these services mainly in the sub-region. So, it is important to identify potential partners for each country by the analysis of importation needs.

4.2 Services Importations Effects on Structural Transformation in ECOWAS

As we observed in the preceding sections, econometric results show a differentiated picture of ECOWAS countries regarding the impact of the import of services on structural transformation. Considering the ratio of value added shares, no services category proved significant enough in Burkina Faso, Guinea Bissau, Nigeria, Senegal and Sierra Leone. This would certainly imply that the levers of structural transformation are elsewhere and particularly in services on which information are not available (communication services, financial services, informatics/information services ...). In other ECOWAS countries, a number of service categories significantly affect structural transformation or improve the relative contribution of industrial sector to GDP.

Table 6 shows that, taken as a whole, imports of services positively affect structural transformation in Côte d'Ivoire and in Gambia. Specifically, Table 6 reveals a differentiated snapshot of ECOWAS. In Benin, imports of insurance services promote structural transformation. In Cape Verde services to enterprise as well as personal and cultural services (education, health, culture ...) significantly contribute to structural transformation. In Côte d'Ivoire, tourism as well as personal and cultural services (education, health, culture ...) promote structural transformation. In Gambia, import of FDI, travel/tourism, transports, public services and insurance services prove to stimulate structural transformation. In Ghana, imports of tourism/travel are important for structural transformation. The same work for imports of public services in Guinea and Mali. In Togo, imports of travel/tourism and transports are significant for structural transformation. In Niger, the set of pro-structural transformation imports services is diversified (travel, services to enterprises, public services, personal and cultural services, insurance services).

Table 6 Impact of services importations on structural transformation in ECOWAS

	Total imports	FDI	Travel	Transport	Other services	Public services	Cultural services	Insurance services
Benin								•
Burkina Faso								
Cape Verde					•*		•*	
Cote d'Ivoire	•*		•				•*	•*
Gambia	•*	•*	•*	•*		•*		•*
Ghana			•					
Guinea						•*		
Guinea Bissau								
Mali						•		
Niger			•		•	•*	•*	•
Nigeria								
Senegal								
Sierra Leone								
Togo			•*	•				

Note: A star is added near the point to indicate a two lagged effect
Source: WDI (2016) and UNCTADstat (2016)

Finally, Table 6 proves that there is, for identified countries, at least one category of services which can foster structural transformation when imported. Results in Table 6 allow identification of intra-ECOWAS pairs of partners to improve trade in services integration. For example, Sierra Leone needs to export transportation services while Gambia and Togo need to import transportation services. Therefore, Sierra Leone may look for means to meet transportation needs in Gambia and Togo. According to Tables 4 and 6, Gambia, Senegal and Togo should exports services to enterprises while Cape Verde and Niger must import such services so they could put in place a common strategy to uphold intra-ECOWAS trade in this category of services.

Considering the speed of industrial value added growth rate, we observe that at least 60% of results in Table 6 are found in Table 7 (in red). Like in the previous table, importation of services has no effect in Guinea Bissau and in Nigeria. For this indicator (s_{it}), importations of services have no effects in Benin. By cons, in Burkina Faso, in Senegal and Sierra Leone Table 7 points out the existence of some pro-structural transformation imported services.

Using this indicator implies that structural transformation is measured by the speed of increase in relative growth rate of industrial sector value added, or simply, an increase in the speed of wealth creation in the industrial sector. Table 7 shows that, taken globally, importations of services ameliorate structural transformation in

Table 7 Impact of services importations on structural transformation (s_t) in ECOWAS

	Total imports	FDI	Travel	Transport	Other services	Public services	Cultural services	Insurance services
Benin								
Burkina Faso	•*			•*	•			•*
Cape Verde				•	•			
Cote d'Ivoire	•	•					•	•
Gambia	•*	•	•*	•*				•
Ghana			•*					
Guinea				•*				
Guinea Bissau								
Mali			•*				•	
Niger			•*		•*			•*
Nigeria								
Senegal	•*							
Sierra Leone			•			•*	•	
Togo				•*			•*	

Note: A star is added near the point to indicate a two lagged effect
Source: WDI (2016) and UNCTADstat (2016)

Burkina Faso, in Côte d'Ivoire, in Gambia and in Senegal. In detail, imports of particular services are able to improve and to modernize production apparel in industrial sector. Those results corroborate the idea that services are input in the production system. That is why importation of services can accelerate wealth creation in industrial sector.

For now, in most ECOWAS countries, transport services and other business services represent the largest share of imports of service. This fact supports the structural transformation in Cape Verde where imports of transportation services represent on average 39% of total imports; and the structural transformation of Guinea where imports account for about 37.8% of total imports. Other ECOWAS countries have to make efforts to raise the weight of this sector in their economy. These results also underline existence of trade in services integration opportunities in ECOWAS.

4.3 *Economic Growth, Structural Transformation and Trade in Services*

Table 8 reveals that, despite the previous results where services exports improve the speed of wealth creation in industrial sector (in Ghana), service exports do not affect economic growth in Ghana and Sierra Leone. Total exports of services have a significant impact on economic growth in Cape Verde and Niger but, as mentioned previously, no effect on structural transformation in Cape Verde. These results

Table 8 Services exportations for economic growth in ECOWAS

	Total exports	FDI	Travel	Transport	Other services	Public services	Cultural services	Insurance services
Benin			•	•*	•*	•*	•	
Burkina Faso					•*			
Cape Verde	•*					•	•	
Cote d'Ivoire				•*	•*			•*
Gambia				•*				
Ghana								
Guinea		•			•	•*		
Guinea Bissau				•*				
Mali		•*	•	•*	•	•*		
Niger	•*		•*				•	•*
Nigeria								•*
Senegal								•
Sierra Leone								
Togo					•			•

Note: A star is added near the point to indicate a two lagged effect
Source: WDI (2016) and UNCTADstat (2016)

support the postulate that there is a difference between economic growth and structural transformation. A more detailed analysis is useful to identify the category of services in each country for which exports enhance economic growth. In this perspective, it is shown that travel/tourism services work for economic growth in Benin, Mali and Niger. The same applies to cultural and personal services in Benin, Cape Verde and Niger. FDI are significant in Guinea and Mali.

When it comes to total imports of service, we note that they do not have a significant impact in all countries. Thus, in Benin, in Cape Verde, in Ghana and in Guinea Bissau total imports of services enhance economic growth rate. In Burkina Faso, in Côte d'Ivoire, in Gambia, in Guinea, in Mali, in Niger, in Nigeria, in Senegal, in Sierra Leonne and in Togo, imports of services have not the expected effect or sign. This can be explained by the mismatch between the needs of these economies and imported services.

In a categorical perspective (Table 9), it is observed that imports of services contribute in economic growth. This empirical result confirms the intuition that services are inputs in the production function of a country (Francois and Reinert 1996; Arnold et al. 2008). Unlike imports which can improve the effectiveness and efficiency of the production system or reduce production costs, exportations are supposed to induce currency inflows to finance development and growth.

Table 9 Services importations for economic growth in ECOWAS

	Total imports	FDI	Travel	Transport	Other services	Public services	Cultural services	Insurance services
Benin	•*	•			•*	•*	•	•
Burkina Faso			•				•*	
Cape Verde	•*	•		•			•	•*
Cote d'Ivoire		•			•*		•*	•*
Gambia								
Ghana	•		•			•		•
Guinea		•				•		
Guinea Bissau	•	•			•			•
Mali			•		•			•
Niger			•*				•*	
Nigeria								
Senegal					•			
Sierra Leone								
Togo					•			•

Note: A star is added near the point to indicate a two lagged effect
Source: WDI (2016) and UNCTADstat (2016)

Finally, global or partial trade in services contributes significantly to economic growth and/or structural transformation in almost all ECOWAS countries, in short and long term. In long term, FDI imports, travel/tourism imports, imports and exports of transportation services, total imports and total exports in services ameliorate structural transformation as well as economic growth. The long run results are common to all ECOWAS countries. In the short run, in each country, there are particular categories of services to be imported and particular ones to be exported to foster structural transformation. Since all countries may not import and export the same services, there are opportunities for intra-ECOWAS trade in services. In order to take advantage of these opportunities, it is necessary to put in place common strategies that help exporters to meet the needs of importers.

5 Conclusion

The objective of this paper was to identify the categories of services likely to foster structural transformation and economic growth in ECOWAS. In our analysis, 14 ECOWAS countries were studied (with the exception of Liberia because of missing data) between 1995 and 2015 using a dynamic panel model estimated with the panel mean group estimator. Theoretically, this study confirms two assumptions: (1) implications for structural transformation depend on the chosen measure; (2) economic growth and structural transformation are two distinct processes that can be connected or not. Practically, our results show that each of the ECOWAS countries can define its services trade strategy. Indeed, there is always at least one category of services that promotes economic growth and/or structural transformation. Services trade (imports and/or exports) could be a powerful tool for economic growth and structural transformation if each country relies on the appropriate service for this purpose. The results also indicate that the dynamics of long-term, which links institutions (quality of regulation, political stability) and trade in some categories of services to structural transformation, is identical to all ECOWAS countries. Results also points out existence of trade in services integration opportunities based on reciprocal commercial relationships involving countries from ECOWAS. On political economy plan, following Cuyvers and Viviers (2012), this paper suggests that it is actually possible to build export/imports of services promotion plan that will serve economic growth and structural transformation in ECOWAS countries.

References

Alcalá, F., & Ciccone, A. (2004). Trade and productivity. *The Quarterly Journal of Economics, 119* (2), 613–646.

Arnold, J. M., Mattoo, A., & Gaia, N. (2008). Services inputs and firm productivity in Sub-Saharan Africa: Evidence from firm-level data. *Journal of African Economies, 17*(4), 578–599.

Cadot, O., & De Melo, J. (2016). Introduction. Vers une transformation structurelle en Afrique. *Revue d'économie du développement, 2*(4), 5–17.

Cuyvers, L. (1997). Export opportunities of Thailand: A decision support model approach. Centre for International management and development and centre for ASEAN studies. *CAS Discussion Paper, 9*, 3–21.

Cuyvers, L. (2004). Identifying export opportunities: The case of Thailand. *International Marketing Review, 21*(3), 255–278.

Cuyvers, L., De Pelsmacker, P., Rayp, G., & Roozen, I. T. (1995). A decision support model for the planning and assessment of export promotion activities by government export promotion institutions—The Belgian case. *International Journal of Research in Marketing, 12*(2), 173–186.

Cuyvers, L., & Viviers, W. (Eds.). (2012). *Export promotion: A decision support model approach* (276 p). Stellenbosch: Sun Press.

Dabla-Norris, E., Thomas, A., Garcia-Verdu, R., & Chen, Y. (2013, July). *Benchmarking structural transformation across the world*. IMF Working Paper WP/13/176.

Duarte, M., & Restuccia, D. (2010). The role of the structural transformation in aggregate productivity. *Quarterly Journal of Economics, 125*(1), 129–173.

Fink, C., Mattoo, A., & Neagu, I. C. (2002). Trade in international maritime services: How much does policy matter? *The World Bank Economic Review, 16*(1), 81–108.

Francois, J. F., & Reinert, K. A. (1996). The role of services in the structure of production and trade: Stylized facts from a cross-country analysis. *Asia-Pacific Economic Review, 2*(1), 35–43.

Gadrey, J. (2003). *Socio-Economie des Services* (3e ed.p. 128). Paris: La Découverte « Repères ». isbn:9782707139511.

Gallouj, C., & Djellal, F. (2007). *Introduction à L'économie des Services*. Presses Universitaires de Grenoble. Collection « Economie en + », France.

Gelb, A., Meyer, C., & Ramachandran, V. (2016). Pays pauvres, pays bon marché? Regard comparatif sur le coût de la main-d'œuvre dans le secteur industriel en Afrique. *Revue d'économie du développement, 24*(2), 51–92.

Ghani, E., & O'Connell, S. D. (2016). Les services peuvent-ils devenir un escalator de croissance pour les pays à faible revenu. *Revue d'économie du développement, 24*(2), 143–173.

Han, L., Li, D., Moshirian, F., & Tian, Y. (2010). Insurance development and economic growth. *The Geneva Papers, 35*, 183–199.

Herrendorf, B., Rogerson, R., & Valentinyi, A. (2013). Two perspectives on preferences and structural transformation. *American Economic Review, 103*(7), 2752–2789.

Herrendorf, B., Rogerson, R., & Valentinyi, A. (2014). Growth and structural transformation. In P. Aghion & S. Durlauf (Eds.), *Handbook of economic growth* (Vol. 2B). Amsterdam: North-Holland.

Hoekman, B., & Mattoo, A. (2011). *Services trade liberalization and regulatory reform: Reinvigorating international cooperation*. Policy Research Working Paper, WPS5517.

Inklaar, R., Timmer, M. P. & Van Ark, B. (2006, August). *Mind the gap: International comparisons of productivity in services and goods production*. University of Groningen GGDC Research Memorandum GD-89.

Inklaar, R., Timmer, M. P., & van Ark, B. (2008). Services trade liberalization and regulatory reform: Re-invigorating international cooperation. *International Productivity Monitor, 16* (Spring), 71–81.

Kose, M. A., Prasad, E. S., & Terrones, M. E. (2006). How do trade and financial integration affect the relationship between growth and volatility? *Journal of International Economics, 69*(1), 176–202.

Kuznets, S. (1966). *Modern economic growth*. New Haven: Yale University Press.

Nyunt, K. M. (2009, August). An empirical study of the effects of services infrastructure on trade efficiency and growth in Myanmar. *Chulalongkorn Journal of Economics, 21*(2), 89–109.

Rigobon, R., & Rodrik, D. (2005). Rule of law, democracy, openness, and income: Estimating the interrelationships. *The Economics of Transition, 13*(3), 533–564.

Rodriguez, F., & Rodrik, D. (2001). Trade policy and economic growth: A skeptic's guide to cross-national evidence. In B. S. Bernanke & K. Rogoff (Eds.), *NBER macroeconomics annual 2000* (pp. 261–325). Cambridge, MA: MIT Press.

The African Center for Economic Transformation. (2014). *Growth with depth*. African Transformation Report.

Triplett, J. E., & Bosworth, B. P. (2004). *Productivity in the U.S. services sector*. Washington, DC: Brookings Institution.

UNCTAD. (2015). *Economic development in Africa: Unlocking the potential of Africa's services trade for growth and development*. Report, United Nation.

UNWTO. (2015). *UNWTO annual report 2014* (88 p). Madrid: World Tourism Organization.

Viviers, W., & Pearson, J. J. A. (2007). *The construction of a decision support model for evaluating and identifying realistic export opportunities for South Africa*. Report prepared for the statistical analysis and modelling unit at the DTI. DTI, Pretoria.

Viviers, W., Rossow, R., & Steenkamp, E. A. (2009, February). *The sustainability of the DSM for identifying realistic export opportunities for South Africa: 2007–2008*. Unpublished report prepared for the department of trade and industry, South Africa.

Viviers, W., Steenkamp, E. A., & Rossouw, R. (2010). *Identifying realistic export opportunities for South Africa: Application of a decision support model (DSM) using HS 6-digit level product data*. Final report: September 2010. Report prepared for the statistical analysis and modelling unit at the DTI. DTI, Pretoria.

WDI. (2016). *World development indicators 2016*. Washington, DC: The World Bank Group.

Wilson, J., Mann, C., & Otsuki, T. (2003, March). *Trade facilitation and economic development: Measuring the impact*. Policy research working papers.

Ypma, G. (2007). *Productivity levels in transport, storage and communication: A new ICOP 1997 dataset*. Groningen Growth and Development Center, Research Memorandum GD-85.

Zoltan, R. (1969, September). A note on measuring structural changes. *The Review of Income and Wealth, 15*(3), 265–268.

Part III
Macroeconomics and Political Economy

Macroeconomic Effects of Commodity Price Shocks on ECOWAS Members

Moses K. Tule, Udoma J. Afangideh, Adegoke I. Adeleke, and Augustine Ujunwa

Contents

Abstract The current global commodity price shocks have generally affected many commodity dependent countries and also raised serious questions on the viability of regional blocks whose member countries are predominantly commodity-based economies. ECOWAS sub-region typifies evidence of primary export as the main source of foreign exchange to member countries, thereby making them susceptible to commodity price shocks. This paper examines the effect of commodity price shocks on ECOWAS member countries using a panel data of 13 member countries for the period 2000–2015. Dynamic General Method of Moment (GMM) technique was adopted using an instrumental variable (IV) regression model. The results showed that precious metals were positively but insignificantly related to gross domestic product per capita which the study adopted as a measure of macroeconomic indicator. Also, there was a positive and statistically significant relationship between energy prices and the dependent variable. However, a negative relationship was observed between non-energy prices and gross domestic product per capita. In addition, the results showed that 87% of the economy is susceptible to energy

M. K. Tule · U. J. Afangideh (✉) · A. I. Adeleke · A. Ujunwa
Monetary Policy Department, Central Bank of Nigeria, Abuja, Nigeria

D. Seck (ed.), *The External Sector of Africa's Economy*, Advances in African Economic, Social and Political Development,
https://doi.org/10.1007/978-3-319-97913-7_8

price shocks. This result forces a rethink of the integration agenda not only along monetary lines, but also along diversification integration.

1 Introduction

Extensive studies have focused on identifying the macroeconomic effects of commodity prices for commodity importing and exporting countries. The literature suggests that commodity exporting economies will earn more foreign exchange during periods of high commodity prices while importing economies will pay more. Invariably, commodity price hikes will have adverse negative effects on commodity importing countries and positive effects on exporting countries (Kose and Riesmanb 2001; Allegret et al. 2015; An et al. 2014). Several studies provide important insights into the sources of the adverse effect on commodity importing economies including: depletion of external reserves, recession effect, higher input cost, slowdown in economic activities, decline in potential output, income shift, current account and fiscal imbalances, among others (Ftiti et al. 2014; Ayres and Voudouris 2014; Global Economic Prospects 2015).

In contrast, some studies provide extensive evidence to validate the argument that fluctuations in commodity prices have adverse effects on commodity producing and commodity importing countries which causes global imbalance. Specifically, the studies agree with Ftiti et al. (2014) that hike in commodity prices "will transmit to a higher input cost for firms, reducing aggregate supply ... labour decline and potential output fall". However, since most oil exporting countries depend on developed economies for their final products (consumption), increase in prices of final output could negatively affect the potential gains of commodity price hikes for the commodity exporting countries. Similarly, declining commodity prices could "support economic activity and reduce inflationary, external, and fiscal pressures in oil-importing countries, but weaken fiscal and external positions of commodity exporting countries". Slowdown in economic activities in commodity exporting countries could adversely affect aggregate demand, business cycle fluctuations, global imbalances and economic slowdown (Global Economic prospects 2015; Kilian and Lewis 2011).

In this paper, we examine the macroeconomic effects of commodity prices on ECOWAS member countries. The justification for the study is threefold. First, previous studies along this line concentrated on developed economies, with much emphasis on commodity importing countries. Little is known on the macroeconomic effects of commodity price swings on commodity importing developing countries. Second, ECOWAS region is targeting monetary integration by 2020. Importantly, the process of monetary integration in ECOWAS started in 1987 with the objective of a single monetary zone envisaged by 2003. The continuous extension of the timeline to the current target of 2020 has been blamed on the inability of member countries to meet the primary and secondary convergence criteria. It would be important to determine the degree and direction of commodity shocks to the region, and whether that would explicitly or implicitly explain the inability of the region to meet the convergence criteria. Third, most studies on commodity exporting economies concentrate on oil exporting countries and mostly at individual country level. The ECOWAS sub-region presents a good case for studying the macroeconomic effects of commodity prices because of certain peculiarities of the region. For instance, ECOWAS member countries are commodity-exporting economies, and import dependent on Western and Asian countries for their manufactures consumption. The region presents a good case for estimating the two conflicting theories on commodity price shocks and macroeconomic nexus.

The rest of the paper is organized as follows. Section 3 presents the stylized facts of commodity prices movement between 1999 and 2016 and the macroeconomic environment of ECOWAS member countries. Section 4 deals with the review of related literature. In Sect. 4, we present the data and outline of our methodology. Results and policy implications are presented in Sect. 5, while Sect. 6 concludes the paper.

2 Stylized Facts

The economies of ECOWAS member countries are generally underdeveloped, except for Nigeria which could be classified as developing economy. These economies are commodity-based, since the major source of export earnings are commodities. For instance, energy (coal, crude oil and gas) is the major source of foreign exchange earnings for countries such as Nigeria, Ghana, Cote d'Ivoire and Niger. Countries like Ghana, Guinea, Liberia and Sierra Leone export precious metals such as gold, platinum and silver. Additionally, all ECOWAS member countries export agricultural products. The volatility of commodity prices therefore, is expected to impact either negatively or positively on member countries, with implications on government revenue, and especially on macroeconomic management like in any typical commodity-exporting economy.

Upswings and declines in international commodity prices, particularly crude oil between 1973 and 2013 have been attributed to major episodes that coincide with changes in oil market and global economy. The earliest episodes of commodity price shocks was the Yom Kippur War of October 6, 1973—when the Organization of Arab Petroleum Exporting Countries (OAPEC) issued a warning of its intention to cut crude oil production by 5% on October 16 until Israeli soldiers were "completely evacuated from all the Arab territories occupied since the June 1967 war and the legitimate rights of the Palestinian people restored" (Hamilton 2009). Others are the Iranian revolution in the fall of 1978; Iraq and Iran crisis of September 1980; change in OPEC policy (1985–1986); and Iraq and Kuwait crisis (1990); recession in U.S. (1990–1991 and 2001); the 1997–1998 Asian crisis; and the 2007, 2008 global financial crisis (see Hamilton 2009; Global Economic Prospects 2015). However, from 2011 to the later part of 2014, commodity prices maintained an upswing (see

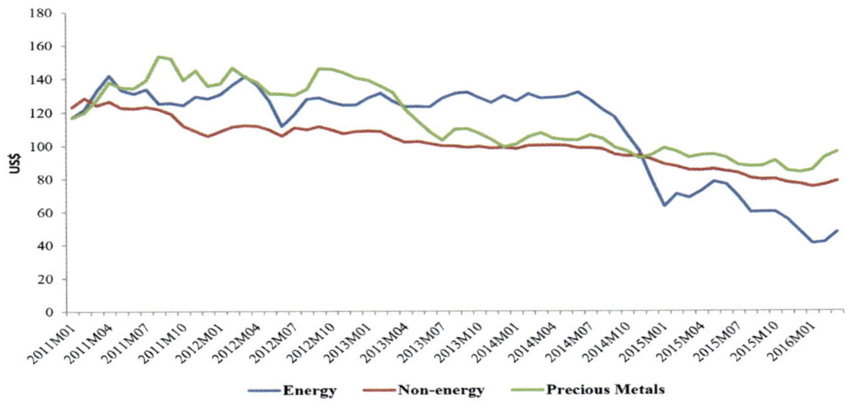

Fig. 1 Trends on energy, non-energy and precious metal prices (January 2011–March 2016)

Fig. 1 below for details). For instance, between January 2011 and June 2014, average monthly oil price was between \$93 and \$118 per barrel. These upswings have been attributed to sustained strong growth in Asia and other emerging economies.

Since July 2014, commodity prices have declined sharply following 4 years of relative stability which saw the price hover around \$105.23 per barrel (bbl) until it bottomed out at \$29.78 per barrel in January 2016. For the same period, overall energy prices have declined sharply from \$126.93 to \$40.50. The non-energy component of commodity prices also dropped from a high of \$98.28 to \$74.64. The precious metal also fell from \$103.02 to \$84.73. Several reasons have been adduced for the decline in commodity prices from their peak and these include weaker demand and increased supply from improved technology and massive investment by developed economies especially U.S. What is clear is that recent weaknesses of commodity prices have dampened growth forecasts for commodity-exporting countries, with the sharpest impact among energy exporters (see Fig. 2).

Sudden declines in commodity prices have inspired a huge literature on the macroeconomic implications of oil and other commodity price fluctuations on macroeconomic variables. As expected, the decline in commodity prices is synonymous with stark slowdown in growth in emerging markets' commodity exports that enjoyed prolonged growth during hike in commodity prices. In most cases, these commodity-exporting countries have, beside declines in growth, seen downgrades in their medium-term growth prospects. However, it is crucial to diagnose how actual and potential growth is influenced by commodity price fluctuations in order to enhance the formulation of macroeconomic policies in commodity exporting economies.

Although greater attention has been focused on crude oil because of its importance in the global economy, many other commodities which are equally essential have been affected by the recent slump in global commodity prices. Some of these commodities which constitute the mainstay of the economies of West African

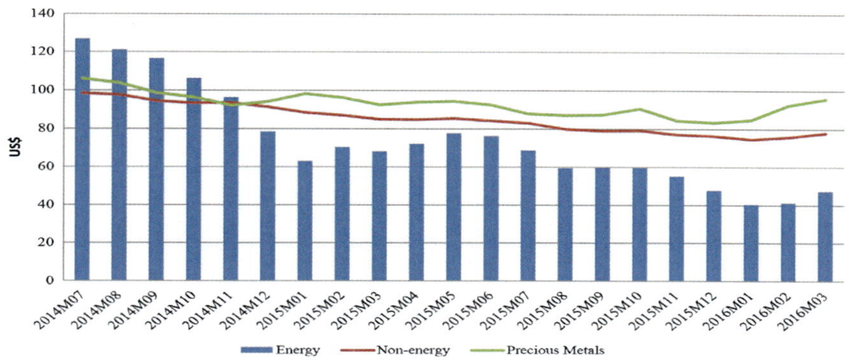

Fig. 2 Trends of prices of energy, non-energy and precious metals (August 2014–March 2016)

countries can be categorized into energy (crude oil), non-energy (agriculture, fertilizers, metals/minerals) and precious metals. The fall in prices for these commodities has macroeconomic implications for the sub-region. For oil exporting countries like Nigeria, Ghana, Cote d' Ivoire and Niger, which depend on oil for their foreign exchange earnings, the consequences of a persistent fall in prices can be devastating. For instance, the robust economic growth of the last decade in these countries, is under threat and the same impact goes for other countries which are depending on one commodity or the other such as cocoa, groundnut, diamond, etc. The case for the sub-region in the face of this downward prices worsened by the fact that these prices are internationally determined as the region remains a price taker with no capacity to influence global prices for their exports.

As observed in the introduction of Chap. 2 Article 3 of its Revised Treaty, ECOWAS objective is to achieve the integration of the sub-regional economy based on trade liberalization among member states, ensure free mobility of factors of production by removing all impediments, as well as harmonizing national economic and fiscal policies of member states. However, the mainstay of the economies of the sub-region is agriculture and its related activities, thereby making the region vulnerable to adverse natural environmental conditions. Particularly, the subregion depends on primary commodities which are the products of agriculture and its related activities. For instance, Petroleum is found in large quantities in Nigeria and other precious metals such as diamond, gold are commercially exploited in countries such as Ghana, Guinea, and Sierra Leone.

Thus, the export of primary raw materials, mainly agricultural commodities for foreign exchange earnings, is still the dominant aspect of domestic and international trade. Also, the sub-region constitutes a small open economy, and therefore, a price taker, with no influence in determining the price of its products at international market. It exports predominantly primary products to developed/industrial countries in exchange for consumer goods, equipment and raw materials for industrial development. Indeed, member countries of ECOWAS depend on this narrow range of

Table 1 Primary commodities (less fuel) by countries in ECOWAS sub-region

Country	Product
Burkina Faso	Cotton, sesame, peanuts, shea nuts, sorghum, millet, corn, rice, livestock, hides and skins
Benin	Cotton, corn, cassava, yams, beans, palm oil, peanuts, livestock (lint and seed)
Cote d'Iviore	Cocoa beans, coffee, bananas, palm kernels, corn, rice, manioc, sweet potatoes, sugar, cotton, rubber, timber
Cape Verde	Bananas, corn, beans, sweet potatoes, sugarcane, coffee, peanuts, fish
Ghana	Cocoa, rice, cassava, peanuts, corn, shea nuts, bananas, timber
Gambia	Rice, millet, sorghum, peanuts, corn, sesame, cassava, palm kernels, cattle, sheep, goats
Guinea	Bauxite, alumina, coffee, rice, pineapples, palm kernels, cassava, bananas, sweet potatoes, cattle, sheep, goats, timber
Guinea-Bissau	Cashew nuts, wood, cotton, fish, cassava, rice, palm kernels, corn, peanuts, beans, timber
Mali	Cotton, millet, rice, corn, vegetables, peanuts, cattle, sheep, goats
Liberia	Rubber, coffee, cocoa, rice, cassava, palm oil, sugarcane, bananas, sheep, goats, timber
Niger	Cowpeas, cotton, peanuts, millet, sorghum, cassava, rice, cattle, sheep, goats, camels, donkeys, horses, poultry, tobacco, onions, beans
Nigeria	Cocoa, peanuts, palm oil, corn, rice, sorghum, millet, cassava, yams, rubber, cattle, sheep, goats, pigs, timber, fish
Sierra-Leone	Coffee, cocoa tobacco, rice, palm kernels, palm oil, peanuts, poultry, cattle, sheep, pigs, fish
Senegal	Groundnuts, phosphate, cotton, peanuts, millet, corn, sorghum, rice, tomatoes, green vegetables, cattle, poultry, pigs, fish
Togo	Coffee, cocoa, cotton, yams, cassava, corn, beans, rice, millet, sorghum, livestock, fish
Niger	Cowpeas, cotton, peanuts, millet, sorghum, cassava, rice, cattle, sheep, goats, camels, donkeys, horses, poultry, tobacco, onions, beans

Source: Extracted from Nationmaster Statistics (2012)

primary commodities for export earnings. Table 1 below shows the various products apart from fuel that could be found within the sub-region. The table shows that most of the products are homogenous, thereby giving credence to the fact that almost all the countries in the subregion are likely to face similar shocks in the event of global commodity price shock.

Thus, for a period of global decline in commodity prices, the associated fluctuations in prices and of terms of trade are likely to have great repercussions for the sub-region. Additionally, other development options available to the sub-region for this period are constrained by the small size and poor economic base of the sub-region. For any balanced development to take place therefore under these conditions, there is need for structural transformation and diversification of economic base to increase production of additional products that would attract new export locations as well as increase value addition.

In Table 2, the performance of key macroeconomic indicators is highlighted. The GDP growth rate and per capita growth rate decline from the peak of 7.1% and 4.2% respectively in 2010 to 5.79% and 2.94% respectively in 2014. The net foreign direct investment peaked in 2011 with 18,956 million US dollars and subsequently decline to 12,763 million US dollars in 2014. Trade balance for the sub-region recorded a deficit for the period 2009 to 2013; same was observed for UEMOA group of countries for the same period. The balance of payment was declining from 7825 in 2009 to negative 940 in 2014. Trade balance for all the years under review was negative. Although export of goods and services was rising from 2009 to 2011, it started declining in 2013 and 2014. Import of goods and services on the other hand, was rising except in 2012 when it recorded a decline. Accordingly, total merchandize trade growth experienced both positive and negative growth for the period.

3 Review of Related Literature

Commodity shocks are exogenously determined and shifts the economy temporarily or permanently from its equilibrium position through multiple transmission mechanisms such as trade channel, financial channel, integration of international market channel, and investment channel, among others. Commodity shocks have been exacerbated due to the effects of globalization and improvements in information communication technology, which eliminated some trade barriers, increased economic interconnectedness, and accelerated the spread of economic risk across national boundaries (Cunado and Perez de Gracia 2003, 2005).

Commodity shocks could be positive—economic boom and improved welfare—or negative—distressed economy and declined welfare (Canova 2005). Since commodity prices are exogenously determined, the study assumes that declining commodity prices will adversely affect countries in West Africa. Though, empirical findings whether external shocks accounts for higher variability in output or macroeconomic fundamentals than internal shocks is inconclusive. For instance, Raddatz (2007) used the VAR approach to estimate the impact of external shocks on output volatility. The result showed that exogenous shocks could partly explain a minute fraction of output variance, while internal shocks are the major sources of fluctuations. The external shocks considered in the study are natural disasters, changes in international interest rates, terms-of-trade shocks, volatility in commodity prices, changes in the state of international economy, and fluctuations in aid flows.

In contrast, Jimenez-Rodriguez and Sanchez (2005) and Lilien (1982) used the dispersion hypothesis to demonstrate the negative impact of external shocks on macroeconomic variables. In their view, external shocks such as aid volatility, international conditions, natural disaster and terms-of-trade fluctuations are responsible for macroeconomic fluctuations. Similarly, multilateral institutions such as the World Bank (2004), UNCTAD (2012) and IMF (2003) noted that exogenous shocks stymie economic growth. Specifically, they argued that exogenous "shocks ... can have a significant negative impact on developing countries' growth, macroeconomic

Table 2 ECOWAS: Key macroeconomic indicators and their performance (2009–2014) in US dollars at current prices in millions

Key indicators	2009	2010	2011	2012	2013	2014
Gross domestic product (GDP)	383,748	489,472	549,425	604,512	675,406	725,243
GDP growth rate (%)	5.93	7.1	4.85	5.05	5.64	5.79
GDP growth rate per capita (%)	3.07	4.2	2.02	2.2	2.79	2.94
Net foreign direct investment (inward flows)	14,725	12,008	18,956	16,322	14,208	12,763
Total trade in goods and services	−1429	466	−1035	4843	6160	−10,547
Trade balance	−22,777	−25,655	−28,877	−29,307	−30,451	
Trade balance UEMOA	−3662	−4060	−4262	−4516	−5965	
Balance of payment	7825	6453	2950	6976	3623	−940
Consumer price index (all item) base year = 2005	138.8	154.4	169.2	186.7	201	215.5
Gross fixed capital formation	68,492	88,031	95,888	101,235	110,691	123,189
Export of goods and services	87,864	131,905	180,271	200,098	151,215	162,278
Import of goods and services	94,585	115,075	148,974	127,806	140,000	140,345
Total merchandise trade growth rate (%)	−25.46	37.9	35.08	0.31	−5.89	−6.18

Source: Authors calculations from UNCTADSTAT (2016) Online Database stability, debt sustainability and poverty", and "low-income countries are particularly vulnerable to natural disasters, terms-of-trade shocks, and other adverse shocks", and that the level of volatility in world commodity prices are important influence on economic growth and the incidence of poverty in less developed countries".

In the opinion of 'exogenous shocks causing negative growth" theorists, since the events are unpredictable, it could threaten large-scale private sector defaults, trigger distressed assets sales, high bank insolvency, depletion of external reserve, currency crisis and loss of market confidence. A classic example was the 2007/2008 global financial crises that originated in United States, but ravaged the entire architecture of the global financial system.

There is a consensus on the sources of external shock which include natural disasters, energy costs, commodity prices, geopolitical crisis, famine, war, economic policies and market dynamics, fluctuations in aid flows, among others. The severe external shocks hitting the world economies could be traced to financial and productive integrations between various countries and regions following the formation of blocs since the 1970s. The increase in economic interrelatedness across in the form of cross-border movement capital, technology and goods and service a result of globalization is associated with risks broadly classified into economic risk, social risk, environmental risk, technological risk, geopolitical risk and regional risk (Kilian 2008; Jimenez-Rodrigues and Sanchez 2005; Mehara 2006).

Several theoretical frameworks have been used to examine the effect of shocks on macroeconomic variables. Some of the theories are the structuralist theory, the classical theory and Keynesian theory. The structural theorists for instance argue that structural shocks such as sudden changes in the prices of food and oil could be attributed to macroeconomic fluctuations (Sommer 2002). However, there is a sharp disagreement among the structuralist theorists on the amplitude effect of structural shocks. One school argues that supply shocks are in the short-run and have only transitory effect on the macro economy (Ball and Mankiw 1995). They further argue that since the role of policy makers is to ensure favourable macroeconomic environment in the long term, policy makers should not respond to adverse pressures from food and oil prices that are highly volatile in the short-run, in order not to drive the economy into recession (Armando 2009). They opine that policy makers should rather, focus on mitigating "the second round effect", which is likely to be more prolonged and could result in economic recession (Inflation Report 2006). Fischer (1985) argues that as long as there is no real wage resistance by workers, supply shock by themselves do not require policy response.

Another school documented extensive evidence from Latin America and developing countries to show that structural shocks could be persistent, and are rooted in bottlenecks of inelastic supply in the agricultural and oil sectors (Watcher 1979). In their view, agriculture, oil, foreign trade, and government sectors suffer from institutional rigidities that cause prices to rise with economic developments. They advocated for the elimination of such institutional rigidities by the fiscal authorities as a measure for curbing the adverse effects of structural shocks.

The above views have been counteracted by some scholars using the rational expectation theory.

They argue that the amplitude of supply-side is contingent on behaviour of expectation (Sommer 2002). For instance, when agents believe that the effects of shocks will be permanent, shocks feed into their expectations, and the persistence of shock is thus large. In the same vein, when agents believe that the effects of shocks are only temporary, macroeconomic fundamentals quickly return to their initial position. They therefore argue that, knowing whether shocks are permanent or transitory, and what determines the magnitude of the effects is important in formulating policy. This theory essentially influenced the theoretical framework for this study.

The effects of external shocks at regional and country-level have been extensively documented in the empirical literature. These studies focus predominantly on the effect of increasing commodity prices on developed economies and the transmission channels. Literature on the impact of declining commodities prices on commodity-exporting countries, especially, developing economies appears scant. Literature that clarifies our understanding of the impact of declining commodity prices on commodity-exporting countries such as the West African SubRegion is very important, since empirical studies that reconcile theory with practical reality is lacking.

Similarly, the bulk of the studies also focus only on oil shocks. According to Blanchard (2009), the 1970s oil shocks resulted in an increase in inflation and a decrease in output. However, the 2000 and 2007 larger increases in the oil price resulted in milder movements in inflation and output. Blanchard argued that "the milder movements in 2000s and 2007 were attributed to two changes in the structure of the economy that moderated or modified the transmission mechanism of the oil shock such as vanishing wage indexation and an improvement in the credibility of monetary policy". Jimenez-Rodriguez and Sanchez (2005) used Vector autoregressive (VAR) analysis to empirically investigate the effect of oil shocks on the economic activity of industrialized OECD countries. They found significant interaction between oil prices and macroeconomic variables. The results showed asymmetric effect of oil price on real GDP. Oil price hike had larger impact on real GDP growth than decline in oil price. Increase in oil price was largely found to have a negative impact on economic activity among oil importing countries.

Dibooglu and Aleisa (2004) employed structural vector auto regression methods to investigate the sources of macroeconomic fluctuations in Saudi Arabia. The study focused on oil prices and changes in terms of trade, while controlling for supply, balance of payments, aggregate demand, and monetary shocks. Their findings are twofold. First, the result showed the vulnerabilities of real exchange rate, price level and to a lesser extent output to trade shocks. Second, the drivers of terms of trade are aggregate demand shocks, trade balance and output.

Bhattachary and Kar (2009) developed a "macro-modelling framework that allows for evaluating the impact of two domestic shocks (rainfall shortfall and fiscal profligacy) and three external shocks (oil price hike, world trade shock and capital flow shock) that affect Indian economy through various channels". Their results revealed that, "capital flow shock and fiscal profligacy show strong pervasiveness, the rainfall shock is moderately pervasive, while the economy is much more resilient to the world trade shock in the long run".

Kose and Riezman (2001) constructed a calibrated stochastic, dynamic multi-sector equilibrium model, to investigate the effect of external shocks on the African economy. The study modeled trade shocks modeled as "fluctuations in the prices of imported capital goods, exported primary commodities and intermediate inputs; and financial shock, modeled as fluctuations in the world real interest rate". Sectoral productivity was used to capture domestic factors in generating macroeconomic fluctuations. Their results indicated that the role of financial shocks is minor, while trade shocks is responsible for 45% of fluctuations in aggregate output. Additionally, they found that prolonged recession could be induced by adverse trade shocks since they induce a significant decrease in aggregate investment.

Ncube et al. (2012) investigated the impact of the 2007/2008 global financial shock on the South African economy based on structural VAR models. Their results showed that the financial shock led to Rand appreciation, bond yield decline, weaker consumer inflation, and fall in monetary aggregates and real rate of interest in South Africa, despite weak trade channel evidence. Sosa and Adler (2012) examined the impact of shocks stemming from Brazil to other Latin America economies using Vector Auto Regression. They used descriptive statistics to show that trade linkages with Brazil are significant for Argentina, Bolivia, Chile, Paraguay, and Uruguay, but weak for the other countries. The econometric estimation also showed that countries with significant trade linkages are vulnerable to output shocks from Brazil compared to other countries with less trade linkages. Canova (2005) studied how external shocks from the United States are transmitted to eight Latin American countries, using individual country and average effects posterior estimates. Their results showed that United States monetary shocks are responsible for significant fluctuations in Latin America, while supply and demand shocks do not have such effects. Based on their findings, they argue that "financial channel plays a crucial role in the transmission and US disturbances explain important portions of the variability of Latin American macro-variables, producing continental cyclical fluctuations and, in two episodes, destabilizing nominal exchange rate effects".

Focusing on commodity supercycle, Gangelhoff (2015) sees it as occurring when prices of many significant primary commodities rise and then fall in concert over an extended period, around some slow-moving underlying trend. The paper links global economic fluctuations as playing critical roles in generating these correlated price movements, by exerting demand pressures to first ensure first boom, followed by bust, among a cross section of countries for a variety of commodity prices. On the other hand, supply-side shocks are less associated with super-cycles because they are so often commodity-specific. But an exception on the supply side is energy which constitute an important proportion in the production of goods and services with the capability to impact on the prices of other commodities through cost of production and consumer purchasing power. This is the reason why energy and non-energy are often analyzed separately. Within the last century, Erten and Ocampo (2012) detect four super-cycles in non-fuel commodities. The first three occurred in 1917, 1951, and 1973 while the last began in 2000 and appears to have peaked between 2008 and 2011 (Gangelhoff 2015).

Yuan et al. (2014) investigated the dynamics of frequent price shocks of crude oil markets. The price shocks were represented by inter-event times and series of counts and the study focused on its price shocks' sequences to study temporal properties in markets for crude oil. Findings from the paper showed that time dynamics of price shock sequences represent a fractal process indicating a high degree of time-clusterization events. This outcome provides useful information in crude oil markets in terms of nature and dynamics.

An et al. (2014) adopted a nonlinear Factor-Augmented Vector Autoregressive (FAVAR) model to investigate the asymmetric effects of oil price shocks on real activity in the United States. The paper simulated the effect of negative and positive oil price shocks on the United States macroeconomy using impulse response function (IRF). Their findings showed that higher oil price has more negative effect than the positive effects of lower oil prices. Furthermore, more evident of asymmetric effect is when oil price shocks are larger.

Valadkhani (2014) focused on dynamic relationship, using Markov-regime switching model and Bai-Perron sequential method, between CPI energy price sub-index in the U.S and Canada and crude oil price. Although the paper does not dispute the previous findings that crude oil price does not currently affect the aggregate CPI as was the case in the 1970s, the paper's sequentially determined break date and time-varying regime-switching probabilities, brought about two new findings: a rise in speed of adjustment particularly in U.S. and consistent and instantaneous increase in marginal effects on consumer energy prices due to changes in price of oil.

Cunado et al. (2015) used VAR model to discuss macroeconomic effect of structural oil shocks in four major Asian oil-consuming economies. Three different structural oil shocks were identified based on sign restrictions and they include an oil-specific demand shock, oil supply shock and a global economic activity driven oil demand shock. Key findings indicate different responses of prices and economic activity to oil price shocks conditional on the categories. It was observed that the shock from oil supply had limited effect but a shock associated with demand from global economic activity had a substantial positive effect on all the four Asian economies that were examined.

As the 1986 oil boom could not bring about the expected economic boom, many researchers became interested and developed a huge literature on the asymmetric effects of oil price movement on economic activity. Uncertainty, costly factor allocation and asymmetric response by monetary authority were identified as factors bringing about such asymmetry. For instance, the U.S. Federal Reserve often respond strongly to rise in inflation brought about by higher oil prices but less to unanticipated fall in inflation due to decline in oil price (Kilian 2014; Bernanke et al. 1997). Thus, large increase in oil price is often linked with lower output in the U.S. and a fall in oil prices is reckoned to have a much smaller, and statistically insignificant, contribution to economic activity (Hamilton 2003; Jimenez-Rodrıguez and Sanchez 2005).

4 Methodology

4.1 Methodology and Data

In estimating the macroeconomic impact of commodity price shocks in ECOWAS, we adopted gross domestic product per capita as the dependent variable. The shocks on the macro-economy are felt or measured in the sub-region through fluctuations in commodity prices such as energy, non-energy and precious metals which are the major source of income for major economies in the sub-region. We measure the commodity price fluctuation in the model by converting the level variables into their standard deviations. Apart from these prices serving as explanatory variables, we also adopted other control variables which impact on the economy such as capital account (ca), Consumer price index (cpi), dependency ratio (depr), foreign direct investment (fdi), openness, real effective exchange rate (reer), real interest rate (rir) and savings (sav). Our empirical study is based on panel dataset covering the thirteen (13) ECOWAS countries except Cape Verde and Liberia due to paucity of data in the two countries. The period of the study is from 1980 to 2015 and data used for the study are from secondary sources such World Bank Commodity price index and Central Bank of Nigeria. The countries were chosen because the focus of the study is to look at the impact of declining commodity prices given that almost all the countries in the sub-region are depending on primary commodity export. As T > N, we are dealing with macro-panel data study (panel time series) and we are adopting both the static panel as well as dynamic general method of moment (GMM) estimation procedure to account for the heterogeneous effects between countries. As is standard in other studies, we report both the static and dynamic results in order to show the departure and flow from one method/technique to another.

4.2 Empirical Approach

The general framework for panel study as shown in Eq. (1) below is adopted for the study

$$Y_{it} = \alpha_{it} + \mu_{it} + \beta X_{it} \tag{1}$$

Where:

Y_{it} is the dependent variable and X_{it} is a vector representing the explanatory variables. The cross-sectional and time series dimensions are represented respectively by i and t subscripts. The composite error term μ_{it} can be decomposed into specific effects and the remainder disturbance term. Hereafter i will be referred to as individual observations which in this instance, refers to the member countries of

ECOWAS.[1] To capture the individual country specific effects, we decompose μ_{it} by re-writing Eq. (1) as follows:

$$Y_{it} = \alpha_{it} + \beta X_{it} + \eta_i + \lambda_t + \varepsilon_{it} \quad (2)$$

Where Y_{it} is defined as the macroeconomic variables; X_{it} is a vector of commodity prices. η_i is the country specific effects; λ_t is the time specific effect; and ε_{it} is the disturbance term that captures the effects of the omitted variables. With the exception of inflation that is not transformed, all other variables are in ratio and or natural logarithm forms.

From Eq. (2) above, we can specify the empirical model depicting the effect of the three broad categories of commodity prices (Energy, Non-Energy and precious Metals) on macroeconomic variables (output and inflation).

Applying the baseline model in Eq. (2), we compare estimates from both panel fixed effects (FE) and random effects (RE) models. The Hausman test is used to compare estimates from the RE with that of the FE. Ezeoha (2013), Buch and Kuckulenz (2009), and Adams (2009) established that most macroeconomic variables are endogenous. To address the probable endogeneity problems that might be present in Eq. (2) in line with Ezeoha (2013) and Bauch and Kuckulenz (2009), we apply an instrumental variable (IV) regression model, based on the Dynamic General Method of Movement (GMM) technique. We validate the instruments by adopting Roodman (2009) through the imposition of lags to reduce the proliferation of instruments. The lag of the dependent variable is used to indicate the dynamics in the model as shown in Eq. (3) below:

$$y_{it} = \alpha_{it} + y_{it-1} + \beta X_{it} + \mu_{it} \quad (3)$$

Where the variables are as previously defined.

5 Discussion of Empirical Results

Three broad techniques were employed in the estimation, namely the static mode comprising pooled OLS, FE, and OLS dummy variable (see Appendix 3), difference GMM (see Appendix 4) and System GMM (Table 3).

The system generalized method of moment (SGMM2) has shown that column 4 is the most robust result. This is because, unlike the first three columns, the predictions of the Sargan and Hansen tests are closed at 1 and 0.787, respectively. The validity of

[1]The countries that make up ECOWAS are Nigeria, Ghana, Benin, Togo, Niger, Mali, Burkina Faso, Cote d' Ivoire, Liberia, Sierra Leone, Guinea, Guinea Bissau, the Gambia, Cape Verde, Senegal.

Table 3 The aggregate results—dynamic panel data analyses-system GMM

Variables	(1) SGMM1	(2) SGMM1−CL[a]	(3) SGMM2	(4) SGMM2−CL[b]
L.gdpc	0.847***	0.868***	0.567	1.267***
	(0.0244)	(0.0913)	(0.667)	(0.152)
premet1	−0.360***	−0.381***	1.310	0.0687
	(0.0943)	(0.126)	(1.250)	(0.315)
enegy1	0.336**	0.249*	−0.0784	1.319*
	(0.140)	(0.134)	(1.382)	(0.698)
noeneg1	0.364	0.661	−0.550	−1.130
	(0.319)	(0.402)	(3.637)	(1.464)
ca	0.239	0.530	−41.42	4.144
	(0.694)	(0.848)	(44.13)	(3.786)
cpi	0.0901	0.0532	1.605	−2.318
	(0.0865)	(0.105)	(3.383)	(1.571)
depr	−3.402	−1.835	0	0
	(4.630)	(5.790)	(0)	(0)
fdi	2.217**	1.477	0	0
	(0.997)	(1.149)	(0)	(0)
lnopen	−54.56***	−69.11***	0	0
	(13.71)	(23.32)	(0)	(0)
reer	−0.00205	−0.00236	−0.123**	0.0384
	(0.00243)	(0.00287)	(0.0609)	(0.0291)
rint	−0.339	−0.906	−6.151	−0.495
	(0.396)	(0.713)	(5.505)	(1.043)
sav	0.449	0.354	−9.522	1.483
	(0.305)	(0.495)	(14.52)	(1.880)
Constant	−25.01	−57.64	0	0
	(42.17)	(44.58)	(0)	(0)
Observations	306	306	306	306
Number of id	9	9	9	9
Firm effect	Yes	Yes	Yes	Yes
Year effect	No	No	No	No
Hansen_test	0	0	0	0
Hansen Prob	1	1	1	1
Sargan_test	388.4	2.427	388.4	2.427
Sargan Prob	0.000156	0.787	0.000156	0.787
AR(1)_test	−2.366	−2.426	−1.321	−2.912
AR(1)_P-value	0.0180	0.0153	0.187	0.00359
AR(2)_test	−1.340	−1.357	−1.009	−1.265
AR(2)_P-value	0.180	0.175	0.313	0.206
No. of instruments	306	18	306	18

Robust standard errors in parentheses. SGMM1 & SGMM2 denote One-Step & Two-Step GMM respectively. Regressions with suffix "CL" follow Roodman (2009) and collapse the instrument matrix

***$p < 0.01$, **$p < 0.05$, *$p < 0.1$

[a]lag(1 5); [b]lag(2 4)

our model is further reinforced by the significance of the AR(1) test while the number of instruments, based on Roodman (2009), has reduced from 306 to just 18.

Accordingly, the result shows that precious metals are positively but insignificantly related to the dependent variable, gross domestic product per capita in the sub-region. Thus, a 10% increase in precious metal prices will bring about a 0.69% rise in gross domestic product per capita, a proxy for the standard of living of the people. Further, energy is also positively and significantly related to gross domestic product per capita. This implies that a 10% rise in the price of energy will bring about a 13.19% rise in the dependent variable, gross domestic product per capita. However, the non-energy shows a negative relationship with the dependent variable as a 10% increase will result in a 11.3% fall in the dependent variable. This is against a priori expectation but could be explained by the well-known Dutch Disease or resource curse hypothesis which result in negative impact on the economy as rent seeking activities of the people results in the abandonment of other products because they have become less competitive due to currency appreciation brought about by inflow from the natural resource.

The implication of the result of precious metals and energy which have both confirmed the a priori expectation is that a period of declining commodity prices (which has been the trend since July 2014) is associated with a fall in gross domestic product per capita (standard of living) in the ECOWAS sub-region. The recent trend of downward fall in the prices of commodities such as energy (oil) and non-energy (agricultural) is welfare-reducing in the sub-region. For instance as shown by our results, a 10% fall in the price of precious metal will bring about a 0.69% decline in standard of living, proxied by gross domestic product per capita while the same 10% fall in energy price will result in 13.19% fall in the standard of living. However, the same 10% fall in non-energy price will result in a 11.30% rise in welfare though not statistically significant.

Curiously, all the control variables (capital account, consumer price index, real effective exchange rate, real interest rate and saving) were not statistically significant with varying degrees of magnitude.

6 Conclusion

The global slump in prices of commodities has serious macroeconomic implications for a typical commodity dependent region like ECOWAS. It is expected that varying degrees of impact across countries in the sub-region will require macroeconomic response to ameliorate adverse consequences. The findings of our paper show a positive and significant relationship between energy prices but only positive and insignificant relationship with precious metals. The relationship with non-energy prices was negative and insignificant. The results also indicate that the ECOWAS sub-region is susceptible to exogenous commodity price shocks as energy producing countries constitute 87% of total gross domestic product of the region. Thus, a likely energy price shock to the region has the potential of affecting more than 80% of the region's economy. Therefore, there is urgent need to re-think integration within the context of monetary integration and diversification integration for the region to withstand any adverse external shocks.

Disclaimer The views expressed in this paper are those of the authors and do not represent the official position of the Central Bank of Nigeria or its Board of Directors.

Appendix 1: Trends in Balance of Payments in ECOWAS (% of GDP)

	2012	2013	2014[a]	2015[b]
ECOWAS	**3.7**	**3.4**	**2.2**	**1.7**
UEMOA	**−5.2**	**−7.0**	**−8.1**	**−8.1**
Benin	−7.6	−8.1	−8.2	−8.5
Burkina	−1.5	−11.1	−10.5	−11.9
Cote d'Ivoire	−1.2	−1.9	−3.4	−2.9
Guinea-Bissau	−7.8	−4.5	−3.8	−5.4
Mali	−2.6	−3.4	−7.9	−7.6
Niger	−15.3	−15.5	−19.6	−22.0
Senegal	−10.9	−10.5	−10.3	−9.1
Togo	−7.6	−13.6	−10.8	−11.4
WAMZ	**5.2**	**5.1**	**3.9**	**3.4**
The Gambia	−17.9	−17.0	−11.9	−13.5
Ghana	−11.8	−11.7	−9.5	−7.0
Guinea	−17.0	−17.8	−16.4	−16.7
Liberia	11.6	−46.7	−33.1	−40.2
Nigeria	7.3	7.4	5.7	4.9
Sierra Leone	−24.7	−11.2	−7.7	−13.2
Cape-Verde	−10.9	−4.9	−7.7	−9.6

Sources: WAMA/ECOWAS Central Banks
[a]Estimates, [b]Projections
The values in bold represent sub-regional average

Appendix 2: Summary Statistics

	(1)	(2)	(3)	(4)	(5)
Variables	N	Mean	sd	min	max
id	315	7.111	4.074	1	13
year	315	1,997	10.12	1,980	2,014
ca	315	−7.822	7.262	−65.26	11.79
cpi	315	63.53	34.61	−52.60	174.7

(continued)

Variables	(1) N	(2) Mean	(3) sd	(4) min	(5) max
nfa	315	−80.55	51.95	−283.8	36.03
sav	315	9.983	10.30	−24.11	45.35
reer	315	719.1	1,166	0.520	7,858
exp	315	23.77	10.30	4.900	59.90
imp	315	35.98	11.05	12.41	71.58
lextdeb	315	20.94	0.788	18.44	22.45
lintdeb	315	16.29	1.181	12.75	18.83
fdi	315	1.886	3.812	−28.62	32.77
rint	315	11.34	17.46	−75.75	45.72
gdpc	315	420.7	197.7	130.2	1,095
gdpgr	315	3.537	5.075	−28.10	26.27
pop	315	6.189	4.309	0	17.40
popg	315	2.744	0.813	−0.910	5.860
depr	315	5.924	0.752	4.560	7.690
open	315	0.169	0.0871	0.0600	0.460
enegy	315	53.17	36.37	19.54	129.1
noeneg	315	62.85	22.33	41.13	119.8
premet	315	47.40	32.37	22.40	138.5
enegy1	315	37.67	49.18	0	164.8
noeneg1	315	16.88	31.42	0.01000	126.7
premet1	315	30.79	46.99	0.0700	207.8
Number of id	9	9	9	9	9

Appendix 3: Static Panel Data Analyses

Variables	(1) OLS	(2) FE	(3) LSDV	(4) RE
premet1	−0.114	−0.145	−0.297*	−0.114
	(0.235)	(0.149)	(0.179)	(0.235)
enegy1	0.625*	0.546**	0.598**	0.625*
	(0.350)	(0.224)	(0.270)	(0.350)
noeneg1	0.751	0.964**	1.440***	0.751
	(0.642)	(0.417)	(0.500)	(0.642)
ca	−2.705**	−0.955	−1.109	−2.705**
	(1.066)	(0.697)	(0.841)	(1.066)
cpi	−0.0454	0.236	0.408	−0.0454
	(0.285)	(0.212)	(0.255)	(0.285)
depr	−33.79***	−23.39**	−34.01***	−33.79***
	(10.32)	(10.30)	(12.37)	(10.32)

(continued)

Variables	(1) OLS	(2) FE	(3) LSDV	(4) RE
fdi	0.468	−0.254	−1.152	0.468
	(2.118)	(1.358)	(1.636)	(2.118)
lnopen	−239.1***	−236.5***		−239.1***
	(15.57)	(12.25)		(15.57)
reer	−0.0161**	0.00104	−0.00624	−0.0161**
	(0.00641)	(0.00532)	(0.00637)	(0.00641)
rint	1.250***	−0.478	−0.371	1.250***
	(0.440)	(0.339)	(0.411)	(0.440)
sav	1.425**	1.876***	2.238***	1.425**
	(0.668)	(0.439)	(0.531)	(0.668)
Constant	98.83	42.45	733.4***	98.83
	(72.00)	(71.78)	(82.26)	(72.00)
Observations	315	315	315	315
R-squared	0.705	0.825	0.835	
Firm effect	No	Yes	Yes	Yes
Year effect	No	No	No	No
F-test	65.94	126.1	78.68	
Prob > F	0	0	0	
Number of id		9		9
Wald-chi2				725.4
Prob > chi2				0

Standard errors in parentheses
***p < 0.01, **p < 0.05, *p < 0.1

Appendix 4: Dynamic Panel Data Analyses-Difference GMM

Variables	(1) DGMM1	(2) DGMM1−CL[a]	(3) DGMM2
premet1	−0.113	−0.131	−0.880*
	(0.230)	(0.0848)	(0.522)
enegy1	0.648***	0.505**	−1.134*
	(0.244)	(0.247)	(0.611)
noeneg1	0.732	0.0424	5.555
	(0.903)	(0.542)	(3.389)
ca	−0.878	−0.681	30.77
	(1.154)	(0.783)	(53.34)
cpi	0.110	0.520	5.209
	(0.450)	(0.429)	(4.217)
depr	−36.55***	−66.59**	0
	(11.93)	(27.86)	(0)

(continued)

Variables	(1) DGMM1	(2) DGMM1−CL[a]	(3) DGMM2
fdi	0.193	−0.159	−23.69*
	(1.785)	(0.993)	(12.24)
lnopen	−236.5***	−173.8***	0
	(38.33)	(31.11)	(0)
reer	0.00106	0.0201	0.0617
	(0.0113)	(0.0128)	(0.258)
rint	−0.551	0.104	9.305
	(0.476)	(0.437)	(8.650)
sav	1.856**	1.462	14.03*
	(0.735)	(0.896)	(7.782)
Observations	306	306	306
Number of id	9	9	9
Firm effect	Yes	Yes	Yes
Year effect	No	No	No
Hansen_test	0	0	0
Hansen Prob	1	1	1
Sargan_test	1070	69.47	1043
Sargan Prob	0	0	0
AR(1)_test	−2.174	−1.201	−0.864
AR(1)_P-value	0.0297	0.230	0.388
AR(2)_test	−2.193	1.180	−0.448
AR(2)_P-value	0.0283	0.238	0.654
No. of instruments	281	16	272

Robust standard errors in parentheses. DGMM1 and DGMM2 denote One-Step and Two-Step Diff-GMM respectively. Regressions with suffix "CL" follow Roodman (2009) and collapse the instrument matrix

***$p < 0.01$, **$p < 0.05$, *$p < 0.1$

[a]lag(1 5)

References

Adams, R. H. (2009). The determinants of international remittances in developing countries. *World Development, 37*(1), 93–103.

Allegret, J., Mignon, C. C. & Razafindrabe, T. (2015). *Oil currencies in the face of oil shocks: What can be learned from time-varying specifications?* CEPII Working Paper. Available http://www.cepii.fr/PDF_PUB/wp/2015/wp2015-18.pdf

An, L., Jinb, X., & Ren, X. (2014). Are the macroeconomic effects of oil price shock symmetric? A factor-augmented vector autoregressive approach. *Energy Economics, 45*, 217–228.

Armando, F. D. (2009). Latin American structuralism and economic theory. *CEPAL Review, 98*, 175–195.

Ayres, R., & Voudouris, V. (2014). Economic growth engima: Capital, labour and useful energy? *Energy Policy, 64*, 16–28.

Ball, L., & Mankiw, N. G. (1995). Relative-price changes as aggregate supply shocks. *Quarterly Journal of Economics, 110*(1), 161–193.

Bauch, C. M., & Kuckulenz, A. (2009). Worker remittances and capital flows to developing countries. *International Migration, 48*(5), 89–117.

Bernanke, B., Gertler, M., & Watson, M. (1997). Systematic monetary policy and the effects of oil price shocks. *Brookings Papers on Economic Activity, 28*(1), 91–157.

Bhattacharya, B. B., & Kar, S. (2009). *Shocks, economic growth and the Indian economy.* Washington, DC: International Bank for Reconstruction and Development.

Blanchard, O. J. (2009). *Why are the 200s so different from the 1970s? A structural interpretation of changes in the macroeconomic effects of oil prices*. Cambridge, MA: National Bureau of Economic Research.

Canova, F. (2005). The transmission of US shocks to Latin America. *Journal of Applied Econometrics, 20*, 229–251.

Cunado, J., & Perez de Gracia, F. (2005). Oil prices, economic activity and inflation: Evidence for some Asian countries. *The Quarterly Review of Economics and Finance, 45*(1), 65–83.

Cunado, J., & Perez de Gracia, F. (2003). Do oil price shocks matter? Evidence for some European countries. *Energy Economics, 25*(2), 137–154.

Cunado, J., Jo, S., & Gracia, F. P. (2015). Macroeconomic impacts of oil price shocks in Asian economies. *Energy Policy*, forthcoming.

Dibooglu, S., & Aleisa, E. (2004). Oil prices, terms of trade shocks, and macroeconomic fluctuations in Saudi Arabia. *Contemporary Economic Policy, 22*(1), 50–62.

Erten, B. & Ocampo, J. A. (2012). *Super-cycles of commodity prices since the mid-nineteenth century.* United Nations Department of Economic and Social Affairs Working Paper 110, New York. http://www.un.org/esa/desa/papers/2012/wp110_2012.pdf

Ezeoha, A. E. (2013). Financial determinants of international remittance flows to the sub-Saharan African region. *International Migration, 12061*, 1–14.

Fischer, S. (1985). Supply shock, wage stickiness and accommodation. *Journal of Money, Credit and Banking, 17*, 1–15.

Ftiti, Z., Tivari, A., & Fatnassi, I. (2014). *Oil shocks and economic growth in OPEC countries.* IPAG Working Paper 064.

Gangelhoff, G. (2015). *The end of the commodity super-cycle? Implications for USAID presence countries.* Economics Brief, USAID.

Global Economic Prospects. (2015). *Understanding the plunge in oil prices: Sources and implications* (pp. 155–168).

Hamilton, J. D. (2003). What is an oil shock? *Journal of Econometrics, 113*(2), 363–398.

Hamilton, J. D. (2009). Causes and consequences of the oil shocks of 2007–2008, Brookings papers on economic activity, Economic studies program. *The Brookings Institution, 40*(1), 215–283.

IMF. (2003). *Fund assistance for countries facing exogenous shocks.* Policy Development and Review Department, International Monetary Fund.

Inflation Report. (2006). Retrieved March 31, 2014, from http://www.bot.or.th/English/MonetaryPolicy/Inflation/PaperInFrame/061_RoleOfMonetPolicy_jul06e.pdf

Jimenez-Rodrigues, R., & Sanchez, M. (2005). Oil price shocks and the real GDP: Empirical evidence for some OECD countries. *Applied Economics, 37*(2), 201–228.

Kilian, L. (2008). Exogenous shocks: How big are they and how much do they matter for US economy. *The Review of Economics and Statistics, 90*(2), 216–240.

Kilian, L. (2014). Oil price shocks: Causes and consequences. *Annual Review of Resource Economics, 6*(1), 133–154.

Kilian, L., & Lewis, L. T. (2011). Does the Fed respond to oil price shocks? *The Econometrics Journal, 121*, 1047–1072.

Kose, M. A., & Riesmanb, R. (2001). Trade shocks and macroeconomic fluctuations in Africa. *Journal of Development Economics, 65*(1), 55–80.

Lilien, D. (1982). Sectoral shifts and cyclical unemployment. *Journal of Political Economy, 90*, 777–793.

Mehara, M. (2006). Energy consumption and economic growth: The case of oil exporting countries. *Energy Policy, 35*(5), 2939–2945.

Nationmaster Statistics. (2012). *Country profiles*. Available https://www.nationmaster.com/countryinfo/Profiles

Ncube, M., Ndou, E., & Gumata, N. (2012). *How are the US financial shocks transmitted into South Africa? Structural VAR evidence*. African Development Bank Group Working Paper Series No. 157.

Raddatz, C. (2007). Are external shocks responsible for the instability of output in low income countries? *Journal of Development Economics, 84*(1), 155–187.

Roodman, D. (2009). How to do xtabond2: An introduction to difference and system GMM in Stata. *The Stata Journal, 9*(1), 86–136.

Sommer, M. (2002). *Supply shocks and persistence of inflation*. Retrieved March 31, 2014, from http://econ.jhu.edu/wp-content/uploads/pdf/papers/WP485SommerInflation_1202.pdf

Sosa, S., & Adler, G. (2012). *Intra-regional spillovers in South America: Is Brazil systemic after all?* IMF Working Paper WP/12/145. Washington, DC: International Monetary Fund.

UNCTAD. (2012). *United Nations conference on trade and development annual report 2012*. Available https://unctad.org/en/PublicationsLibrary/dom2013d1_en.pdf

UNCTADSTAT. (2016). United Nations trade and development statistics for 2016. Available http://unctadstat.unctad.org/EN/Infographics.html#&gid=2018&pid=Total%20merchandise%20trade%2C%202017%20(Final%20figures).

Valadkhani, A. (2014). Dynamic effects of rising oil prices on consumer energy prices in Canada and the United States: Evidence from the last half a century. *Energy Economics, 45*, 33–44.

Watcher, S. M. (1979). Structuralism vs monetarism: Inflation in Chile. In J. R. Behrman & J. Hanson (Eds.), *Short-term macroeconomic policy in Latin America* (pp. 227–256). Cambridge, MA: NBER.

World Bank Global Monitoring Report. (2004). *Policies and actions for achieving the millenium development goals and related outcomes*. Washington, DC: International Bank for Reconstruction and Development.

Yuan, Y., Zhuang, X., Liu, Z., & Huang, W. (2014). *Analysis of the temporal properties of price shock sequences in crude oil markets*.

Is Currency Devaluation Appropriate for Improving Trade Balance in the WAMZ Countries?

Abwaku Englama, Momodou Sissoho, Olukayode Odeniran, and Ozolina Haffner

Contents

Abstract The paper examines the appropriateness of devaluation in improving trade balance in the six WAMZ countries. The motivation is largely derived from the need to reverse the deteriorating external sector of these countries which has become worrisome particularly from the latter half of 2014 on the backlash of slump in commodities prices and tight global monetary condition. The study employs descriptive analysis, granger causality technique, and Vector Error Correction Model (VECM) to analyze the impact of devaluation on trade balance in these countries. Two other control variables, domestic and global output, are included in the model to capture the impact of domestic and global shock while the data covers the period 1980–2014. The trend analysis reveals considerable volatility in real exchange rate in all the countries with the exception of the Gambia while there is

A. Englama (✉) · M. Sissoho · O. Odeniran · O. Haffner
West African Monetary Institute, Accra, Ghana
e-mail: aenglama@wami-imao.org

D. Seck (ed.), *The External Sector of Africa's Economy*, Advances in African Economic, Social and Political Development,
https://doi.org/10.1007/978-3-319-97913-7_9

a virtual absence of co-movement between devaluation and trade balance in all the countries. All the series are integrated to the first order while Johansen cointegration test indicates the existence of long run relationship among the variables employed in the study.

Results of the normalized long run model indicates that the coefficient of real exchange rate is positively significant in only Liberia while it is negatively significant in the Gambia only. Real exchange rate is not significant in the remaining four countries, suggesting that devaluation may not lead to an improvement in trade balance in the WAMZ countries except probably in Liberia. Results from the models further suggest that external condition like expansion in global output tends to have positive impact on trade balance though the effect is not significant in all the countries. The variables are virtually not significant in the short run models for all the countries while the vector error correction term is suggestive that the impact of shock to trade balance does not wane rapidly. The study recommends, among others, that devaluation may not be the most appropriate policy option to improve trade balance in these countries while these economies should endeavor as much as possible to improve the export content of Gross Domestic Product in order allow local economic condition drive trade balance.

1 Introduction

The WAMZ countries comprising Nigeria, Ghana, Gambia, Sierra Leone, Liberia, and Guinea experienced a fairly robust macroeconomic performance in the decade preceding 2014, resulting largely from developments in global environment. Diverse kinds of factors ranging from economics, geo- political tension, and actual conflicts in different regions of the world provided tailwinds for the prices of commodities exported by these countries with the ensuing improvement in terms of trade leading to favorable trade balances cum improved output growth. By mid-2014, most of the initial favorable conditions commenced significant slowdown while complete reversals were experienced in some cases. For example in oil exporting countries such as Nigeria, resolution of conflicts between Iran and UN as well as commencement of oil export by the US considerably expanded the supply space while softness in economic activity in key industrialized and emerging economies such as China reduced export demand, leading to slump in price.

In addition, global monetary policy has been less supportive, with the resumption of tight monetary conditions in key advanced economies fuelling capital flight from emerging and developing economies. As a result, rising trade imbalances coupled with capital outflows put pressure on external reserves leading to a rise in fiscal deficit with the attendant increased public debt and interest rates. The cumulative effects of these developments in the WAMZ countries is a slowdown in economic growth, elevated unemployment and poverty rates.

Against this perspective, some academics and policymakers in these countries are beginning to look at the direction of devaluation of currencies as a viable option for stimulating export performance and invariably restoring sustainable improvement in trade balances in these countries. This view finds theoretical foundation from the orthodoxy that devaluation could improve external sector performance because weakening currency would boost export demand while simultaneously reducing import demand. Early proponents of this thesis include Prebisch (1950, 1964) and Keesing (1967) who argue that export oriented industrialization should not only be a critical component of economic growth but more fundamentally, the strategy should include expansion in market share through comparative cost advantage like cheap labor or weak exchange rate.

Other proponents in recent times include Mussa and Rosen (1978) and Kaiser and Wroughton (2010). The strength of their argument lies in the fact that a relatively weak exchange rate would improve the competitiveness of countries' exports and help them achieve higher prosperity. In addition, it is recognized that switching of expenditure from import to domestically produced goods would increase aggregate demand, raise domestic output (GDP), and eventually per capita income. Also relevant in this context is the logic that devaluation may be more appropriate in stimulating export performance in developing and emerging economies than in the matured economies. A new strand of economics, efficiency-driven economies, posits that the use of devaluation to gain global competitiveness is more relevant to developing industrializing nations for whom export sectors contribute substantially to domestic output (Porter 1998).

A number of economists, on the other hand, have expressed reservations about unqualified acceptance of this school of thought (Alejandro 1963; Cooper 1971; Krugman and Taylor 1978). Their argument hinges on the fact that trade balance is a critical function of elasticity of demand for export which is a major burden to most emerging and developing economies. Beside, exchange rate risk from a falling currency may constrain inflows of foreign capitals that could be used to finance trade deficit thereby pushing up interest rate and heighten the risk of recession. In addition, there is the burden of foreign debt and debt service repayment which could also increase trade gap. Moreover, perception by speculators regarding imminent devaluation could trigger offloading of domestic currency, put pressure on the external reserves, and ultimately fostering balance of payment crisis.

In light of this salient and unresolved issue, the mind boggling questions include whether devaluation of currencies could be used to stimulate exports and invariably trade balance in these countries? What is the type of relationship between devaluation and trade balance in the WAMZ countries? What is the short and long run impacts of devaluation on trade balance in the WAMZ countries? Most of the previous studies on the subject have revealed inconclusive and sometimes contradictory results (Musila and Newark 2003; Auer and Chaney 2009; Frankel et al. 2005; Berman and Berthou 2009). Again, most of these studies generally consider developed and developing countries as a group. Though this approach has its merits, it definitely excludes certain country specific characteristics which could have significant influence on the results. This study, therefore, attempts to provide insight into this issue by employing both trend and econometric tools to analyze the relationship between currency devaluation, trade balance in each of the WAMZ countries. Specifically, the study examines the short and long run impacts of currency devaluation on trade balance in the WAMZ countries as well as trace the time path of response of trade balance to exchange rate shock by testing the validity of the J-curve hypothesis.

The remaining part of the study is organized as follows: Sect. 2 is on both theoretical and empirical literature while Sect. 3 focuses on empirical methodology. Sections 4 and 5 present results from trend analysis and Vector Error Correction Model, respectively, while the last Section summarizes and proffers policy recommendations.

2 Literature Review

2.1 Theoretical Literature

The impact of devaluation on trade balance has a long history in economic literature as a number of theories have been propounded in the quest to examine the relationship. The conclusions from these theories are as diverse as the heterogeneity in economic conditions of various parts of the globe. One of the earliest theories is the absorption theory which is basically an extension of Keynesian short run model with devaluation having both nominal and real effects. The theory emerged from the works of authors like Harberger (1950) and Meade (1951). The key argument is that devaluation leads to deterioration in a country's terms of trade and ultimately national income through a two-stage process. In the first stage, devaluation induces expenditure-substituting process in which the composition of general goods and services shifts from foreign goods towards domestic good. Given the usual assumption of unemployment in the Keynesian theory, the process would increase domestic output, hence income. In the second stage, the resultant increases in income would enhance absorption thereby reducing trade balance. The major critique of the theory however is that the whole export component of the balance of payment is reduced to trade balance and is largely applicable to big advanced economies. In addition, the theory assumes that export volumes are independent of national income while imports, on the other hand, depends on national income.

Another important theory is the monetarist approach which now has a number of variants due to the dynamics of macroeconomic environment. The main argument is that trade imbalance is largely due to excess money demand or supply because excess money would increase demand for goods and services including import demand and thereby leads to deficit in the balance of payment (Alexander 1952). Consequently, the performance of balance of payment could be analyzed within the framework of demand and supply. Devaluation is expected to constrain import demand by reducing the real value of cash balances and thereby improve the balance of payment. The significant shortfall of the main monetarist approach, however, is that it ignores the role of relative prices on trade balance. Economists like Polak (1957) and Hahn (1959) attempted to fill this gap by recognizing that devaluation could reduce the price of export in foreign currency while the price of imports remain constant and thereby stimulate export demand such that the balance of payments will ultimately improve. One of the main variants of monetarist approach is the Keynesian view, which is also referred to as the "global monetarist" (Whitman 1975). The theory rests on three important assumptions namely existence of significant level of unemployment, price rigidities, and high substitutability of money for other assets. The key argument is that increases in money supply would increase real balances above the optimum level required by economic agents and thereby increase the level of expenditure above the normal ratio from a fixed income which ultimately increase import demand and deterioration in balance of payments.

The other major theory is the elesticities approach which is largely premised on what is commonly referred to as the BRM (Bickerdike 1920; Robinson 1947; Metzler 1948) model. The elesticities approach posits that the impact of devaluation on trade balance is a function of four elesticities: the foreign elasticity of demand for exports; the home elasticity of supply; foreign elasticity of import supply, and home elasticity of import demand (Robinson 1950). The theory recognizes the long and short run behavior of both import and export. Devaluation could negatively impact on export in the short run, leading to imbalance in trade, but this initial outcome would create adjustment in both export and import in the long run due to reduction in the foreign price of devaluing country's export and increases in the price of her imports. The ultimate outcome therefore is an improvement in trade balance. Other scholars like Marshall (1923), Lerner (1944), and Krueger (1983) further expounded the BRM theory by identifying the conditions under which devaluation could improve trade balance. In their contribution, they argue that the level of improvement in trade balance is contingent upon the degree of elasticity of imports and exports. Marshal and Lerner in particular developed a hypothesis normally termed MarshalLerner's condition which postulates that devaluation could only improve trade balance if the sum of export and import elasticities exceeds unity. Some other scholars have attempted to rationalize the performance of trade balance under the elasticity approach into a J-curve behavior. Junz and Rhomberg (1973), Magee (1973), Meade (1988) provide an explanation to the J-time path of trade balance by stressing that devaluation always triggers an instant adjustment in the exchange rate, while producers and consumers, on the other hand, takes time to adjust to changes in relative prices. The elasticity approach has been critiqued on a number of grounds. Among others, the structural model, which is defined by import demand and export supply function, is based on nominal prices instead of relative prices and relevant scale variables like real income, real expenditure, and real money balances (Alexander 1952). The other major critique is from the work of Williamson (1983) who argues that devaluation induced higher import prices could have a spillover to the domestic prices of non-traded goods and thereby pose upside risk to inflation.

A likely inference from the theories as well as their shortcoming therefore is that the overall net impact of devaluation on export or trade balance is yet to be settled in economic theory.

2.2 Empirical Literature

Issues bordering on currency devaluation and trade balance have attracted attention in the empirical literature as much as the theoretical literature. Just like the theoretical issues, empirical results have also revealed diverging outcomes. Findings from most of the empirical studies could be broadly dimensioned along three main lines: those that lend credence to the relevance of devaluation in promoting favorable trade balance; those that reject the hypothesis that devaluation could enhance trade performance; and those with neutral outcomes. Among studies with negative impact of devaluation on trade balance is the work of Obonye Galebotswe and Tshimologo Andrias (2011) on small open import-dependent economy of Botswana. The authors test the contractionary devaluation hypothesis in the context of a small open import-dependent economy using an error-correction model that controls for monetary policy, fiscal policy, base country output and interest rates. The study finds that currency devaluations are contractionary in the long run and expansionary in the short-run. The result tends to lean towards the absorption theory in the sense that the contraction in output in the long run would eventually constrain improvement in trade balance. Based on this finding, the authors cautioned that the monetary authority in Botswana should guide against the use of currency devaluation in stimulating economic activities. Another study with similar outcome is the work of Miteza (2006) who examined the effects of devaluation on income in a group of five transition economy, using panel unit root and panel cointegration test. The finding from the study indicates that devaluation had contractionary effects on output in the long run. This would invariably affect the capacity of the country to improve its trade performance. Nicola Kim Rowbotham et al. (2014) examined the impact of exchange rate movement on export performance in a sample of nine efficiency-driven economies that were operating under floating exchange rate regimes. The study employed a fixed effects model under panel data framework. The result shows that weakening of the exchange rate does not necessarily improve export performance but improvement in merchandise export seems to be associated with stronger exchange rates.

Relatedly, Raza et al. (2013) investigated the impact of currency depreciation on trade balances in selected South Asian countries while they also attempted to assess the validity of Marshal-Lerner conditions in these economies. Their results show that the cumulative elasticity of demand for export and import is relatively inelastic for all countries except Nepal, suggesting that devaluation of currency exchange rate has inverse relationship with trade balance. They stress that real exchange rate increases trade deficit to developing economies due to inelasticity of their exports. On the basis of this, the study maintains that devaluation of currencies increase the value of imports in these countries in general and thereby places heavy burden over balance of trade. Furthermore, Rose in the examination of the effect of devaluation on 29 countries finds that devaluation is insignificant in 28 of these countries while it is negatively significant in the remaining one country. In the light of this result, the study concludes that devaluation does not necessarily lead to improvement in trade balance. The findings of Upadhyaya and Dhakal (1997) is almost similar to that of Rose as they find that devaluation improves trade balance in only one country out of eight countries employed in their study. Equally supporting this position is Agbola (2004) who employed the Johansen multivariate co-integration procedure and Stock-Watson dynamic Ordinary Least Square (DOLS) to examine the impact of devaluation on trade balance in Ghana with the results indicating that devaluation does not improve trade balance. In supporting this finding, Acharya (2010) provides an explanation about the channel through which devaluation leads to deterioration in trade balance in Nepal. The study shows that both industrial and agricultural sectors which produce for export markets in Nepal are highly dependent on imported inputs while devaluation induced increases in price of these imported items would ultimately cause a decline in trade balance.

On the other hand, some studies have shown that devaluation could have a salutary impact on trade balance. Among others, Rawlins and Pravern (1993) examine the influence of devaluation on trade balance in 19 sub Saharan African countries by employing an Almon Distributed lag model based on annual data. Their result shows that devaluation improves trade balance in seventeen of the nineteen countries. Similarly, Bahmani-Oskooee and Rhee (1997) based on Johansen's cointegration and error-correction technique show that depreciation has a positive impact on income in Korea although the positive effects appeared only after three quarters. In the same vein, Onafowora (2003) finds that devaluation improves trade balance of three Asian countries in their bilateral trade relationship with the USA though the improvement usually comes after some lags. Furthermore, Nunnenkamp and Schweickert (1990) examine the influence of devaluation on growth and performance of merchandise export in 48 developing economies. The result on external sector shows that devaluation has a long run positive effect on export performance in countries where manufactured goods account for a substantial part of export while the positive effect is observed in both the short and long run in countries where agriculture constitutes the bulk of exports.

A reasonable number of studies have equally shown that the impact of devaluation on trade balance is neutral. Authors who have results that tend towards this line include Genye (2011) and Ayen (2014). In his work on Ethiopia, Ayen (2014) used a vector auto regression (VAR) model based on quarterly time series data to assess the impact of currency devaluation on output growth and export performance. He finds that by controlling the monetary and fiscal policies, currency devaluations has a neutral effect on output in the short-run but a contractionary effect in the long run. With respect to the external sector, the study shows that devaluation does not have significant impact on export because the Ethiopian export is dominated by primary agricultural products and thus insensitive to exchange rate change. This finding, however, appears as a puzzle given that it contradicts the conclusion of Nunnenkamp and Schweickert (1990) for developing countries. In a closely related study,

Kalyoncu et al. (2008) examined the influence of movement in real exchange rate on GDP in 23 Organization of Economic and Cooperation Development (OECD) countries based on error-correction model. They find that devaluation tends to reduce output in six countries, raised output in three and had no effect on output in fourteen countries. The major shortcoming of the study, however, is that exchange rate was the only independent variable as other key control variables such as the stance of monetary and fiscal authorities were excluded in the model. Similarly, Bahmani-Oskooee (1998) finds that devaluation has a neutral effect on output in a study involving 23 least developing economies.

The overall trend from the empirical literature suggests that the impact of devaluation on trade balance is not completely settled as it varies from one jurisdiction to the other and more fundamentally on the nature of the economy.

3 Methodology

Both descriptive and econometric techniques are employed in the study. The descriptive analysis examines the movement in real effective exchange rate and trade balance in the six WAMZ countries. Econometrics tools involve cointegration models which examine the impact of movement in in exchange rates on trade balance in these countries.

3.1 Measurements of Devaluation

There are two broad measures of devaluation in the literature namely gross devaluation and net devaluation. Gross devaluation is defined as percentage change in the nominal or parity rate. The parity rate is the number of units of local currency per unit of foreign currency or the unit of domestic currency. The other measure is net devaluation which is percentage change in effective exchange rate (EER). The effective exchange rate could be defined as the addition of various pricing charges to the basic rate, thus, it is the rate at which units of domestic currency translates into foreign currency for different categories of transactions. In an environment devoid of quantitative restrictions, the effective exchange rate for a particular commodity times the foreign price should translate to the domestic price exclusive of domestic handling charges. Thus, the difference between gross and net devaluation is commonly referred to as replacement component of a parity charge. In line with notable empirical works like Krueger (1978), the estimation in this study employs net devaluation.

3.2 Econometric Specification

The econometric specification is in tandem with the model adopted by Rose and Yellen (1989) in which a country's trade balance is specified as a function of real exchange rate, real domestic and foreign incomes. Consequently, we specify a trade balance equation for each of the six WAMZ countries as follow:

$$\mathrm{TB_t = f(REER, RDY, RFY)} \tag{1}$$

where TB_t is trade balance at a given period, REER is the real effective exchange rate, RDY is the real domestic income, and RFY is the real foreign income. In line with Hsing (2003) and Grigoryan (2015), we employ the ratio of imports and exports (imexp) as proxy for trade balance given that it gives us the additional flexibility to obtain the natural logarithm which is impossible in an environment of trade deficit. The empirical model for each of the countries is therefore specified as follows:

$$\mathrm{imexpt = f(REER, RDY, RFY)} \tag{2}$$

Equation (2) could also be specified as follows:

$$\mathrm{Y_t = f\ (ReeR_t, X_t, U_t)} \tag{3}$$

In Eq. (3), Y_t is a measure of trade balance while $ReeR_t$ is effective exchange rate. X_t is a vector of the two main control variables that capture the influence of domestic and external shocks. With respect to foreign shock, it is recognized that developments in foreign output particularly in key trading partners could independently trigger devaluation. Thus, if the effects of these variables are not controlled, it could lead to distortion in the relationship between exchange rate and the key endogenous variables under consideration (Kamin and Klau 1998). All the variables are in natural logarithmic form which permits the interpretation of the parameters estimates as elasticities.

Given that our objectives include the estimation of both the short and long run impact of exchange rate devaluation on trade balance, we employ a Vector Autoregressive Model (VECM) to estimate Eq. (3). VECM has been widely used to model macroeconomic variables that are not stationary individually but have long run relationship. Hendry and Juselius (2000) have shown that VECM is most appropriate if the variables are integrated of order one (I1). Thus, the empirical analysis would proceed by first testing the order of integration using the ADF and Phillip Peron test statistics. Following the test of stationarity, a cointegration test is done using Johansen cointegration techniques with a view to confirming that the variables are cointegrated as well as determining the number of cointegrating equations. The Johansen's cointegration is very sensitive to lag length, thus the optimal lag structure is determined with the aid of Schwarz criterion (SC) and Likelihood Ratio (LR) tests.

We proceed by defining a vector X_t of n potentially endogenous variables in which X_t is modeled as an unrestricted vector auto regression (VAR) up to k lags.

$$X_t = A_{1Xt-1} + \cdots + A_k X_{it-k} + U_t \tag{4}$$

$$U_t \sim IN\,(0, \varepsilon)$$

X_t is n × 1 matrix while A_1 is n × n matrix of parameters. Sims (1980) advocated this type of VAR as a means to estimate dynamic relationship among jointly endogenous variable without imposing strong apriori restriction. Given that the system is a reduced form with each variable in X_t regressed on only lagged values of both itself and all other variables in the system, OLS could give an efficient and consistent estimate of each equation in (3). Equation (4) could be reformulated into VECM form as follows:

$$\Delta X_t = \Gamma_1 \Delta X_{t-1} + \cdots + \Gamma_{k-1} \Delta X_{t-k+1} + \Pi X_{t-k} + U_i \tag{5}$$

Where

$$\Gamma_1 = (1 - A_1 - \cdots - A_i)$$

$$I = 1 \ldots k - 1$$

$$\Pi = -(1 - A1, \ldots - Ak)$$

The short and long run adjustment to changes in X_t is captured by the estimates of Γ_1 and Π_i, respectively.

Essentially, Π is β where U_i is speed of adjustment to disequilibrium and β is the matrix of long run coefficient. Thus the term $\beta X_{t\,-\,k}$ embedded in Eq. (5) represents up to (n − 1) cointegtrating relationship in the multivariate model, which makes X_t converges with their long run steady state solution. If we assume that X_t is a vector of I(1) variables, then for U_i to be white noise, in other words, $U_i \sim I(0)$, all the terms in Eq. 4 that involve $\Delta X_{t\,-\,i}$ as well as $\Pi X_{t\,-\,k}$ must be I(0).

There are three possible scenarios under which the requirement $\Pi X_{t-k} \sim I(0)$ could be met. First, when all the variables in X_t are stationary, in other words, there are r = n linearly independent columns, thus Π is adjudged to have full rank. The second extreme scenario is when the rank of Π is zero, in which case there are no linear combinations of the X_t that are I(0). In this case, the most appropriate model is a VAR in first-differences involving no long-run elements. This implies no cointegrating relationship. The third scenario is when r columns of β forms r linearly independent combinations of the variables in X_t, each of which is stationary. In this particular case, there is $r \leq (n - 1)$ cointegrating vectors in β. Thus, the issue in focus under Johansen approach is the determination of the number of $r \leq (n - 1)$ cointegrating vectors in β, commonly referred to as testing for the reduced rank of Π.

Two statistics are commonly used in applied empirical works to determine the rank of Π and we shall employ these statistics in this study. These are Trace test statistics and Maxima Eigen value or λ-max statistics.

The trace statistics computes a standard likelihood ratio test by comparing the log of the maximized likelihood function for the restricted model against the log of the maximized likelihood function of the unrestricted model.

$$\Lambda_{\text{trace}} = -2\log(\mathrm{Q}) = -\mathrm{T}\sum\nolimits_{i=r+1}^{n} \log(1 - \lambda i) \tag{6}$$

$$\mathrm{r} = 0, 1, 2, \ldots, \mathrm{n} - 2, \mathrm{n} - 1.$$

Where

$$\mathrm{Q} = \frac{\text{Restricted Maximized likelihood}}{\text{Unrestricted Maximized likelihood}}$$

Λ = Eigen vectors obtained from the maximum likelihood estimate of Eq. (6). The null hypothesis that there are at most r cointegration vectors is given by:

$$\mathrm{H}_0 : \lambda_1 = 0 \qquad\qquad \mathrm{i} = \mathrm{r} + 1, \ldots\ldots., \mathrm{n}.$$

Where only the first r Eigen values are non-zero.

The maximal Eigen value or λ-max statistics is represented by Eq. (7).

$$\Lambda_{\max} = -\mathrm{T}\log\left(1 - \lambda_{\mathrm{r}+1}\right) \tag{7}$$

$$\mathrm{r} = 0, 1, 2, \ldots\ldots.., \mathrm{n} - 2, \mathrm{n} - 1$$

Equation (7) tests that there are r cointegrating vectors against the alternative of r + 1.

3.3 *Trends in Exchange Rate, Export and Growth in the WAMZ Countries*

The trends in devaluation and trade balance in the WAMZ countries is presented in this section. The analysis is on country by country basis while trade balance is measured in terms of percentage growth.

Sierra Leone The trend of exchange rates in Sierra Leone reveals significant swings during the entire review period, 1980–2014, while trade balance equally exhibited varying degrees of fluctuations during the period (Fig. 1).

The fluctuations in the real effective exchange was relatively mild in the eighties up to the early-nineties and indeed some levels of revaluation could be observed during the period. Devaluation, however, was highly pronounced in the two decades

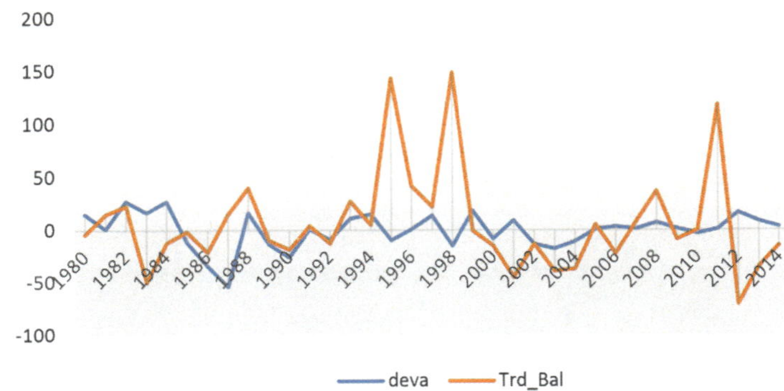

Fig. 1 Trend analysis of devaluation and trade balance in Sierra Leone

spanning 1994–2014 as net devaluation of about 150% was recorded particularly between 1994 and 1998 as well as between 2010 and 2012. The development in 2012 could be attributed to the general slump in commodities prices which severely hit diamond, the main export commodity of Sierra Leone. Trade balance, on the other hand, did not show much spikes like the real exchange rate but there was a preponderance of negative growth during the period particularly in the era preceding 2004. The relative improvement in the post 2004 era could equally be ascribed to the boom in commodity prices that characterized that period.

In terms of co-movement, devaluation and positive trade balance do not appear to move together. This is clearly shown between 1994 and 1998 when a wide divergence existed between two variables. In addition, improvement in trade balance seems to coincide with revaluation in domestic currency between 2012 and 2014.

The Gambia The trend in trade balance and net devaluation in the Gambia from 1980–2014 is presented in Fig. 2.

The chart shows that the exchange rate in the Gambia revolved along the zero line in the review period except in few cases like 1984 to 1986 and 2000–2004. This suggests that devaluation or revaluation of currency was not a common phenomenon in the Gambia with the implication that the country is practically employing a fixed exchange rate regime. The Gambia could have been able to sustain this level of

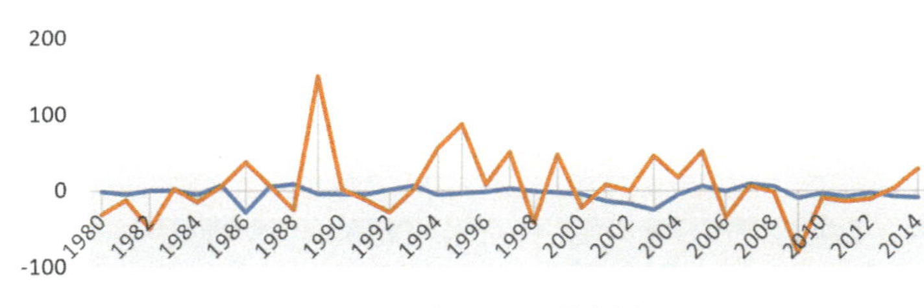

Fig. 2 Trend of devaluation and trade balance in the Gambia (1980–2014)

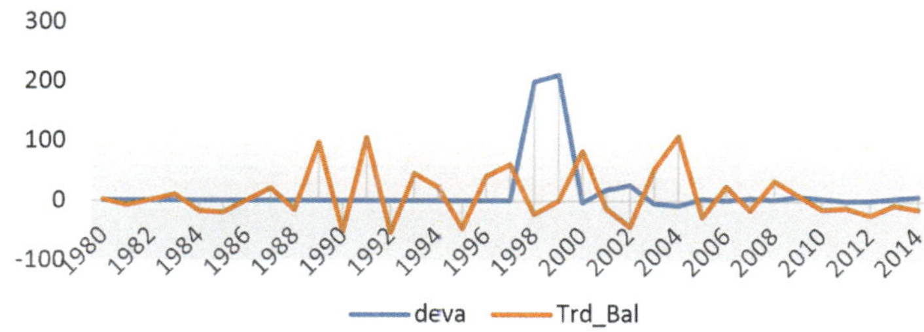

Fig. 3 Trend of devaluation and trade balance in Liberia (1980–2014)

fixed exchange rate regime because of limited trade with the outside world as the country does not practically have any mineral resource. Re-export trade normally constitutes a major component of economic activity but this has almost been taken over by the Senegalese consequent upon the 50% devaluation of CFA franc in 1994. Trade balance, however, exhibited considerable volatility that spanned the entire review period but worth of note is that the periods with positive growth dominated the negative growth periods. The highest growth in trade balance of about 160% was recorded in the late eighties and early nineties. In terms of co-movement, given that exchange rate was almost flat during the period, no serious co-movement was visible between net devaluation and trade balance.

3.4 *Liberia*

The trend in net devaluation and trade balance from 1980 to 2014 in Liberia is shown in Fig. 3.

As revealed in Fig. 3, exchange rate in Liberia was almost flat except for a sharp devaluation in 1998 when the Liberian dollar was devalued by over 200%. Apart from the sharp devaluation of 1998, there was further devaluation of about 20% in 2001 while there was no significant devaluation thereafter. The major issue in exchange rate management is that the country is highly dollarized to the extent that the US dollar is used for most economic transactions. Trade balance, on the other hand, exhibited a lot of fluctuations most especially from 1998 to the end of the review period. As in the Gambia in which exchange rate was flat, trade balance did not show any co-movement with devaluation during the review period in Liberia.

3.5 *Nigeria*

The trend in net devaluation and trade balance from 1980 to 2014 is shown in Fig. 4.

Like in all the other countries, there was a considerable swings in real effective exchange rate in Nigeria during the entire review period. It is however, striking that

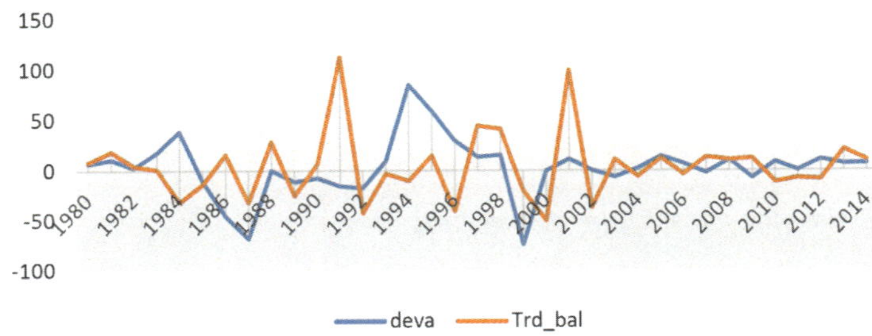

Fig. 4 Trend analysis of devaluation and trade balance in Nigeria (1980–2014)

the highest episode of devaluation in real effective exchange rate occurred in 1994 despite the fact that the Structural Adjustment Programme (SAP), which entailed devaluation of nominal exchange rate, commenced in 1986. The real effective exchange rate recorded a devaluation of about 100% in 1994 and remained fairly high up to 1998. This points out the fact the devaluation in the nominal exchange rate at the commencement of SAP did not filter into the real exchange rate while simultaneously showing that stability in the nominal exchange rate prior to the adoption of the SAP was more of exchange rate misalignment. The sharp devaluation in the real exchange rate between 1994 and 1998 could be largely attributed to the political crisis which engulfed the country given that it was a period he country witnessed a botched general election and series of military interventions in the polity. These developments must have affected investors' confidence with far reaching implications on key macroeconomic indicators. Trade balance exhibited volatility throughout the entire period but with significant positive spikes in the early 1990s and 2000s. The early 1990s was the period of gulf war in which the disruption of oil production in the oil rich Middle East, particularly Kuwait, provided significant tailwinds for the price of crude oil and thereby constituted a major boost to trade balance in the country. Similarly, the significant improvement in trade balances in the early 2000s could be attributed to commencement of positive investment climate as the country returned to democratically elected government in mid-1999. As in most other countries, the picture from the chart does not support the thesis that devaluation has any impact on trade balance.

3.6 Ghana

Figure 5 shows the trend in devaluation and trade balance in Ghana from 1980 to 2014.

The trend from the chart shows that real exchange rate experienced considerable devaluation in the early eighties up to 1984 when the currency witnessed a strong revaluation while the level of volatility moderated from 2002 up to the end of the

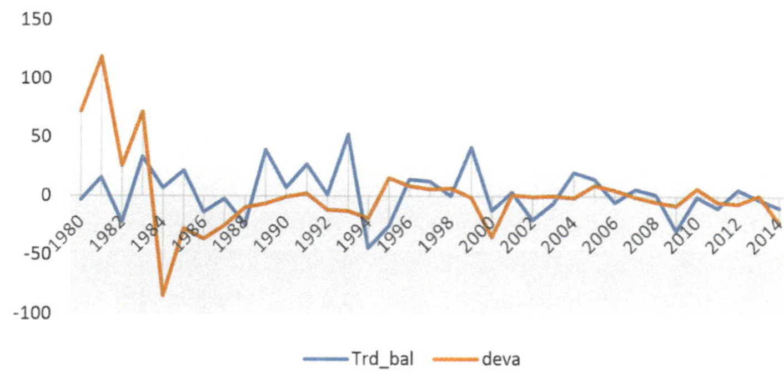

Fig. 5 Trend of devaluation and trade balance in Ghana (1980–2014)

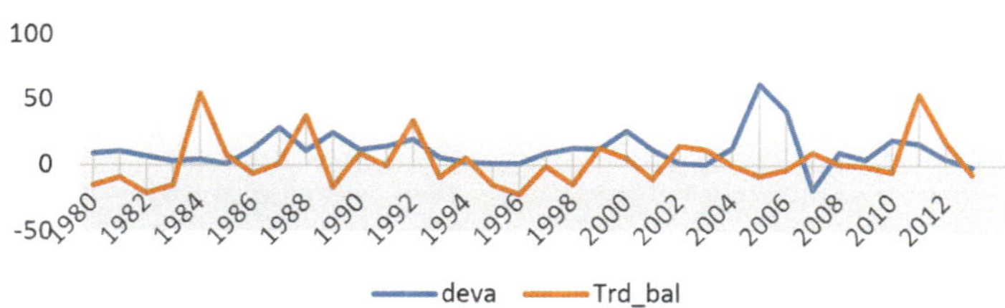

Fig. 6 Trend of devaluation and trade balance in Guinea (1980–2014)

review period. The volatility in trade balance, on the other hand, did not follow any defined pattern and it pervaded the entire review period. In terms of comovements, there was some kinds of synchronized movement between the two variables in the early part of the review period (1980–2014) while a clear divergence in trend could be seen from 1985 up to the end of the review period.

3.7 *Guinea*

The trend in devaluation and trade balance from 1980 to 2014 in Guinea is presented in Fig. 6.

The trend reveals that real exchange rate was relatively stable in Guinea for most part of the review period as there were only three major instances of devaluation. The highest episode of devaluation of about 50% occurred between 2004 and 2008 followed by a mild degree of devaluation from in the late eighties to early nineties while the last instance from 2010 to 2012. Trade balance, on the other hand, shows a very high volatile regime that persisted through the entire review period. The relatively high volatility of trade balance in Guinea is closely linked to the type of major export commodities. The three major export items are gold, crude petroleum, and iron ore in which the prices are highly vulnerable to the vagaries of global business cycles. Given the persistence of volatility in trade balance, there was no discernible co-movement between trade balance and devaluation through the entire review period. In summary, the trend analysis reveals varying degree of fluctuations in the real exchange rate for all the countries of the zone with the exception of the Gambia. This is largely a reflection of high dependence of these countries on primary commodities as export items, while the exceptional case of the Gambia could be attributed to a considerable low level of participation in international trade as re-export items accounts for a significant component of exports. Similarly, trade balance exhibited a high degree of volatility in all countries and even in countries where exchange rate was fairly stable. On the whole, the trend analysis does not show much support to co-movement between changes in the exchange rate and trade balances in all the six countries.

4 Estimation Results

In order to avoid estimating a spurious regression, we proceed by testing for the stationarity of the various variables. The details of the unit root test for all the countries are provided in Appendix while the summary is presented in Table 1.

The unit root test, based on both Augmented Dickey Fuller and Phillip Perron tests, shows that none of the variables is stationary at the level in all the six WAMZ countries. The variables, however, are stationary at the first difference, confirming that they are integrated of order one. Since the variables are not stationary at the level, we test for the existence of long run relationship among the variables by employing Johansen cointegration test. In view of the fact that the underlying VAR for the Johansen Cointegration test is very sensitive to lag length, the optimum lag length was selected based on Akaike Information Criterion (AIC) and Schwarz Criterion (SC). The result is presented in Table 2.

The optimum lag length revolves around the first and second lags among the various countries. The Schwarz criterion indicates an optimum lag length of one in all the countries while the AIC suggests a lag length of two in Nigeria and Liberia and lag length of one in the remaining four countries. On the basis of appropriate lag length for each country, the study employs Wald exogenous test to determine if exchange rate granger causes trade balance. The result of the test is shown in Table 3.

Table 1 Results of unit root test

	S/Leone		Guinea		The Gambia		Liberia		Ghana		Nigeria	
	ADF	PP	ADF	PP	ADF	PP	ADF	PP	ADF	PP	ADF	PP
limexpt	I(1)	I(1)	I(1)	I(1)	I(1)	I(1)	I(1)	I(1)	I(1)	I(1)	I(1)	I(1)
lreer	I(1)	(1)	I(1)	(1)	I(1)	(1)	I(1)	(1)	I(1)	(1)	I(1)	(1)
lrdy	(1)	(1)	(1)	(1)	(1)	(1)	(1)	(1)	(1)	(1)	(1)	(1)
lrfy	(1)	(1)	(1)	(1)	(1)	(1)	(1)	(1)	(1)	(1)	(1)	(1)

Table 2 Result of lag length selection criteria

	S/Leone		Guinea		The Gambia		Liberia		Ghana		Nigeria	
	AIC	SC	AIC	SC	AIC	SC	AIC	SC	AIC	SC	AIC	SC
lag1	−5.526	−4.601[a]	−6.608[a]	−5.867[a]	−6.919	−5.985[a]	−2.194	−1.454[a]	−9.099[a]	−8.174[a]	−5.474	−4.549[a]
Lag2	−4.994	−3.329	−6.276	−4.798	−6.774	−5.093	−2.479[a]	−0.998	−8.783	−7.117	−5.700[a]	−4.034
Lag3	−4.988	−2.583	−5.786	−3.566	−6.875	−4.448	−2.150	0.070	−8.513	−6.107	−5.448	−3.043
Lag4	−5.947[a]	−2.801	−5.573	−2.612	−7.050[a]	−3.874	−1.890	1.070	−8.565	−5.419	−5.460	−2.316

[a]Optimum lag

Table 3 VEC granger causality/block exogeneity wald tests

Dependent variable: trade balance	S/Leone (Prob.)	Guinea (Prob.)	The Gambia (Prob.)	Liberia (Prob.)	Ghana (Prob.)	Nigeria (Prob.)
lreer	0.483	0.042*	0.375	0.153	0.216	0.699
ldgdp	0.129	0.026*	0.291	0.803	0.730	0.114
lfgdp	0.131	0.518	0.219	0.304	0.231	0.004**
Joint	0.377	0.130	0.468	0.427	0.325	0.008**

*, ** Significant at 5% and 1%, respectively

The granger causality test as reported in Table 3 shows that real effective exchange rate, without the influence of other variables, is not significant in granger causing trade balance in all the countries except in Guinea. Similarly, the block Exogeneity Wald test shows that the joint influence of real effective exchange rate and other variables is not significant in granger causing trade balance except in Nigeria. This implies that there is virtually little evidence to support the thesis that devaluation precedes improvement in trade balance either through its own influence alone or in combination with other variables.

The Johansen cointegration test was conducted based on a lag corresponding to the optimum length for each country. The result of the cointegtrating test is presented in Table 4.

The trace test statistics from Table 4 shows that the number of cointegtrating relations vary across the countries of the zone. It shows that there are two cointegtrating relations in the Gambia, Guinea and Liberia while there is only one cointegtrating relation in the remaining three countries. The maximum Eigen value statistics, on the other hand, indicates that there is no cointegtrating relation in the Gambia while it suggests one cointegtrating relation for the remaining five countries of the zone. Based on the result of trace statistics for Guinea as well as the results of the two statistics for the remaining five countries, we reject the null hypothesis of no cointegration among the variables which implies that the variables have a long run relationship though they are not stationary at the level. Consequently, we employ the cointegtrating equation to identify the long-run coefficients by normalizing on trade balance. The result of the normalized long run cointegration test is presented in Table 5.

The long run determinants of trade balance show a fair degree of variation among the WAMZ countries as reflected in the behavior of the variables. The key variable of interest, the real effective exchange rate (lreer), is not significant in four countries namely Sierra Leone, Nigeria, Guinea, and Ghana. Real effective exchange rate is significant in the remaining two countries though the coefficient is positive in only one of the countries, namely, Liberia with the elasticity indicating that a devaluation of Liberian dollar by 1% would improve trade balance by 0.21%. The coefficient of the real effective exchange rate is negative in the Gambia with elasticity suggesting that a devaluation of the Gambian Dalasi by 1% would worsen trade balance by 6.88%. One major inference from the results, therefore, is that devaluation of currencies in the WAMZ countries may not improve their trade balances in the

Table 4 Johansen cointegration test

		S/Leone		Guinea		The Gambia		Liberia		Ghana		Nigeria	
H0	Ha	Trace (Prob.)	M-Eigen (Prob.)	Trace (Prob.)	M-Eigen (Prob.)	Trace (Prob.)	M-Eigen (Prob.)	Trace (Prob.)	M-Eigen (Prob.)	Trace (Prob.)	M-Eigen (Prob.)	Trace (Prob.)	M-Eigen (Prob.)
r = 0	r = 1	0.001*	0.001*	0.013	0.250	0.000	0.009*	0.006	0.091*	0.003*	0.007*	0.043*	0.470
r = 1	r = 2	0.227	0.395	0.020**	0.113	0.017*	0.071	0.032*	0.163	0.149	0.267	0.180	0.408
r = 2	r = 3	0.320	0.497	0.058	0.074	0.93	0.308	0.064	0.124	0.253	0.273	0.231	0.176

*Significant at 5%
**Significant at 1%

Table 5 Results of long-run (normalized cointegtrating coefficients)

	S/Leone		Liberia		Nigeria		Guinea		The Gambia		Ghana	
	Coef.	t-stat.	Coef.	t-stat.	Coef.	t-stat.	Coef.	t-stat.	Coef.	t-stat.	Coef.	t-stat.
C	373.14	–	1.64	–	–	–	72.96	–	127.49		111.83	–
T	–	–	0.01	0.22	–	–	–	–	−0.95	−3.85**	–	–
lreer	0.59	0.29	0.21	2.65**	−0.05	−0.56	−2.57	−0.75	−6.88	−4.37**	0.05	1.06
lrdy	−13.82	−2.98**	0.03	0.27	−0.25	−6.56	3.14	0.95	3.75	4.77**	−0.79	−6.32**
lnrfy	11.34	1.33	0.19	0.13	0.42	8.39**	0.27	0.08	3.42	0.70	4.47	6.20**

**Significant at 1%

long run, except probably in Liberia. This results tilt towards the findings of many authors on emerging economies notably that of Agbola (2004). The underlying reason may vary from one country to another but the common ones include the fact that the structure of exports tilt heavily in favor of primary commodities in these economies as explained by Ayen (2014).

A major characteristic of primary product is that the producers do not have much influence in determining the international price given that the price is determined in a currency outside the control of the exporting country. Invariably, devaluation of the home currency does not in any way exert influence on the international price and as such does not provide incentives to trade more of such commodity to the extent of having a salutary impact on the balance of trade. In Nigeria, for instance, export of crude oil accounts for about 95% of total exports but the price and production quota are determined outside the country and as such devaluation of the Naira cannot have any impact on the real value of export revenue. On the other hand, import items in these countries are basic essentials which in most cases are used for further production within the economies. In essence, devaluation does not necessarily reduce the volume of import items except the country is in recession. The exceptional case of Liberia could be partly explained by the fact that the country is highly dollarized to the extent that devaluation could in practical sense be construed as loss of value of the US dollar.

The performance of domestic income, one of the control variables, also reveals contrasting behavior across the countries. Domestic income is negative and significant in three countries namely Sierra Leone, Nigeria, and Ghana while it is significantly positive in only the Gambia. The coefficient is, however, not significant in the remaining countries namely, Liberia and the Guinea. Nigeria and Ghana, indicating that improvement in domestic income does not translate to improvement in trade balance in most of the WAMZ countries. The result reflects the structure of these economies in which tradable goods constitute a small component of gross domestic product domestic product while the countries simultaneously have high preference for foreign consumption. In Ghana for instance, export to GDP ratio was about 34% in 2014 while import to GDP ratio was about 38% in the same period. Thus, improvement in domestic income normally skew in favor of import and ultimately weaken trade balance. Foreign income, on the other hand, shows a fairly uniform result across the zone given that the coefficient is positive in all the countries. The coefficient is however significant in only Nigeria and Ghana with the elasticity is indicating that an increase in foreign income by 1% would improve trade balance by 0.42% and 4.47%, in Nigeria and Ghana, respectively.

The result of the short run determinants of trade balance is presented in Table 6.

The behavior of real exchange rate in the short run model shows some level of similarity with the long run model. The coefficient of real exchange rate is not significant in three countries namely Sierra Leone, Liberia, and Ghana while it is significant in the remaining three countries albeit with different signs. In tandem with the result of the long run model of the Gambia, the coefficient of real effective exchange rate is negative and significant at 5% while for Nigeria and Guinea, the coefficient is positively significant in the short run model in contrast to

Table 6 Results of the short run dynamics of trade balance in the WAMZ countries

	S/Leone		Liberia		Nigeria		Guinea		The Gambia		Ghana	
	Coef.	T-Sta.	Coef.	T-Sta.	Coef.	T-Sta.	Coef.	T-Sta.	Coef.	T-Sta.	Coef.	T-Sta.
C	0.55	1.26	1.63		–	–	−0.07	−0.34	−0.18	−0.81	0.17	1.53
T			0.01	0.21			–	–	–	–	–	–
D(limexpt(−1))	0.11	0.53	−0.18	−0.98	−0.65	−3.45**	−0.37	−1.83	−0.45	−2.89	0.18	0.88
D(limexpt(−1))	0.02	0.13	–	–	−0.23	−1.14	−0.19	−1.02	−0.15	−0.97	–	–
D(lrdy(−1))	−0.35	−0.51	0.06	0.25	−0.43	−1.35	−1.37	−2.65**	−1.39	−2.80**	−0.10	−0.34
D(lrdy(−2))	–	–	–	–	−0.06	0.22	0.04	0.07				
D(lreer(−1))	−0.32	−0.58	−0.14	−1.42	0.32	2.16**	1.26	2.49**	−1.73	−1.69*	−0.11	−1.23
D(lreer(−2))	−0.19	−0.33	–	–	−0.09	−0.59	−0.11	−0.19	−0.61	−0.91	–	–
D(lrfy(−1))	2.69	0.57	−2.67	−1.02	−5.66	−1.97**	−0.35	−0.15	9.72	2.61**	−2.78	−1.19
D(lrfy(−2))	−9.51	−2.14**	–	–	−0.39	−0.13	2.23	1.15	0.83	0.25	–	–
Vecm(−1)	−0.06	−1.57*	−0.67	−2.96**	−0.33	−1.58*	−0.04	−2.28**	−0.27	−4.35**	−0.78	−3.39**
Adj.R^2	0.23		0.33		0.32		0.26		0.44		0.25	

**, *, Significant at 1% and 5%, respectively

non-significance in the long run model. The results suggest that devaluation of real effective exchange rate may likely worsen trade balance in both the short and the long run in the Gambia while it could have a salutary impact, albeit in the short run, in both Nigeria and Guinea. The underlying reason in both Guinea and Nigeria could be mainly attributed to the nature of production system in developing countries.

The production system particularly the manufacturing sector depends heavily on imported intermediate materials, thus the demand for these imported items is highly price inelastic. Devaluation could initially spur a reduction in all kinds of imported items including the intermediate raw materials thus, promotes a favorable balance of trade. Such scale back in the level of import may however be short-lived as the compelling need to avert recession would lead to restoration of import to the initial level, and perhaps at a higher cost. This was exactly the phenomenon at work in Nigeria in the mid to late eighties when the Structural Adjustment Programme (SAP) was introduced. The initial high cost of imported raw materials forced most industries particularly those in the agro-allied sector which used wheat and malt barley as raw materials to reduce their level of imports. The ensuing slowdown in economic activities and slide to recession eventually forced these companies to resume importation of those items.

The impact of the lag level of trade balance is not significant in any of the countries except in Nigeria where the first lag is negative and significant at 1% level. Domestic income (lrdy) is significant and negative in only two countries namely the Gambia and Guinea while it is not significant in the remaining four countries. The results tend to suggest that improvement in domestic income tends to increase the level of imports than exports in the short run in these two countries. As in domestic income, the influence of foreign income on trade balance is also limited in the short run. The coefficient is not significant in three of the countries namely Liberia, Guinea, and Ghana while it is significant but with different signs in Sierra Leone, Nigeria, and the Gambia. The coefficient is negatively significant in both Sierra Leone and Nigeria, suggesting that improvement in foreign income could worsen trade balance in the short run. The result, however, appears as a puzzle but the fact that it is not significant in the long run model lends credence to the fact that positive net trade balance the WAMZ countries depends more favorable external conditions. The vector error correction coefficient is negative and significant in all the countries. The coefficient is however, relatively small across these countries except in Ghana and Liberia, suggesting that the process of correcting a shock to external trade is very slow in the WAMZ countries except in Ghana and Liberia. The impulse response function for the various WAMZ countries is presented in Fig. 7.

The impulse response shows that trade balance slows down as a result of a unit shock to real effective exchange rate in all the countries except in Liberia. The extent of the slowdown however, varies across the countries, being extremely sharp in Nigeria and the Gambia while it is relatively mild in Ghana, Guinea, and Sierra Leone. Besides, the slowdown does not show sign of reversal during the review period except in Sierra Leone and Guinea where the impact of the shock eventually wanes. Although the impact of the shock eventually dies out in these two countries the trend does not show significant improvement in trade balance after reversion to

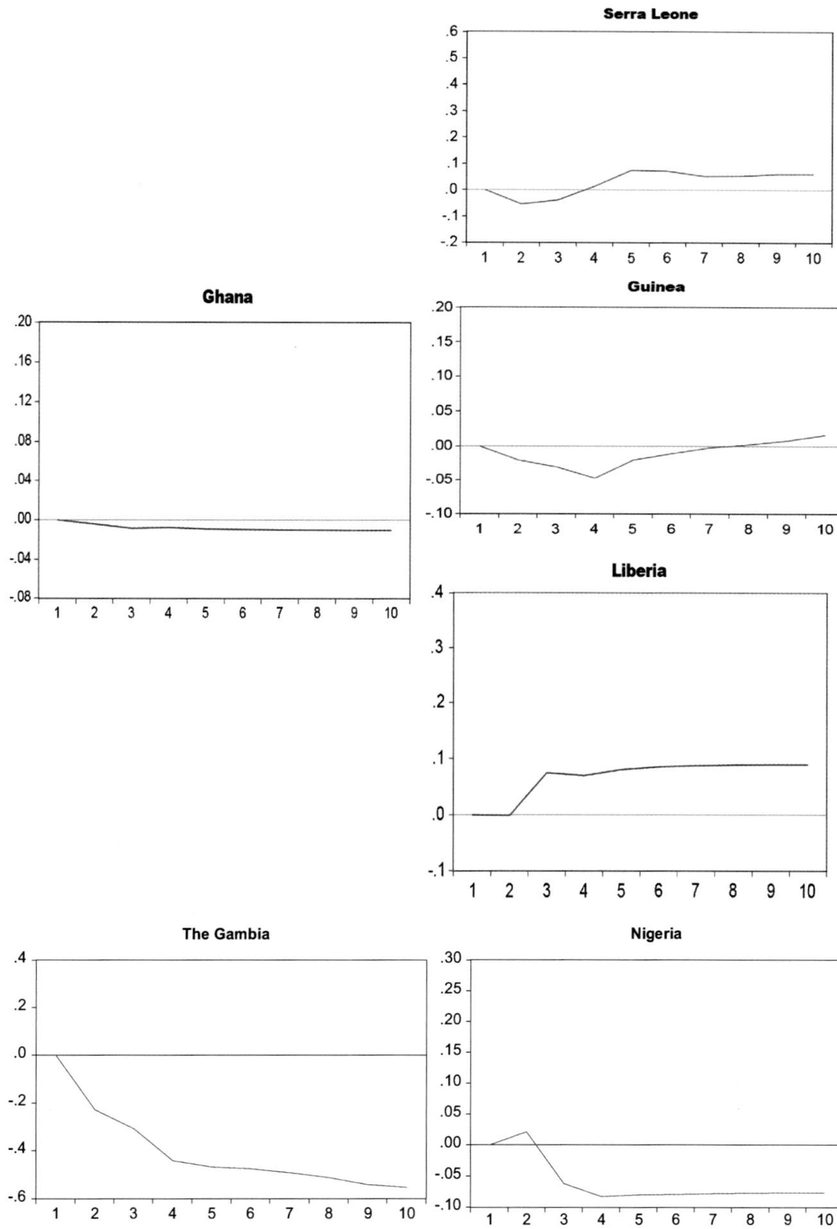

Fig. 7 Impulse response function

the initial equilibrium as suggested by the J-curve thesis. The response in Liberia shows that trade balances experiences an upward trend following a unit shock to the real effective exchange rate. Contrary to the J-curve thesis, however, trade balance does not show an initial decline before commencing the upward trend. In all, the impulse response function shows that devaluation of real exchange rate does not translate to improvement in trade balance in the WAMZ countries except in Liberia and more fundamentally, the J-curve thesis does not hold in any of the countries.

5 Summary and Recommendations

The study examines the impact of exchange rate devaluation on trade balance in the six WAMZ countries, using data that from 1980 to 2014. Both descriptive and vector error correction model are employed. Preliminary trend analysis shows considerable swings in real effective exchange rate in all the countries during the review period with the fluctuations showing more of devaluation than revaluation. The trend in trade balance is equally highly volatile with preponderance of negative trade balances in virtually all the countries. The trend analysis largely reveals an absence of co-movement in real exchange rate and trade balances in all the countries.

The unit root test confirms that the series are integrated of order one while result of the granger causality test does not support the thesis that devaluation precedes improvement in trade balance. The Juselius cointegrating result suggests the existence of long run relationship among the variables although the number of cointegrating equations vary for each country.

The long run normalized result on trade balance shows that exchange rate is positively significant in only one country, Liberia, while it is negatively significant in another one country, the Gambia. Exchange rate is not significant in the remaining four countries, therefore, pointing to the fact that devaluation of exchange rate does not improve trade balance in the WAMZ countries with the probable exception of Liberia. The likely reason for the deviation in Liberia may be due to the fact that the country is highly dollarized such that devaluation is more of loss of value in the US dollar. This is not easily applicable to other countries in which the local currencies do not have strong fixed rate to the dollar. More fundamentally, the export commodities in these countries are denominated in foreign currencies such that devaluation of domestic currencies does not have any impact on the foreign price. The result further indicates that improvement in domestic income does not really translate to improved trade balance in the WAMZ countries, reflecting the fact that structure of GDP in these countries skews largely in favor of non-tradable. One variable that appears to show a consistent behavior across the zone is foreign income with results indicating that it could positively influence trade balance in the WAMZ countries although the effect is not significant in some countries.

In the short run, devaluation could positively influence trade balance in Nigeria and Guinea but it worsens trade balance in the Gambia while the effect is not significant in the remaining countries. The two control variables are generally not significant in most of the countries, indicating that trade balance in the WAMZ countries respond to macroeconomic variables mostly in the long run. The error correction term is negative and significant in all models but relatively small in magnitude except in Ghana, suggesting slow adjustment process to external shocks. The impulse response reveals that shocks to exchange rate causes a downward movement in trade balances in almost all the WAMZ countries with the probable exception of Liberia. Though the exchange rate induced downward movement reverts to the initial steady state in two countries, Sierra Leone and Guinea, the trend does not show significant upward trend thereafter, suggesting that the J-curve thesis does not hold in the WAMZ countries.

Based on the results from both the trend and econometric model, we are of the view that devaluation of domestic currency may not be the appropriate tool for improving trade balance in these countries given the poor performance of real exchange rate in both the short and long run models. Trade balance appears to depend more on global economic condition than domestic conditions in these economies. We are also inclined to recommend that these countries should endeavor to build shock mitigating mechanisms for trade balances as the impact of shocks does not die out quickly.

In conclusion, the WAMZ economies should endeavor as much as possible to improve the export content of Gross Domestic Product in order allow local economic condition drive trade balance. Reliance on global economic condition is a clear signal that the zone's export commodities are not final goods but such commodities are used for further production in the importing countries. It is therefore expedient for countries in the WAMZ to explore the possibilities of adding value to their export commodities.

Appendix: Results of Unit Root Test

		Augmented Dickey Fuller (ADF)		Phillip Perron (PP)		
		Level	1st difference	Level	1st difference	Remarks
Sierra Leone	limexpt lreer ldgdp lfgdp	0.607	0.000**	0.428	0.002**	I(1)
		0.536	0.001**	0.501	0.001**	I(1)
		0.061	0.047*	0.208	0.051	I(1)
		0.068	0.002**	0.000**	0.003**	I(1)
Guinea	limexpt lreer ldgdp lfgdp	0.184	0.000**	0.181	0.000**	I(1)
		0.886	0.000**	0.886	0.000**	I(1)
		0.872	0.000**	0.872	0.000**	I(1)
		0.930	0.000**	0.937	0.000**	I(1)
The Gambia	limexpt lreer ldgdp lfgdp	0.590	0.000**	0.539	0.001**	I(1)
		0.911	0.000**	0.916	0.000**	I(1)
		0.296	0.000**	0.276	0.003**	I(1)
		0.069	0.004**	0.000**	0.003**	I(1)

(continued)

		Augmented Dickey Fuller (ADF)		Phillip Perron (PP)		
		Level	1st difference	Level	1st difference	Remarks
Nigeria	limexpt lreer ldgdp lfgdp	0.957	0.000**	0.951	0.000**	I(1)
		0.327	0.001**	0.265	0.000**	I(1)
		0.959	0.000**	0.959	0.001**	I(1)
		0.068	0.002**	0.000**	0.000**	I(1)
Liberia	limexpt lreer ldgdp lfgdp	0.632	0.000**	0.363	0.000**	I(1)
		0.822	0.000**	0.822	0.000**	I(1)
		0.608	0.035*	0.722	0.035*	I(1)
		0.068	0.002**	0.000**	0.002**	I(1)
Ghana	limexpt lreer ldgdp lfgdp	0.0538	0.000**	0.086	0.000**	I(1)
		0.512	0.000**	0.606	0.000**	I(1)
		0.098	0.000**	0.025*	0.000**	I(1)
		0.068	0.029*	0.000**	0.002**	I(1)

*, **, Significant at 5% and 1%, respectively

References

Acharya, S. (2010). Potential impacts of the devaluation of Nepalese currency: A general equilibrium approach. *Journal of Economic Literature, 34*(4), 413–436.

Agbola, F. (2004). Does devaluation improve trade balance of Ghana. In *International conference on Ghana's economy at the half century* (pp. 18–20)

Alejandro, C. F. D. (1963). A note on the impact of devaluation and the redistributive effect. *Journal of Political Economy, 71*(6), 577–580.

Alexander, S. S. (1952). Effects of devaluation on the trade balance. *International Monetary Fund Staff Papers, 2*(April), 263–278. (Reprinted in Caves, Richard and Johnson, Harry G., eds. (1968). *Readings in international economics*. Homewood, Ill.: Irwin).

Auer, R., & Chaney, T. (2009). Exchange rate pass-through in a competitive model of pricing-to-market. *Journal of Money, Credit and Banking, 41*(S1), 151–175.

Ayen, Y. (2014). The effect of currency devaluation on output: The case of Ethiopian economy. *Journal of Economics and International Finance, 6*(5), 103–111.

Bahmani-Oskooee, M. (1998). Are devaluations contractionary in LDCs. *Journal of Economic Development, 23*, 131–144.

Bahmani-Oskooee, M., & Rhee, H.-J. (1997). Response of domestic production to depreciation in Korea: An application of Johansen's cointegration methodology. *International Economic Journal, 11*, 103–112.

Berman, N., & Berthou, A. (2009). Financial market imperfections and the impact of exchange rate movements of exports. *Review of International Economics, 17*(1), 103–120.

Bickerdike, C. F. (1920). The instability of foreign exchange. *The Economic Journal, 30*(117), 118–122.

Cooper, N. C. (1971). *Currency devaluation in developing countries*. Essays in International Finance. No. 86. Princeton, N.J.: International Finance Section, Princeton University.

Frankel, J., Parsley, D., & Wei, S.-J. (2005). *Slow pass-through around the world: A new import for developing countries?* NBER working paper no. 11199. Cambridge, MA: NBER.

Galebotswe, O., & Andrias, T. (2011). Are devaluations contractionary in small import-dependent economies? Evidence from Botswana. *Botswana Journal of Economics, 8*(12), 86–98.

Genye, T. (2011). *Currency devaluation and economic growth the case of Ethiopia*. Stockholm: Stockholms Universitet.

Grigoryan, G. (2015). The J curve effect on the trade balance in Armenia. *International Journal of Economics, Finance and Management, 3*(3), 270–278.

Hahn, F. (1959). The balance of payments in a monetary economy. *Review of Economic Studies, 26*(70), 149–158.

Harberger, A. C. (1950). Currency depreciation, income and the balance of trade. *Journal of Political Economy, Lviii*, 47–60.

Hendry, D. F., & Juselius, K. (2000). Explaining cointegration analysis: Part 1. *Energy Journal, 21*, 1–42.

Hsing, Y. (2003). Impacts of the exchange rate and interest rate policies on output in South Korea: A VAR model. *International Review of Economics and Business, 50*, 279–288.

Junz, H., & Rhomberg, R. R. (1973). Price competitiveness in export trade among industrial countries. *American Economic Review, Papers and Proceedings, 63*, 412–418.

Kaiser, E., & Wroughton, L. (2010). *Global currency war: Currency war fears tinge IMF meetings*. Reuters. Accessed September 25, 2013, from http://bit.ly/o725t8

Kalyoncu, H., Artan, S., Tezekici, S., & Ozturk, I. (2008). Currency devaluation and output growth: An empirical evidence from OECD countries. *International Research Journal of Finance and Economics, 14*, 232–238.

Kamin, S. B., & Klau, M. (1998). *Some multi-country evidence on the effects of real exchange rates on output*. International Finance Discussion Papers, No. 611.

Keesing, D. B. (1967). Outward-looking policies and economic development. *The Economic Journal, 77*(306), 303–320.

Krueger, A. O. (1978). *Liberalization attempts and consequences*. Cambridge, MA: National Bureau of Economic Research.

Krueger, A. O. (1983). *Trade and employment in developing Countrie, 3: Synthesis and conclusions*. Chicago, IL: University of Chicago Press.

Krugman, P., & Taylor, L. (1978). Contractionary effects of devaluation. *Journal of International Economics, 8*, 445–456.

Lerner, A. P. (1944). *The economics of control: Principles of welfare economics*. London: Macmillan.

Magee, S. P. (1973). Currency, pass-through and devaluation. *Brookings Papers on Economic Activity, 4*(1), 303–325.

Marshall, A. (1923). *Money credit and commerce*. London: Macmillian.

Meade, J. E. (1951). *The balance of payments*. Oxford: Oxford University Press.

Meade, J. E. (1988, October). Exchange rates, adjustment and the J-Curve. *Federal Reserve Bulletin, 74*, 633–644.

Metiza, I. (2006). Devaluation and output in five transition economies: A panel cointegration approach of Poland, Hungary, Czech Republic, Slovakia and Romania, 1993–2000. *Applied Econometrics and International Development, 6*(1), 77–86.

Metzler, L. A. (1948). *Three lags in the circular flow of income. Income, employment, and public policy: Essays in honor of Alvin H Hansen* (pp. 11–32). New York: W.W. Norton Company Inc.

Musila, J. W., & Newark, J. (2003). Does currency devauation improve the trade balance in the long run? Evidence from Malawi. *African Development Review, 15*(2–3), 339–352.

Mussa, M., & Rosen, S. (1978). Monopoly and product quality. *Journal of Economic Theory, 18*(2), 301–317.

Nicola, K. R., Saville, A., & Mbululu, D. (2014). *Exchange rate policy and export performance in efficiency driven economies*. Economic Research Southern Africa.

Nunnenkamp, P., & Schweickert, R. (1990). Adjustment policies and economic growth in developing countries – Is devaluation contractionary? *Weltwirtschaftliches Archive, 126*, 474–493.

Onafowora, O. (2003). Exchange rate and trade balance in East Asia: Is there a J-Curve. *Economic Bulletin, 5*(18), 1–13.

Polak, J. (1957). An international economic system. *South African Journal of Economics, 25*(4), 309–309.

Porter, M. E. (1998, November–December). Clusters and the new economics of competition. *Harvard Business Review, 76*(6), 77–90.

Prebisch, R. (1950). *The economic development of Latin America and its principal problems*. New York: United Nations Department of Economic Affairs, Economic Commission for Latin America (ECLA). http://archivo.cepal.org/pdfs/cdPrebisch/002.pdf

Prebisch, R. (1964). *Nueva politica comercial para el desarrollo*. Mexico City: Fondo de Cultura Económica.

Rawlins, G., & Pravern, J. (1993). *Devaluation and trade balance: The recent experiences of selected African countries*. Montclair, NJ: Centre for Economic Research on Africa, School of Business, Montclair State University.

Raza, A., Larik, A., & Tariq, M. (2013). Effects of currency depreciation on trade balances of developing economies: A comprehensive study on south Asian countries. *IOSR Journal of Humanities and Social Science (IOSR-JHSS), 14*(6), 101–106.

Robinson, J. (1947). The foreign exchanges. In *Essays in the theory of employment*. Oxford: Blackwell.

Robinson, J. (1950). The foreign exchanges. Reprinted in Ellis and Metzler, eds (pp. 83–103).

Rose, A. K., & Yellen, J. L. (1989). Is there a J-curve? *Journal of Monetary Economics, 24*(1), 53–68.

Sims, C. (1980). Macroeconomics and reality. *Econometrica, 48*, 1–48.

Upadhyaya, K., & Dhakal, D. (1997). Devaluation and the trade balance: Estimating the long run effect. *Applied Economics Letters, 4*(6), 343–345.

Whitman, M. V. (1975). Global monetarism and the monetary approach to the balance of payments, brookings. *Papers on Economic Activity, 3*, 491–536.

Williamson, J. (1983). *The exchange rate system*. Cambridge, MA: MIT Press for the Institute of International Economics.

The ECOWAS–EU Economic Partnership Agreement: Towards Inclusive Development?

Theophilus Acheampong and Ernest Amoabeng Ortsin

Contents

Abstract The Economic Partnership Agreement (EPA) continues to court controversy. Many ECOWAS countries together with other civil society organizations have expressed concern over the agreement and continue to campaign against it on grounds of possible damage to West Africa's fragile economies from opening

---

T. Acheampong
Department of Economics, Aberdeen Centre for Research in Energy Economics and Finance (ACREEF), University of Aberdeen, Aberdeen, UK
e-mail: theo.acheampong@abdn.ac.uk

E. A. Ortsin (✉)
Legon Centre for International Affairs and Diplomacy (LECIAD), University of Ghana, Accra, Ghana
e-mail: eaortsin@st.ug.edu.gh

D. Seck (ed.), *The External Sector of Africa's Economy*, Advances in African Economic, Social and Political Development,
https://doi.org/10.1007/978-3-319-97913-7_10

their markets to free trade with the European Union (EU). This notwithstanding, the objectives of the EPA highlight fundamental agreement between both EU and ECOWAS countries about the instrumental role that the agreement could play in pursuing sustainable development goals by recognizing the importance of implementing competitiveness, poverty alleviation strategies, ensuring EU assistance for structural transformation and embracing the principles of asymmetrical liberalization. The literature provides evidence to the fact that not every developing country integrating into the global economy may be considered positive because trade liberalization on its own cannot ensure the attainment of development objectives from an economic, social and environmental perspective.

This paper analyses the ECOWAS-EU EPA agreement attempting to answer the question: how does the agreement foster both international trade and inclusive development by promoting investment and sustainable growth? Using evidence from countries in the ECOWAS sub-region, this discussion paper covers the following thematic areas: (1) external sector development impact of the EPA agreement and (2) the impact on fostering inclusive growth and development. Our analyses indicate that the EPAs will pose a number of policy challenges for West African countries as their economies increasingly morph into the global economy. However, the EPA provides an opportunity to fast-track global trade and the regional integration agenda in West Africa. It is important that the EU treats the EPA as an instrument of development cooperation and not a conduit to pursue mercantilist corporate interests as did happen in colonial times. We also find out that balanced growth and poverty reduction are not automatic outcomes from liberalization processes, but rather these objectives must be actively promoted by complementary policies in conjunction with appropriate fiscal adjustments in order to fully gain from trade liberalization.

1 Introduction and Background

International trade has played an essential part in the unprecedented growth and subsequent globalization that the world has witnessed over the past three decades evidenced by the increased flow of goods, services, capital and information between countries. This has been driven by technological revolutions and interconnections as well as the application of liberal economic policies such as deregulation and the lowering of restrictions on international trade, foreign investment and financial transactions (ECLAC 2014). Many ECOWAS countries have experienced remarkable growth over the past decade as they, together with their other sub-Saharan African (SSA) cousins, become ever more integrated into the global economy. Economic growth in West Africa[1] averaged 4.8% from 2007 to 2014 buoyed by

[1]West Africa is defined to include the 15 member states of the Economic Community of West African States (ECOWAS). See: http://www.ecowas.int/member-states/

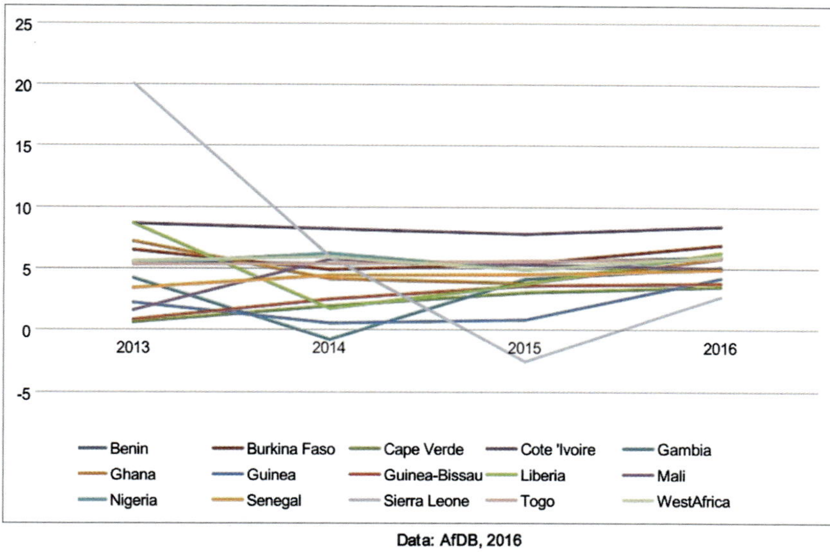

Fig. 1 Real GDP growth rates, 2007–17

the strong demand for primary commodities. Since 2014, West Africa has managed to maintain a 6% growth, which is more than two points above the continental average (AfdB 2015) (Fig. 1).[2]

This growth came under some headwinds in 2015 as commodity prices slumped on the international markets, slowing to less than 5% in 2015. It is however expected to rebound to about 6% in 2016, making West Africa the second most dynamic sub-region in SSA after East Africa.[3] For example, Benin saw 6.5% growth in 2014 compared to 5.6% in 2013; also, Nigeria had a more diversified growth of 6.3% compared with 5.4% in 2013 driven by strong growth in the non-oil sector of the economy in services, manufacturing and agriculture. Côte d'Ivoire also recorded robust growth of 8.3% of GDP in 2014, driven by domestic and external demand.[4]

Economic growth in West Africa has not been without its challenges: it has earned the "jobless growth" tag within many development circles. The paradoxical narrative is that West Africa (and indeed SSA) is rising and its economies are growing steadily, yet unemployment remains massive (Hanson and Leautier 2013; Sy 2014). Structural problems with the region's pattern of growth have seen poverty rates decline but inequality still at an all-time high. It has been argued that this growth, driven mainly by resource extraction tied to long periods of commodity booms and consumption of mostly imported goods, has not been transformative

[2]http://www.afdb.org/en/blogs/measuring-the-pulse-of-economic-transformation-in-west-africa/post/african-economicoutlook-2015-resilient-economies-positive-forecast-for-west-africa-14406/

[3]Ibid.

[4]Ibid.

from a sectoral perspective as there is hardly any shift from low to high-productivity activities (Lisk 2015).[5]

It is against the backdrop of this rising growth and integration of West African countries to the global economy that the European Union (EU) commenced an Economic Partnership Agreement (EPA) with 16 West African states via the Economic Community of West African States (ECOWAS) and the West African Economic and Monetary Union (WAEMU). Negotiations on the EPAs closed on 6 February 2014 in Brussels, Belgium, after almost 10 years of talks and ECOWAS Heads of State endorsed the EPAs in principle on 10 July 2014 (European Commission 2016a, b, c).[6] However, the main agreement is subject to ratification in all the respective West African countries for it to become fully operational. Despite agreeing to the EPA in principle, some member states, particularly Nigeria have raised concerns over technical issues on the potential negative impact of the deal on the country's industrial sector if certain products were allowed tariff-free and quota-free entry into its market.[7]

The EPA promises to be a major achievement from a trade and development point of view as it becomes the main tool through which the EU and ECOWAS countries renegotiate their trade and economic collaboration. The EPAs have an original aim of fostering free trade between the EU and six African Caribbean Pacific regions, covering goods, services and other trade-related issues, with added development support and political dialogue. The West African regional agreement covers goods and development cooperation and includes rendezvous clauses providing for further negotiations on services and rules chapters.[8]

West Africa remains the EU's largest trading partner in SSA with Ivory Coast, Ghana and Nigeria accounting for 80% of West Africa's exports to the EU.[9] West Africa's exports to the EU consist mainly of fuels and food products with EU imports consisting of fuels, food products, machinery, and chemicals and pharmaceutical products. The EU continues to be the most important trade partner for Ghana, for example, accounting for about 30% of Ghana's total external trade in 2012. Foreign Direct Investment (FDI) inflows into Ghana have also increased significantly in the past few years, with the country featuring among the top five recipients of FDI into Africa in 2012 (United Nations Conference on Trade and Development 2015).

The objectives of the EPA highlight fundamental agreement between both the EU and ECOWAS countries about the instrumental role that the Agreement should have in pursuing the sustainable development goals by recognizing the importance of implementing competitiveness, poverty alleviation strategies, ensuring EU

[5]http://www.crepol.org/acria6/boosting-investment-for-transformative-growth-and-competitiveness-in-africaneconomies-a-review-of-t

[6]http://trade.ec.europa.eu/doclib/docs/2009/september/tradoc_144912.pdf

[7]http://agritrade.cta.int/Agriculture/Topics/EPAs/West-Africa-heads-of-state-defer-final-decision-on-the-regional-EPAagreement

[8]http://trade.ec.europa.eu/doclib/docs/2009/september/tradoc_144912.pdf

[9]http://ec.europa.eu/trade/policy/countries-and-regions/regions/west-africa/index_en.htm

assistance for structural transformation and embracing the principles of asymmetrical liberalization.[10] Though the objectives of the EPA remain simple with regard to increasing productive investments and job creation as well intensifying and facilitating trade between ECOWAS countries and the EU, many people have wondered on the extent to which these objectives will result in a 'win-win' developmental relationship more especially for West Africa given the wide information and trade asymmetry as well the many institutional and supply-side constraints.

This paper makes a contribution to the literature by critically analyzing the EPA agreement and its objectives from the perspective of fostering inclusive development in West Africa—i.e. economic, social and environmental perspectives. We attempt to answer the following fundamental question: how does the EPA foster trade and development cooperation by promoting investment, sustainable growth and development? The paper examines the key issues raised in the Agreement, their relationship to the WTO trade rules as well as the domestic reforms that West African countries have to undertake to accompany liberalization of trade with the EU in both goods and services as well as the potential effects of the EPA on regional integration in West Africa.

The development literature provides evidence to the fact that not every developing country's integration into the global economy may be considered positive because trade liberalization on its own cannot ensure the attainment of development objectives from both an economic, social and environmental perspective (Edwards 1993; Frankel and Rose 2005). For example, it has been established that balanced growth and poverty reduction are not automatic outcomes from liberalization processes, but rather these objectives must be actively promoted by policies in conjunction with appropriate adjustment to the opening-up of an economy (Yusuf et al. 2013; Pacheco-López and Thirwall 2011).

Using evidence from the ECOWAS region, this paper covers the following thematic areas: (1) external sector development impact from the trade agreement; and (2) their impact on fostering inclusive growth and development. Section 2 traces the history of ECOWAS-EU trade from colonial times to the recent EPA as well as issues of disagreement between the negotiating parties. Section 3 reviews the trade and development literature with a view of identifying the channels through which trade liberalization affects growth and development. The section ends with a discussion of the relationship between economic growth and development and a summary of recent empirical evidence. In Sect. 4, we present our discussion of the EPAs and inclusive development in West Africa focussed on ECOWAS-EU trade, and the social and environmental dimensions. We finally conclude in Sect. 5 focussing on the policy challenges that the EPA brings to ECOWAS countries and also provide some policy recommendations on fast tracking global trade and the regional integration agenda.

[10]http://www.eeas.europa.eu/delegations/solomon/eu_solomon/trade_relation/epa/index_en.htm

2 West Africa-EU Trade Narrative

West African coastal ethnic groups and land-locked kingdoms further up North to the Sahel region since pre-colonial times traded raw materials mostly cocoa, timber, gold, salt, and a host of other raw and semi-processed goods in exchange for mostly finished products (Acheampong et al. 2014). Trade relations between European and West African states were developed against the backdrop of the colonial conquest starting in the fifteenth century whereby European mercantilist companies quickly developed ties with indigenous states along the coast and erected fortified "factories or warehouses, on coastal areas to store goods and defend their trading rights from foreign encroachment" (Bortolot 2003).[11]

By the turn of the twentieth century all the states in West Africa with the exception of Liberia[12] had come under European colonial control and domination. During this period raw materials exploited from West Africa were uninhibitedly exported to feed the industrializing economies of Europe. Conversely, finished products from Europe were imported into West Africa which served as a surplus market. It is the contention of some scholars that the colonial trade pattern is responsible for the perennial trade imbalances that have persisted till today between the two trading blocs (Rodney 1972).

The advent of independence in the late 1950s and early 1960s did very little to change the trade architecture between West Africa and Europe. The failure of the newly-independent states to pursue rigorous policies of industrialization meant that they had to continue to export raw materials and import finished products from Europe. Equally, the inability of the new states of West Africa to hone cutting-edge strategies to enter the international economic system meant that they had to rely upon their former European masters to hold their hands in the global trading arena. Thus, with the umbilical cord uncut the fortunes of West African States were tied to their European benefactors almost inextricably into the future.

Post-independence EU-West Africa trade relations crystallized in 1975 upon the signing of the Lomé Convention. That same year the Economic Community of West African States (ECOWAS) and the African, Caribbean and Pacific (ACP) group of countries were established. In light of the geopolitical dynamics of the 1970s, the ACP countries that signed the 25-year Lomé Conventions[13] were able to negotiate a non-reciprocal trade agreement with their European counterparts. According to Article 1 of the convention, it was negotiated taking into account the "respective levels of development" of the European Economic Community (EEC) and ACP the member states. In general, the aim of the convention was "to ensure better balance in the trade between the Contracting Parties." Article 2 made provisions for ACP

[11]http://www.metmuseum.org/toah/hd/aftr/hd_aftr.htm

[12]Liberia is the "oldest republic" in Africa. It was the only territory in West Africa that was not colonized. Its capital, Monrovia, was founded in 1822 by freed slaves resettled by the American Colonization Society.

[13]The Lomé Convention was renewed every 5 years until its expiration in 2000.

countries to export products into the EEC market "free of customs duties and charges having equivalent effect". On the flip side, article 3 enjoined the EEC member states "not to apply to imports of products originating in the ACP states any quantitative restrictions or measures having an equivalent effect." Thus, the convention created a preferential trade agreement (PTA) between the EEC and ACP countries lopsided in favour of the latter.

Upon the expiration of the Lomé Convention in 2000, the EU came under intense pressure from some developing countries, particularly in Asia and Latin America, who argued that the provisions of the Lomé conventions were discriminatory and incompatible with Article I of the GATT decision (1979) which required equity in preferential treatment for all least developed countries (LDCs), not just those belonging to the ACP and who had historical ties to European countries (Grynberg 1998). This led to the signing of the Cotonou Agreement[14] in 2000 that was intended to correct the situation. The Cotonou Agreement introduced the Economic Partnership Agreement (EPA) hinged on reciprocal trade between the EU and ECOWAS countries in alignment with World Trade Organization (WTO) rules. A transition period of 7 years (2000–2007) was specified in the Cotonou Agreement, which allowed the preferences to remain during that period. Negotiations for the EPA commenced in 2002 and it was expected to come into force in 2008. However, the negotiations were severally strained due to objections from the ECOWAS negotiators.[15] This continued until February 2014 when a full EPA was agreed upon by all the negotiating parties. It is now awaiting ratification by the respective member states (Table 1).[16]

The preamble to the EPA reaffirms that the Agreement must "be a development tool for promoting, in particular, sustainable development, increasing the production capacity and exports of the West African States and supporting the structural transformation of the West African economies and their diversification and competitiveness, leading to the development of trade, technology, the creation of jobs in the West African States and attracting investment to them".[17] The EPA is based on the principles and essential points of the Cotonou Agreement, as set out in Articles 2, 9, 19 and 35 of the said Agreement. At its core, the Agreement states that trade relations between the two regions shall be based on reciprocity taking into account the difference in levels of development.

Thus, commitments undertaken in this regard are meant to comply with Article 34 of the Cotonou Agreement, which applies special and differential treatment to the two parties. The agreement enjoins ECOWAS and the EU to ensure that they take into account the vulnerability of the economies of the West African region and that the liberalization process incorporates the principles of progressivity, flexibility and

[14]http://ec.europa.eu/europeaid/where/acp/overview/cotonou-agreement/index_en.htm

[15]The delays in the negotiating process precipitated the initialling of an interim Economic Partnership Agreement (iEPA) by Cote d'Ivoire and Ghana in December 2007.

[16]The ratification process is being delayed further as a result of some more objections from Nigeria.

[17]http://trade.ec.europa.eu/doclib/docs/2015/october/tradoc_153867.pdf

Table 1 List of EPA countries

	Central Africa	EAC	ECOWAS	ESA	SADC	CARIFORUM	Pacific
No. of EPA countries	1 out of 8	5	16	4 out of 11	6	15	2 out of 14
Degree of liberalisation	Cameroon: 80%	82.6%	75%	Madagascar: 81% Mauritius: 96% Seychelles: 98% Zimbabwe: 80%	SACU: 80% Mozambique: 81%	86.9%	Fiji: 87% PNG: 88%
Timeframe	15 years	25 years	20 years	10 years	12 years	25 years	15 years

Source: ECDPM

asymmetry in favour of the West African region. ECOWAS exports to the EU in general are governed by these arrangements:

2.1 *Generalized Scheme of Preferences*

(a) **Standard Generalized Scheme of Preferences (GSP):** This offers generous tariff reductions to developing countries. Practically, this means partial or entire removal of tariffs on 66% of all product categories.
(b) **Generalized Scheme of Preferences Plus (GSP+):** The GSP+ provides for duty-free treatment of all products falling under the normal GSP. These are granted to countries which ratify and implement international conventions relating to human and labour rights, environment and good governance.[18] However, for products on which both ad valorem and specific tariffs are applied, the ad valorem but not the specific tariffs are eliminated. The GSP+ is designed to encourage countries to meet certain human and labour rights, environment and good governance standards.
(c) **Everything But Arms (EBA) scheme:** Applicable to least developed countries (LDCs), it grants duty-free quota-free access to all products, except arms and ammunitions.[19] Benin, Burkina Faso, Gambia, Guinea, Guinea Bissau, Liberia, Niger, Senegal, Sierra Leone, Togo and Mali all fall under this scheme.[20]

2.2 *EPAs/iEPAs*

The EPA is modelled on the concept of Free Trade Area (FTA) as defined by guidelines of international trade. The underlying principle of any Free Trade Area is that of reciprocity and the lowering of all barriers to trade therefore fundamentally, trade liberalization cannot be avoided in an FTA.[21]

With the exception of the 11 LDCs from the ECOWAS region which can trade under the EBA scheme, Cote d'Ivoire, Ghana and Nigeria, due to their status as lower middle income countries and to a large extent the regional economic giants, have their trade terms covered under the GSP/GSP+ or the EPAs/iEPAs.

---

[18] Ibid.

[19] http://ec.europa.eu/trade/policy/countries-and-regions/development/generalised-scheme-of-preferences/

[20] http://trade.ec.europa.eu/doclib/docs/2014/october/tradoc_152839.pdf

[21] Ibid.

3 Literature Review

3.1 International Trade and Development

International trade and trade liberalization have been argued to stimulate economic growth, which in turn benefits the poor on average, as one of the pathways that trade liberalization impacts poverty.

The Asian development story of the 1980s to date illustrates the extent to which trade openness played a role in catalyzing their rapid industrial development (Chen 1999; Tahir and Khan 2014; Yusoff and Febrina 2012; Sinha and Sinha 2002). The importance of international trade to a nation's economic welfare and development is widely documented in the economics literature starting from Adam Smith's (1776) pioneering work on the *Wealth of Nations* and David Ricardo's *Principles of Economics* (1817).[22] This is driven by the fact that economies need to export goods and services to generate revenue to finance imported goods and services which cannot be produced indigenously. Neoclassical trade theory dictates that countries are able to gain if each devotes resources to the generation of goods and services in which they have an economic advantage (Ricardo 1817; Smith 1776). This describes the scenario where a country generates goods and services in which it has an advantage, for consumption indigenously, and subsequently exports the surplus (Morgan and Katsikeas 1997).

International trade theory, based on both the static and dynamic versions of traditional trade, suggests that openness to international trade leads to higher national incomes. According to the traditional theory of trade, liberalization of trade by lowering barriers creates welfare enhancing improvements as specialization and exchange gains manifest themselves into higher output than would have been possible under a restrictive trade regime (WTO 2002). Dynamic versions of these traditional models were later developed which suggested that over time, the productivity gains from trade tend to be higher due to acceleration in the accumulation of additional resources—higher savings made possible by higher output levels, or because of enhanced technology, forward and backward linkages in the export sector as well as efficiency gains. These models implied that countries that are more open should experience higher output growth since openness can raise the rate of accumulation of additional resources (Krugman 1986).

With regard to international development, it has been argued that international trade increases the availability and brings down the prices of better quality goods and services which hitherto were not available to the poorest population growth. The fall in prices leads to increased consumption and is one of the most direct links between the international market and the poorest population groups. Overall well-being, thus increases as many of these low-income sectors are able to obtain goods that were previously inaccessible. The channels for the transmission of trade benefits to production and social structures are many and illustrated in Fig. 2. The most

[22]http://www.st-andrews.ac.uk/business/distance/Economics/Reading/Critique_trade_theories.pdf

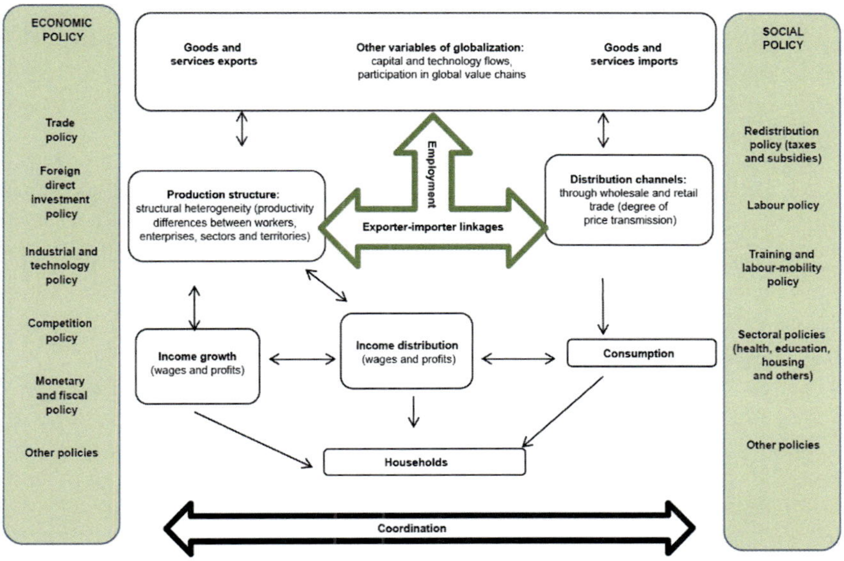

Fig. 2 Channels of transmission between trade, growth and equality. Source: Economic Commission for Latin America and the Caribbean (ECLAC) (2014)

important for the EPA regarding fostering inclusive development is the nexus that exists between trade and income growth via the production structure and distribution channels through exporter-importer and employment linkages. These are important because the EPAs, at their core, seek to increase the production and supply capacity of West African countries by promoting structural processing and economic diversification of their economies while supporting regional integration. Thus the EPAs become instruments of development and anchor for a regional integration agenda.[23]

It has been shown in the literature that the link between international trade, economic growth and development is a highly variable and complex one. It operates through changes in export, import and technology flows (ECLAC 2014). Exports do stimulate growth but for them to stimulate development, the local content levels must be high. For example, a country export model based on the processing of imported inputs delivers less value than one based on manufacturing industries with high local content.[24] With regard to imports, technology imports embodied in goods can raise competitiveness which in turn lowers unit production costs for in-country consumption as well as for exports. This so-called 'transmission mechanism of technological progress and spillovers' featured in the new growth theories of Grossman and Helpman (1991) say that access to a large variety of intermediate

[23]http://www.eeas.europa.eu/delegations/solomon/eu_solomon/trade_relation/epa/index_en.htm

[24]Local content is defined here to include the domestic sourcing of raw materials, labour and other factor inputs to the production process.

goods and new final products will affect a country's productivity growth.[25] Also, a related indirect channel of international trade is the inducement of competition among firms in exportoriented countries. These pro-competitive gains from trade might force domestic firms to innovate by encouraging specialization that would have been unprofitable in smaller markets.

The production structure in all ECOWAS countries suffers from structural heterogeneity to the extent that there are major observable differences in productivity levels between workers, enterprises, sectors and territories. Structural heterogeneity in this context is expressed by the large productivity differences between small and large enterprises operating in the same economic sector, between sectors, and between different geographical areas within a country (ECLAC 2014). This productivity gap is much lower and more perversely skewed in the micro, small and medium-scale enterprises (MSME) sector of the economy which tends to employ a greater majority of the population in these countries. Hence, the cumulative picture at the regional level is one marked by large asymmetries among segments of enterprises and workers, and the fact that the bulk of jobs are concentrated in very low productivity sectors.

This is partly responsible for some of West Africa's social inequality and the wider wage and income distribution gaps. It has been shown that greater social inequality can act as a constraint on economic growth and development (Galor 2009[26]; Ferreira 1999). Inequality has been shown to be associated with lower level of human capital formation, and lower human capital formation is associated with lower levels of economic growth; giving credence to the Galor-Zeira hypothesis (Perotti 1996; Easterly 2007). Hence, for international trade to be inclusive as medium of fostering development, it has been argued that it has to reduce structural heterogeneity and increase equity and not only facilitate economic growth in the broad sense of the word.

3.2 Empirical Evidence on Trade Liberalization and Development

There is still a lot of debate within the vast literature on the links and causality between trade openness, economic growth and income distribution. The debate on whether openness to trade (liberalization) causes higher growth is riddled with these two paradoxes: (1) mixed growth outcomes of developing countries that have undergone extensive trade liberalization; and (2) differences over data, econometric techniques, and model specifications. The latter deals with issues of measurement, reverse causality (faster-growing countries tend to open their markets more quickly),

[25]https://www.cairn.info/revue-economie-internationale-2008-4-page-5.htm

[26]http://www.oecd-ilibrary.org/social-issues-migration-health/trends-in-income-inequality-and-its-impact-on-economicgrowth_5jxrjncwxv6j-en

and omitted variable bias (countries that successfully lower tariffs also adopt other complementary policies).[27]

The empirical evidence despite criticisms and difficulties in interpreting country experiences over the past two decades generally show that in the long run more trade liberal countries register higher economic growth (Sachs and Warner 1995; Frankel and Romer 1999; Lee et al. 2004). Although trade liberalization in and of itself is not enough for economic growth, many studies show that trade reforms and trade policy are most likely to be associated with positive outcomes when it is conducted in a favourable economic environment and effective regulations. For example, a variety of factors reinforced each other for the developing countries that successfully integrated into the global economy in the 1990s. These were a stable investment climate, greater market access, complementary macroeconomic policies, and unilateral or multilateral trade reforms.[28]

3.2.1 Trade Liberalization and Economic Growth

Gries and Redlin (2012) examined the short-term and long-run dynamics between per capita GDP growth and openness for 158 countries over the period 1970–2009 using panel cointegration tests and error-correction models in combination with GMM estimation to explore the causal relationship. Their results suggest a long-run relationship of positive significant causality from openness to growth and vice versa between openness and economic growth, with a short-run adjustment to the deviation from the equilibrium for both directions of dependency.

Yanikkaya (2003) demonstrates that trade liberalization does not have a simple and straightforward relationship with growth using a large number of openness measures for a cross section of countries over three decades. The results for numerous trade intensity ratios were found to be mostly consistent with the existing literature on trade liberalization but contrary to the conventional view on the growth effects of trade barriers, the estimation results showed that trade barriers are positively and, in most specifications, significantly associated with growth, especially for developing countries and they are consistent with the findings of theoretical growth and development literature. That is, some protectionist measures may be growth enhancing in some developing countries.

Chang et al. (2009) show that the effect of trade openness on economic growth may depend on complementary reforms that help a country take advantage of international competition. They presented cross-country, panel data evidence on how the growth effect of openness may depend on a variety of structural characteristics using non-linear growth regression specifications that interacts a proxy of trade openness with proxies of educational investment, financial depth, inflation stabilization, public infrastructure, governance, labour market flexibility, ease of firm

[27]http://www1.worldbank.org/prem/lessons1990s/chaps/05-Ch05_kl.pdf

[28]Ibid.

entry, and ease of firm exit. They concluded by saying that that the growth effects of openness may be significantly improved if certain complementary reforms are undertaken.

Huchet-Bourdon et al. (2011) examined the relationship between trade openness and economic growth focussing on the openness measurement issue. They proposed a more elaborate way of measuring trade openness by taking into account two additional dimensions of countries' integration in world trade: quality and variety. Their results confirmed that countries exporting higher quality products grow more rapidly and found an interesting non-linear pattern between the trade dependency ratio and trade in quality, suggesting that trade may impact growth negatively for countries which have specialized in low-quality products. A non-linear relationship between exports variety, trade ratio and growth is also found, suggesting that countries exporting a wider range of products will grow more rapidly until a certain threshold in terms of dependency of the economy to trade.

3.2.2 Trade Liberalization and Development

The empirics of the impact of trade liberalization on poverty have largely provided a mix picture of the trade-poverty nexus. Recent studies have shown that the relationship between trade liberalization and poverty is largely case- and country-specific (Berg and Krueger 2003). Winters (2002) develops a framework for exploring the links between trade and poverty where trade liberalization reaches households via four channels: Enterprise, distribution, economic growth, government revenue. Trade liberalization has played an important role the economic development of many countries especially in South East Asian countries. Used efficiently, the imports of capital as well as technology and other factors can improve a country's development capacity. For example, imports of modern agriculture equipment and technical services can expand a country's domestic capacity to produce food that enhances the general health of the population and thus contribute to human development.

Eusufzai (1998) examined the relationship between trade openness and 21 measures of economic development using data from 88 developing countries attempting to answer the question: does trade openness result in positive economic growth at the expense of higher income inequality, a higher poverty rate, and other harmful effects on economic development measures? He showed that there is a net positive correlation between openness and measures of economic development, and also trade openness affects economic growth positively and the higher economic growth in turn leads to a higher level of economic development.

Son Le (2014) examined the impacts of trade openness and institutional reforms on rural household welfare at the provincial level through the analysis of the determinants of welfare of rural households in Vietnam using data from the Vietnam Household Living Standards Surveys (VHLSSs) of 2006 and 2010. It directly captured the institutional effect on welfare and found that in the provinces with high institutional reforms and trade openness, the welfare of rural households improved.

Mustafa et al. (2013) examined the interdependence of openness, economic growth, and human development for some Asian countries. Their results suggest that in Asia (1) openness has a strong positive impact on both economic growth and human development; (2) human capital and FDI have a strong positive effect on both economic growth and human development; (3) while human development contributes positively to growth, growth has a negative and significant influence on human development. Thus, they confirmed that the success of trade liberalization policies in the region in achieving higher growth but also suggested that this has had a negative impact on human development. They, therefore, called for distributional policies that would improve income distribution and ultimately human development.

Nourzad and Powell (2003) examined the interaction between openness, growth, and development using a panel of 47 developing countries and 5-year averages for the period, 1965–1990. Using a two-equation simultaneous-equations model of development and growth and three alternative measures of openness, suggested that openness has a positive influence on both economic growth and human development, and also economic growth makes a positive contribution to development.

3.2.3 Sector Experiences

Chandran and Munusamy (2009) investigated the long-run relationship between trade openness and manufacturing growth and further assessed the causal relationship between these variables. Their results suggest that in the long-run, trade openness has positively impacted manufacturing growth in Malaysia. They argued that openness should be viewed as the long-term policy initiative for the manufacturing sector to benefit. They called for further studies to pin down which manufacturing subsectors are affected the most by openness, and importantly, policy makers should understand that leveraging the benefits of openness also depends on whether the liberalized sector has a comparative advantage.

4 The EPAs and Inclusive Development in West Africa

4.1 EPAs and West African Trade

In terms of scope, the EPA covers trade in goods in compliance with WTO rules. West Africa is the EU's most important trade partner in the ACP region. West African countries account for 40% of all trade between the EU and the ACP region with Ivory Coast, Ghana and Nigeria accounting for 80% of West African exports to the EU—hence our choice to use these countries as case studies. All the countries in the West Africa region except for Liberia are members of the WTO. Liberia is currently going through the accession process with full support of the EU. EU exports to the Ivory Coast and Ghana are dominated by industrial goods, machinery, vehicles and transport equipment and chemicals whereas EU imports from West

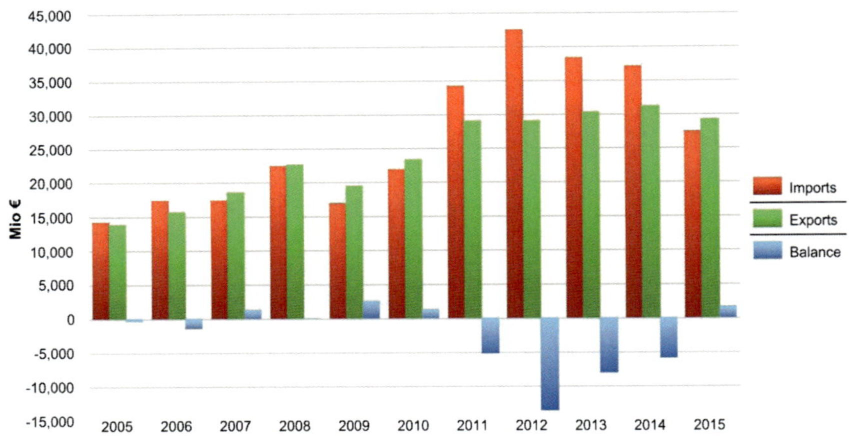

Fig. 3 EU-West Africa Trade Statistics. Source: European Commission (2016a, b, c)

African countries are dominated by a limited number of basic commodities. Nigeria is a major oil exporter, recently followed by Ghana. Ghana and Ivory Coast are the world's two largest cocoa exporters. They also export bananas and, together with Cape Verde and Senegal, processed fisheries products. Other exports from the region include a range of agricultural commodities (mango, pineapple, groundnuts, cotton, etc.) and to a far lesser extent (copper, gold) and diamonds. The balance of trade data from Fig. 3 indicates that EU imports of goods and services from the ECOWAS outstripped exports between 2011 and 2014—a net gain for ECOWAS. The trade balance was however marginally titled in favour of the EU from 2007 to 2010 and in 2015.[29]

4.1.1 Are the EPAs Anti-development?

Several arguments have been made for and against the EPA especially regarding its implications for West Africa's socioeconomic development. There have been major disagreements in the run-up to signing the EPA mainly over whether or not it would contribute to development in the West African region. The EU approach has been primarily from the philosophical perspective that far-reaching trade liberalization reforms trigger economic development. On the other hand, West African countries maintained that protectionism and aid-for-trade are still necessary to address existing supply-side constraints.[30] The arguments against the EPAs have been on the fear of West African nations losing fiscal revenues from import duties—an important source

[29]http://trade.ec.europa.eu/doclib/docs/2013/november/tradoc_151898.pdf

[30]http://www.ictsd.org/bridges-news/bridges-africa/news/the-recent-eu-west-africa-trade-deal-is-noteverybody%E2%80%99s-success

of government revenues, unfair competition from subsidized European products especially agricultural ones and crowding out of small businesses from an already weak manufacturing sector due to competition from European products. Signing the EPA has major implications for many ECOWAS economies through the channels of competition with EU imports in the domestic market, and declines in government revenue. For example, the direct financial impact of the loss of import tariff revenues to Ghana is estimated to affect the fiscal position (trade balance and budget deficit) by a cumulative US$1.13 billion between 2008 and 2022 (2.35% of 2013 GDP).

Perhaps the biggest criticism of the EPAs has been that while its goals, intermediate targets and policy instruments are broadly consistent with ECOWAS countries' economic plans, the major problem has to do with the EPA strategy (Nwoke 2009). It has been argued that the strategy of enforcing substantial trade liberalization within ECOWAS countries before adequate supply response and adjustment mechanisms have been built or sufficiently strengthened is wrongly placed.[31] Nwoke (2009) suggests that the interests of ECOWAS member countries would have been better reflected in the context of a strategy which prioritises supply response capacity building and enhanced market access ahead of import liberalisation.

4.1.2 Local Manufacturing and Local Markets Issues

It is argued that the EPA prohibit the use of import duties and export taxes as a policy tool for industrial development (Bagooro 2014). Governments usually resort to the use of tariffs or import duties as a trade policy tool to differentiate between domestic and foreign products to create an advantage for locally produced goods by increasing the cost of foreign products. The policy objective here being to protect local infant industries; however, sometimes these tariff measures do not necessarily effectively result in outcomes that meet the policy objectives due to the lack of complementary reforms to address supply-side constraints. That is, many of these industries remain uncompetitive even without the imposition of tariffs and duties.

So, under the EPA most ECOWAS countries cannot apply for example the 99% bound tariff rate on EU agricultural products.[32] Ghana, for example, cannot resort to the use of tariffs or import duties to protect local poultry farmers because no new duty can be imposed and the current rate cannot be raised under the EPA (Bagooro 2014). The use of export taxes in a similar vein cannot be employed, and this may deprive some raw material available for use by local industries which are of strategic national interest. For example, Nigeria's long-standing reservations on the EPAs stem around its implications for its domestic agricultural and industrial policy given that Nigerian government actively uses trade measures to restrict trade—i.e. an

[31]Ibid.

[32]Theoretical tariff upper band.

integral part of the national agricultural and manufacturing transformation policy agendas.

It has also been argued that the almost full liberalization of trade over a short span of 20 years will significantly affect manufacturers in the light industrial sector who produce such as goods such as aluminium, insecticides, soap and detergents, wire and metals and wood products which form the basis for heavy industrial development.[33] Industry stakeholders have voiced concerns about the impact of duty removals on imported EU goods have on local competition notwithstanding the supply side constraints. This they argue, is at variance with a regional industrial policy to the extent that prospect of losing the local market to EU imports poses a threat to industries and the very existence of an industrial sector in ECOWAS countries. This is going to be more precarious given that the intraAfrican market for manufactured products is growing at a much faster pace than exports to the EU market and thus opening up the market brings these products in direct competition with relatively cheaper imported EU products.[34]

These issues notwithstanding, we argue that the biggest threat to the industrial sector in most ECOWAS countries remains imports from China and the Far East as well as supply side and technological constraints, which need to be addressed through effective government action such as ensuring reliable energy supply, access to credit, macroeconomic stability (inflation, exchange rates, etc.) and lowering of tax bottlenecks. These policies take time to bear fruit and we are convinced that the resolution of their implementation through a well-structured industrial policy that seeks to address the major supply-side constraints hindering competitiveness with a view of improving economies of scale and scope would go a long way to make local products compete favourably with EU imports or indeed imports from any other region. EU exports to West Africa are mostly semi-finished industrial products which go into the manufacture of finished goods.

4.1.3 Some Opportunities

The issue of losses for local manufacturing and limited protection of local markets notwithstanding, the EPA, effectively implemented, presents some good opportunities for the manufacturing and agricultural value chain in West Africa. This has the potential to achieve the development objectives by improving livelihoods and thus inclusive development. The EPA has the potential to increase access to the EU market for exporters especially for burgeoning non-traditional exports (NTEs) and agro-processed goods in the select West African countries. For example, the NTEs sector in Ghana has seen phenomenal growth over the past decade with the total value of exports quadrupling from approximately US$500 million to over US$2

[33]Supra.

[34]Supra.

billion between 2001 and 2012.[35] In 2012, the sector contributed over US$2 billion to the country's GDP to improve the country's balance of trade. The non-traditional exports sector witnessed a 3.05% growth in 2013, amounting to US$2.5 billion, contributing 17.2% of total exports revenue that stood at US$14.158 billion. About 34% of the country's NTEs end up in the EU market, 10% in other developed countries, and about 32% for the Economic Community of West African States (ECOWAS) market.[36]

The growth of the NTEs sector has been mainly due to the preferential trade terms given under the Cotonou Agreement and government-donor led reform efforts such as the export development assistance development programme aimed at improving local export capacity. Therefore, it is our contention that to the extent that the EPAs facilitate more processed exports with simpler and improved 'rules of origin', then ECOWAS countries could import raw materials to make goods for onward export to the EU, particularly in key sectors that they have comparative advantage in like textiles, fisheries and agriculture. The improved 'rules of origin' have been argued to be superior to those applicable in the Cotonou Agreement and even under the Generalized Scheme of Preferences+, particularly on the degree of tolerance afforded to non-originating inputs.[37]

Exploring the opportunities in the NTEs sector holds truer for a regional giant like Nigeria, which has been majorly dependent on crude oil export proceeds to prop up its economy. The EPAs provide an alternative avenue for ECOWAS countries to aggressively improve their export performance by identifying new markets to target within the context of the respective country's export diversification policy, and to determine the products for which they have a comparative advantage in exporting and their market prospects. It has been shown that whereas developing countries in Latin America that followed import substitution industrialization (ISI) strategies experienced relatively lower growth rates, their East Asian counterparts on the other hand that employed export-promotion policies consistently outperformed other countries (ECLAC 2014).

---

[35]The NTEs sector has overtaken cocoa as Ghana's third highest export earner. The government of Ghana has an annual revenue target of US$5 billion from the export of non-traditional products within the next 5 years, under the Ghana National Strategy for the non-traditional export sector. Total earnings from Ghana's non-traditional export sector were driven by three main sub-sectors: namely agriculture, processed and semi-processed foods, and handicrafts. Cocoa paste, cashew nuts, articles of plastic and canned tuna took the top-four spot for top-10 non-traditional export items, contributing 40.35% to total non-traditional exports. Others were veneers, natural rubber sheets, animal feed, medicinal plants, aluminium plates and iron/steel products. See: http://ghanaports.gov.gh/news/1054/ghana-chalksover-usd2bn-from-non-traditional-exports

[36]http://www.myjoyonline.com/business/2014/February-12th/non-traditional-exports-ghana-faces-eu-ban.php

[37]The "GSP+" enhanced preferences mean full removal of tariffs on essentially the same product categories as those covered by the general arrangement. These are granted to countries which ratify and implement core international conventions relating to human and labour rights, environment and good governance. See: http://ec.europa.eu/trade/policy/countries-and-regions/development/generalised-scheme-of-preferences/index_en.htm

Finally, it is important to stress out that a number of agricultural and non-agricultural products, such as chicken, tomatoes, sugar, cereals and flour, frozen fish, tobacco, beer and industrial plastics, have been excluded from liberalization to protect sensitive sectors. Imported EU food items which already incur tariffs are considered sensitive products and remain on the exclusion list of the market access offer of items prevented from any tariff liberalization. Hence, ECOWAS countries can still impose already existing tariffs or even increase them for anti-dumping reasons subject to reviews with the EU. For example under the interim EPA signed with Ghana, about 1038 items were excluded from liberalization, 32.5% of which are agricultural products already covered by WTO rules. About 85% of the excluded items attract the highest tariff band of 20%, while 10% are within the 10% tariff band (ActionAid 2003).

4.2 Socio-Environmental Perspective and the EPA Development Programme

West Africa ranks as the poorest region in the world. By headcount, Niger has the highest incidence of poverty with as much as 89.3% of its population experiencing multidimensional poverty (United Nations Development Programme 2015).[38] This is followed by Burkina Faso and Sierra Leone at 84% and 81% respectively. The highest ranked country (regarding the human development index is Cape Verde with a ranking of 122 out of 188 countries. Ghana comes next with a ranking 140. All the remaining countries are found at the bottom 25% of the rankings in the low human development category. Agriculture is the mainstay of most economies in West Africa. It is estimated that as much as 60–70% of the labour force is engaged in agriculture. Paradoxically, the populations in the farming areas are among the poorest and most deprived. Recent environmental challenges occasioned by climate change have also compounded the situation for rural dwellers. Aning and Atta-Asamoah (2011) have also indicated that between 1980 and 2005 up to 3.3% of West African forests were lost. Equally, from 1990 to 2000 about 1.2% or 1.3 million hectares of forest vegetation was lost to exploitation from high dependency. For the landlocked countries in the Sahel region desertification is the major environmental challenge that confronts their existence.

With such high incidences of deprivation and inequalities, several questions have been asked as to how the EPA would engender inclusive development in West Africa. Many fear that the EPA would rather worsen an already bad situation. To this extent, we now turn our attention to discussing the development offerings of the EPA Development Programme (EPADP). The EU as part of the EPA deal is pledging

[38]The UNDP describes extreme or multi-dimensional poverty using ten indicators. Where a person falls into three of the indicators, they are said to be in multi-dimensional poverty. See Technical Note 5 at http://hdr.undp.org for more details.

financial assistance from the European Development Fund (EDF), European Investment Bank (EIB) and other sources to support the economies of ECOWAS and other ACP countries. In the period between 2010 and 2014, the EU spent in excess of 8.2 billion euros under the EPADP even before the EPA becomes fully operational. Also, for the period 2015–2016 the EU has budgeted 6.5 billion euros in development assistance to ACP countries.[39] These resources, among other things, are expected to shore up for the differences (losses) in revenue for ACP countries as they gradually eliminate tariffs on imports from the EU.

The Green Paper (1996) on relations between the EU and ACP countries notes that ACP countries (including ECOWAS) failed to take advantage of the preferential treatment offered them under the Lomé Conventions. Rather than increase their share of exports to the EU market, exports to the EU dropped drastically from 6.7% in 1976 to 2.8% in 1994. Meanwhile that of other developing countries in Asia increased from 4.2% to 15.5% within the same period. Critics of the EPA have often cited these statistics as evidence of the fact that if ECOWAS countries could not improve their trade under a non-reciprocal regime, how would they fare under a reciprocal arrangement? In view of this, the EU as part of the EPADP intends to intensify its aid for trade programme for ECOWAS countries. The aid for trade is designed to provide support for developing countries to develop and expand their trade as leverage for growth and poverty reduction. The areas categorized for assistance include: trade policy and regulation, trade and development, trade related infrastructure, building productive capacity, trade-related adjustment and other trade-related needs.

In 2012 and 2013 the EU provided 11.5 billion euros and 11.7 billion euros funding respectively to support its aid for trade programme. Africa received 55% of the 2013 funding which among other things were to correct internal constraints that confront the trade of many developing countries. These include lack of productive capacity, poor infrastructure, inefficient customs procedures, bureaucratic bottlenecks and challenges in meeting technical standards in high-value export markets. It is the argument of EPA advocates that if these supply-side constraints are constructively and comprehensively addressed, ECOWAS countries would this time around derive maximum benefit from its trade with the EU.

5 Conclusions and Policy Recommendations

In concluding, we argue that the EPAs will pose some policy challenges for West African countries as their economies increasingly morph into the global economy. However, the EPA provides an opportunity to fast track global trade and the regional integration agenda in West Africa. It is important for the EU to treat the EPAs as instruments of development cooperation and not a conduit to pursue mercantilist

[39]http://ec.europa.eu/trade/policy/countries-and-regions/development/aid-for-trade/

corporate interests as did happen in colonial times. More fundamentally, the responsibility lies on ECOWAS countries to use this opportunity to implement much-needed economic reforms particularly trade policy reforms that positively impact on regional integration. The latter is of particular importance as implementing these reforms will ensure that the benefits regarding improvements to livelihoods and inclusive development are sustained.

Non-tariff trade measures are often cited as major obstacles to regional trade within the ECOWAS region. These cover a diverse array of policies that countries apply to imported and exported goods such as sanitary and phytosanitary standards (SPS), technical barriers to trade (TBTs), price control measures, import and export licensing, inspections, as well as rules determining the origin of goods for the purposes of tariff treatment.[40] It is interesting to note that the contribution of non-tariff measures to overall trade restrictiveness is significant, and in some estimates, these measures are far more trade restrictive than tariffs account for about 30% of international trade costs.[41] ECOWAS countries need to commit more resources to infrastructural investments to address supply-side constraints as sub-optimal investment productivity will hinder the long-run growth rates necessary for sustained and transformative development. For the EPAs to benefit West African nations, it is imperative to identify and put in place measures that address internal and external structural gaps. To further this, we propose the following policy recommendations:

1. ECOWAS countries must focus on developing their industrial capacity with a renewed emphasis on innovation. There is much room for nation states to leapfrog by adopting and pursuing innovative development strategies. It is important to note that innovation does not occur automatically but countries that have been proactive in implementing a national innovation strategy have generally achieved more equitable development outcomes such as in East Asia. West African nations must adopt and drive technological changes focused on the creation and dissemination of knowledge. The integration of manufacturing industries with high local content delivers more value added and growth than an export model based on the processing of imported inputs.
2. ECOWAS countries must increase support for micro small and medium scale enterprises. This should be anchored on an export-led development strategy geared towards improving their competitiveness. It is well established within the literature that exports and imports of intermediate and capital goods tend to increase the competitiveness of enterprises and economies as a whole. Greater and better integration of West Africa's economies through the elimination of trade barriers can reduce the structural heterogeneity and this in turn will foster productivity gains. Despite advanced regional integration processes in the region, barriers to intra-regional trade remain a challenge for the economies of West

[40]http://www.afdb.org/en/news-and-events/article/itc-afdb-to-hold-roundtable-on-non-tariff-measures-affectingregional-trade-in-ecowas-15835/

[41]https://www.wto.org/english/res_e/booksp_e/anrep_e/wtr12-2d_e.pdf

Africa. Regional trade lags behind trade with developed and emerging countries outside West Africa.

3. ECOWAS countries must ensure that as part of measures to reduce the impact of the EPA on vulnerable populations, social safety nets are put in place to cushion possible hardships. More support would have to be given to rural folks engaged in agricultural production. There would be the need for pro-poor policies that are gender sensitive and also takes care of the needs of people with disability. Overall, there must be deliberate strategies geared towards achieving inclusive growth and sustainable development.

Underpinning these initiatives, we expect ECOWAS states to create the functional links that anchor these policies such as prudent macroeconomic policies of stable real exchange rates and inflation—i.e. the need for macroeconomic stability, trade-related infrastructure and institutional stability. Liberalization of trade can facilitate growth insofar as it is incrementally phased and is accompanied by complementary policies that stimulate in-country competitiveness, along with macroeconomic and institutional stability. The EPAs have the potential to contribute to the creation of quality employment and enhancing productivity levels in West Africa; thus assist in the reduction of inequality. However, these benefits are highly dependent on the quality of public policies that West African nations will pursue in the coming years. Although the form and substance of the EPAs are primarily a continuation of the Yaounde, Lome and Cotonou conventions/agreements, it has been argued that they can be instruments that foster inclusive development. Either way, ECOWAS nations have to trade with the EU and indeed America, China, etc., under some trade agreement that conforms to WTO principles but also takes into account our specific developmental needs. The duty is on governments in West Africa to ensure the safeguards such as the gradual opening of the market (full liberalisation schedule) and some of the anti-dumping measures can be policed effectively.

Finally, we are of the opinion that the transitional period of 20 years should be extended by another 10 years to a total of 30 years with a graduated liberalization approach to allow ECOWAS countries to adequately prepare to fully transition in order to reap the benefits of this trade agreement—i.e. allow enough room for the necessary fiscal and productivity adjustments to take place domestically before fully opening up to the EU. Trade agreements in and of themselves are not a problem. It is their structuring and how that addresses the asymmetrical balance of power between the negotiating parties. So, does the current EPA address that or will our reversion to other WTO trade terms make West African nations worse off? We are of the opinion that reverting to WTO trade rules without some preferential rules will make West African nations worse off. There is a need to concentrate on building inclusive value chains or inclusive business. Inclusive value chains are a set of activities that promote the involvement of SMEs or other vulnerable groups in taking a product or service from the creation and production stage to the end consumer.

Appendix: West Africa Statistics

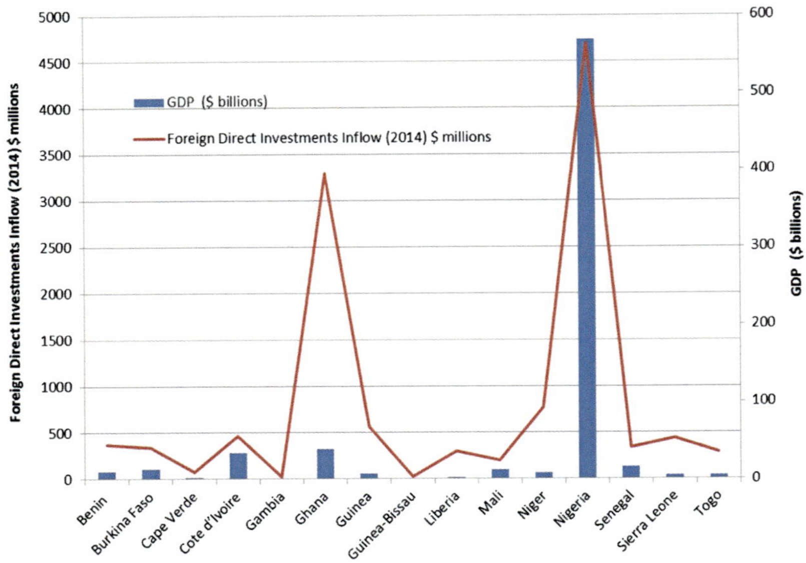

Fig. 4 GDP vs. foreign direct investments. Sources: World Bank (2014) and World Investment Report (UNCTAD 2015)

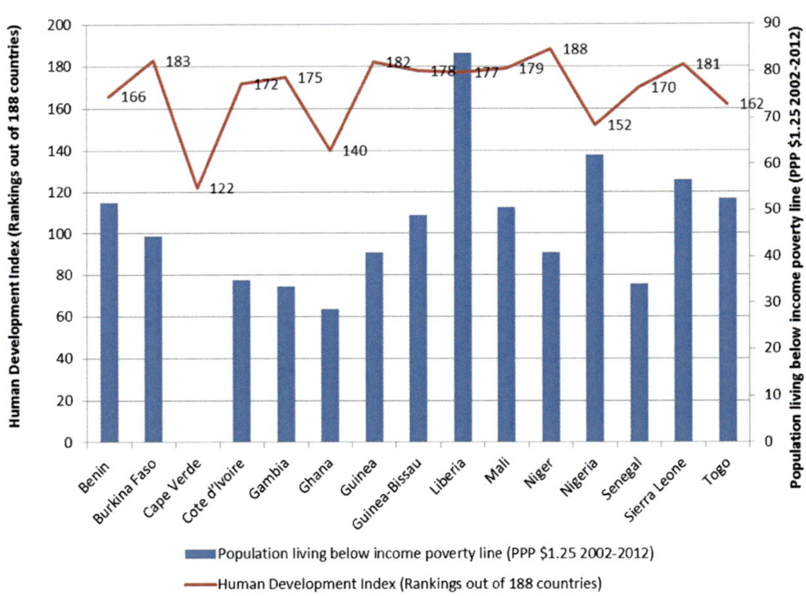

Fig. 5 HDI and Poverty Statistics. Source: United Nations Development Programme (2015)

References

Acheampong, T., Omane-Achamfuor, M., & Anang T. N. (2014). *The economic partnership agreement between Ghana and the European Union: A developmental game changer?* Ghana Growth and Development Platform Working Paper 2. Accessed June 15, 2016, from http://ghanagdp.org/file/2014/08/GGDP_WP2_Ghana-and-EPA.pdf

ActionAid Ghana. (2003). *Ghana under interim Economic Partnership Agreement (EPA): Analysis of socioeconomic development and policy options under the interim EPA regime with the European Union.* Accessed June 18, 2016, from http://www.actionaid.org/sites/files/actionaid/actionaid_ghana_research_-_ghana_under_interim_epa_and_implications_for_socio-economic_development.pdf

African Development Bank. (2015). *African Economic Outlook 2015: Resilient economies, positive forecast for West Africa.* Accessed June 11, 2016, from http://www.afdb.org/en/blogs/measuring-thepulse-of-economic-transformation-in-west-africa/post/african-economic-outlook-2015-resilienteconomies-positive-forecast-for-west-africa-14406/

Aning, K., & Atta-Asamoah, A. (2011). *Demography, environment and conflict in West Africa.* Occasional Paper No. 34. Kofi Annan International Peacekeeping Training Centre. Accessed May 23, 2016, from http://www.kaiptc.org/Publications/Occasional-Papers/Documents/OccasionalPaper-34-Aning-and-Asamoah.aspx

Bagooro, S. (2014). *West Africa and Europe trade: Who will benefit more?* Accessed June 11, 2016, from http://www.aljazeera.com/indepth/opinion/2014/06/west-africa-europe-tradeagree-2014621155835409177.html

Berg, M. A., & Krueger, A. O. (2003). *Trade, growth, and poverty: A selective survey (No. 3-30).* International Monetary Fund.

Bortolot, A. I. (2003) Trade relations among European and African Nations. In *Heilbrunn timeline of art history.* New York: The Metropolitan Museum of Art, 2000. Accessed June 11, 2016, from http://www.metmuseum.org/toah/hd/aftr/hd_aftr.htm

Chandran, V. G. R., & Munusamy. (2009). Trade openness and manufacturing growth in Malaysia. *Journal of Policy Modeling, 31*(5), 637–647.

Chang, R., Kaltani, L., & Loayza, N. V. (2009). Openness can be good for growth: The role of policy complementarities. *Journal of Development Economics, 90*(1), 33–49.

Chen, B. L. (1999). Trade openness and economic growth: Evidence in East Asia and Latin America. *Journal of Economic Integration, 14*, 265–295.

Easterly, W. (2007). Inequality does cause underdevelopment: Insights from a new instrument. *Journal of Development Economics, 84*(2), 755–776.

Economic Commission for Latin America and the Caribbean. (2014). *International trade and inclusive development: Building synergies.* Accessed June 11, 2016, from http://www.cepal.org/en/publications/37040-international-trade-and-inclusive-developmentbuilding-synergies

Edwards, S. (1993). Openness, trade liberalization, and growth in developing countries. *Journal of Economic Literature, 31*, 1358–1393.

European Commission. (2016a). *Aid for Trade – Trade – European Commission.* Accessed June 11, 2016, from http://ec.europa.eu/trade/policy/countries-and-regions/development/aid-for-trade

European Commission. (2016b). *Overview of economic partnership agreements.* Accessed June 11, 2016, from http://trade.ec.europa.eu/doclib/docs/2009/september/tradoc_144912.pdf

European Commission. (2016c). *ACP – The Cotonou Agreement – International Cooperation and Development – European Commission.* Accessed June 11, 2016, from http://ec.europa.eu/europeaid/where/acp/overview/cotonou-agreement/index_en.htm

Eusufzai, Z. (1998). Do more open countries have a higher growth rate but more inequality? *Atlantic Economic Journal, 26*(1), 32–43.

Ferreira, F. H. G. (1999). *Inequality and economic performance: A brief overview to theories of growth and distribution.* Accessed May 8, 2016, from http://siteresources.worldbank.org/INTPGI/Resources/Inequality/ferreira.pdf

Frankel, J. A., & Romer, D. (1999). Does trade cause growth? *American Economic Review, 89*, 379–399.
Frankel, J. A., & Rose, A. K. (2005). Is trade good or bad for the environment? Sorting out the causality. *Review of Economics and Statistics, 87*(1), 85–91.
Galor, O. (2009). *Inequality and economic development: An overview. Inequality and economic development: The modern perspective*. Cheltenham: Elgar Publishing.
Gries, T., & Redlin, M. (2012, June). Trade openness and economic growth: A panel causality analysis. In *International Conferences of RCIE, KIET, and APEA*, March (pp. 16–18).
Grossman, G. M., & Helpman, E. (1991). *Innovation and growth in the global economy*. Cambridge, MA: MIT Press.
Grynberg, R. (1998). *The WTO incompatibility of the Lomé convention trade provisions*. The Asia Pacific school of economics and management. Working Papers 98/3. Accessed April 29, 2016, from https://crawford.anu.edu.au/pdf/wp98/sp98-3.pdf
Hanson, K. T., & Leautier, F. (2013). Jobless economic growth in Africa: Is there a role for agriculture? *Journal of African Development, 15*(2), 1–17.
Huchet-Bourdon, M., Le Mouël, C. L. M., & Vijil, M. (2011). The relationship between trade openness and economic growth: Some new insights on the openness measurement issue. In *XIIIème Congrès de l'Association Européenne des Economistes Agricoles (EAAE)*.
Krugman, P. R. (1986). *Strategic trade policy and the new international economics*. Cambridge, MA: MIT Press.
Le, M. S. (2014). Trade openness and household welfare within a country: A microeconomic analysis of Vietnamese households. *Journal of Asian Economics, 33*, 56–70.
Lee, H. Y., Ricci, L. A., & Rigobon, R. (2004). Once again, is openness good for growth? *Journal of Development Economics, 75*(2), 451–472.
Lisk, F. (2015). *Boosting investment for transformative growth and competitiveness in African economies: A review of trends, policies, development challenges and prospects*. Accessed June 11, 2016, from http://www.crepol.org/_literature_136471/Boosting_Investment_for_Transformative_Growth_and_Competitiveness
Morgan, R., & Katsikeas, C. (1997). *Theories of international trade, foreign direct investment and firm internationalization: A critique*. Accessed June 11, 2016, from http://www.st-andrews.ac.uk/business/distance/Economics/Reading/Critique_trade_theories.pdf
Mustafa, G., Rizov, M., & Kernohan, D. (2013). *Openness, economic growth, and human development: The Asian experience*. Accessed June 11, 2016, from https://editorialexpress.com/cgibin/conference/download.cgi?db_name=GPEN2013&paper_id=52
Nourzad, F., & Powell, J. J. (2003). Openness, growth, and development: Evidence from a panel of developing countries. *Scientific Journal of Administrative Development, 1*, 72–94.
Nwoke, C. O. (2009). *EU-ECOWAS economic partnership agreement: Nigeria's role in securing development-focus and regional integration*. Accessed February 12, 2016, from https://www.afdb.org/fileadmin/uploads/afdb/Documents/Knowledge/2009%20AEC-%20EUECOWAS%20Economic%20Partnership%20Agreement%20Nigeria%27s%20Role%20in%20ensurnig%20Development-Focus%20and%20Regional%20Integration.pdf
Pacheco-López, P., & Thirlwall, A. P. (2011). Has trade liberalisation in poor countries delivered the promises expected? In *Market liberalism, growth, and economic development in Latin America* (pp. 7–25). London: Routledge.
Perotti, R. (1996). Growth, income distribution, and democracy: What the data say. *Journal of Economic Growth, 1*(2), 149–187.
Ricardo, D. (1817). *Principles of political economy* in P. Saffra (Ed.) (1951). The Works and Correspondence of David Ricardo, Vol. 1. London: Cambridge University Press
Rodney, W. (1972). *How Europe underdeveloped Africa*. London: Bogle-L'Ouverture Publications.
Sachs, J. D., & Warner, A. M. (1995) *Natural resource abundance and economic growth*. NBER Working Papers, No. 5398. New York: National Bureau of Economic Research.
Sinha, D., & Sinha, T. (2002). Openness, investment and economic growth in Asia. *Indian Economic Journal, 49*(4), 90–95.

Smith, A. (1776). *An inquiry into the nature and causes of the wealth of nations*, edited by E. Cannan (1961) and reprinted by Methuen, London

Sy, A. (2014). *Jobless growth in sub-Saharan Africa*. The Brookings Institution. Accessed June 11, 2016, from http://www.brookings.edu/blogs/africa-in-focus/posts/2014/01/30-jobless-growth-africa-sy

Tahir, M., & Khan, I. (2014). Trade openness and economic growth in the Asian region. *Journal of Chinese Economic and Foreign Trade Studies, 7*(3), 136–152. https://doi.org/10.1108/jcefts-05-20140006.

United Nations Conference on Trade and Development. (2015). *World investment report: Reforming international investment governance*. Accessed June 10, 2016, from http://www.unctad.org/wir

United Nations Development Programme. (2015). *Human development report: Work for human development*. Accessed June 8, 2016, from http://hdr.undp.org/2015-report

Winters, A. L. (2002). *Trade liberalisation and poverty: What are the links?* Accessed 11 June, 2016, from http://siteresources.worldbank.org/INTAFRSUMESSD/Resources/1729402-1150389437293/Winters_Trade_Lib_and_Poverty_World_Ec_2002.pdf

World Bank. (2014). *Trade liberalization: Why so much controversy?* Accessed June 11, 2016, from http://www1.worldbank.org/prem/lessons1990s/chaps/05-Ch05_kl.pdf

World Trade Organization. (2002). *Annual report*. Accessed May 23, 2016 from https://www.wto.org/english/res_e/booksp_e/anrep_e/anrep02_e.pdf

Yanikkaya, H. (2003). Trade openness and economic growth: A cross-country empirical investigation. *Journal of Development Economics, 72*(1), 57–89.

Yusoff, M., & Febrina, I. (2012). *Trade openness, exchange rate, gross domestic investment, and growth in Indonesia*. Accessed June 13, 2016, from http://iafor.org/archives/offprints/acss2012offprints/ACSS2012_0108.pdf

Yusuf, M., Malarvizhi, C. A., & Khin, A. A. (2013). *Trade liberalization economic growth and poverty reduction in Nigeria*. Available at SSRN 2371117.

Made in the USA
Monee, IL
20 January 2021

16cefb9d-74e8-4fd0-8ca8-45e00598c7e4R01